LIVING in the LAND of the UPRIGHTS

A Story About Thomas Voss Sorensen

by
Kathaleen Sorensen

FriesenPress

One Printers Way
Altona, MB R0G 0B0
Canada

www.friesenpress.com

Copyright © 2024 by Kathaleen Sorensen
First Edition — 2024

Editor: Lorna Stuber

Scripture taken from the New King James Version. Copyright © 1982 by Thomas Nelson. Used by permission. All rights reserved.

Scripture taken from the Holy Bible, New International Version, NIV Copyright ©1973, 1978, 1984, 2011 by Biblica, Inc. Used by permission. All rights reserved worldwide.

All rights reserved.

No part of this publication may be reproduced in any form, or by any means, electronic or mechanical, including photocopying, recording, or any information browsing, storage, or retrieval system, without permission in writing from FriesenPress.

ISBN
978-1-03-830405-6 (Hardcover)
978-1-03-830404-9 (Paperback)
978-1-03-830406-3 (eBook)

1. BIOGRAPHY & AUTOBIOGRAPHY, PEOPLE WITH DISABILITIES

Distributed to the trade by The Ingram Book Company

Table of Contents

Preface — vii
A Fresh Start — 1
A Family of Three — 8
Thomas is Born — 15
The Early Years — 24
More Questions — 31
A Frustrated Toddler — 39
Schooling Begins — 47
Challenges with School — 54
Thomas's Advocacy Begins — 72
Family and Friends — 81
Increasing Demands, Increased Awareness — 90
Junior High School — 98
High School Approaches — 118
High School Days — 127
A New School Year — 136
Continued Struggles and Triumphs — 147
The Dream — 153
Funding the Dream — 164

Camp Horizon 2013	174
A University Student	184
"Home for Christmas"	194
Daily Accounts of the Hospital Stay in Ottawa	205
Last Chance to Be a Kid	230
Bringing Our Boy Home for Good	237
The Final Hospital	245
The News	251
Final Moments	258
Thomas Speaks	265
Planning for a Funeral	267
The Beginning of a Legacy	276
The Funeral	282
Carleton Honours	298
Still Reeling	306
Life Without Thomas	313
Honouring Our Son	320
Afterword	331
Getting to Know More About Thomas	345
Timeline	349
Gratitude	353
For Further Reading and Reference	355

Preface

My full name is Thomas Voss Sorensen, but I go by almost anything. I've been called Tom, T-Dog, T-Bone, T-Moe, T, Mr. T, Tommy Douglas, and everything else in between; don't ask me why, because I don't know. My parents have affectionate nicknames for me like Pumpkin, Goombah, Chicken Louis, and more commonly, Magoo. To most people, I'm just Thomas.

— Thomas, from "Thomas Time," a school project in 2008, age twelve

The following is the story of our son Thomas who had a rare form of muscular dystrophy. At the time of his death in 2014, we were told he was one of three people in the world with this particular form of muscular dystrophy.

We always thought that he would live much longer. Yes, he was having issues, but we were led to believe that he would overcome the "episodes" of gaining fluid within his whole body, which he began to experience toward the end of his life. Thomas's death was unexpected.

Our son led an amazing life. He accomplished much more in his eighteen years than most people do throughout fifty years or more. Thomas also taught so many the importance of spirit, humour, love, and the ability to face life's daily challenges with dignity and determination.

We were a normal family dealing with a child with special needs. Now, since Thomas's passing, we are a family of three, but Thomas still lives in our hearts every day.

We hope you are inspired by his story.

—*Kathy*

A Fresh Start

When I found out that I was pregnant with Thomas, I had mixed emotions. Both Glenn and I were excited and scared about this pregnancy as I had already had two miscarriages. I was anxious to have more children after Jamie, my older son from my first marriage. I was thirty-five years old. The clock was ticking, and I wasn't getting any younger.

Thomas, taken from "Thomas Time"

My father is a bricklayer who owns one of the larger masonry businesses around. It was partly started by my grandfather, who owned a company that merged with another. My grandfather's company was nearly the same size as the other company except for a single wheelbarrow that the other company had, so the other company kept the name. My dad enjoys collecting old Danish oil paintings, cooking, watching documentaries on just about anything, travelling, and playing cards.

Rewind to spring 1991. A small-town girl from New Glasgow, Nova Scotia, living in Lumsden, Saskatchewan, after ten years of marriage I found myself divorced with a young, beautiful son, Jamie. It was time I started a new chapter, and I decided to move to Calgary, Alberta, where one of my sisters who could offer support was living. I also heard of a prospective teaching position that looked appealing. I looked around the house, and when my eyes settled on my sleeping little boy, I knew the two of us would be okay.

Once the school year was over, I ended up selling what I could. I took what I thought Jamie and I needed, mostly his favourite toys and our clothes, and moved over seven hundred kilometres west to Calgary in June 1991.

I bought a small house on a busy street in Calgary and started the job hunt. After the standard interviews with the HR department in the Calgary Board of Education (CBE), I managed to land a temporary job at Dr. E. W. Coffin School, an elementary school close to my home. I was hired to teach music and share a grade 2/3 classroom with the assistant principal.

There was a daycare across the street from my house, and a spot was available for Jamie. Dropping him off the first day was heartbreaking. He cried and cried, holding his arms out for me to take him back. I felt like a bad parent. However, he quickly adapted and even enjoyed himself at the daycare. The daycare workers, however, were not so happy. When nap time came along, all the children would snooze or rest on mats with their pillows and blankets. Instead of napping, Jamie would go around and wake up all the other children. As a result, he had to have a caregiver beside him during nap time. In time, Jamie was able to adapt to the rules with help from his caregivers and friends.

In the meantime, Marj, my sister, was trying to set me up with prospective dates. One of her friends told her to tell me about a new social club. It was the early nineties, and such clubs were a new trend in the dating game. This one was called the Going Solo Travel Club. It was only starting up, but I decided to check it out. My first time attending was on a Sunday at a pub, where the club gathered about once a month. About thirty-five people were there.

The event was okay. The organizers presented information regarding trips of all sorts such as day excursions both in and around the city, evening events like learning how to scuba dive, and week-long all-inclusive trips to Mexico and such—unfortunately, nothing I could afford or take the time to do. I knew no one and the event was a bit out of my comfort zone. However, it forced me to meet a few new people and gave me a chance to have an afternoon of adult time.

A couple of weeks later, the organizer of the club called to see if I would play hostess at the next event and seat attendees according to age. I agreed. This event was on the evening of Sunday, May 3, 1992, at a lounge in a hotel in south Calgary called the Carriage House Inn. I wore a flowered dress with off-the-shoulder sleeves. I distinctly remember Glenn entering. Here was a tall, blond guy with deep-blue eyes. He had a presence, and he was dressed nicely in a button-up dress shirt and jeans. I deviously seated him on his own, as I had full intentions of joining him.

The club again showed videos promoting their upcoming trips. Glenn and I politely ate the steak sandwiches we ordered and watched the videos and presentations. As the evening progressed, Glenn asked if I would be interested in dinner and a movie the following weekend. I was hesitant because I was not really into dating and was quite happy being on my own with Jamie. However, I had opened the door to this invitation by making sure I sat with him, so I said, "Yes."

We exchanged phone numbers, and Glenn left when the presentations were over.

Glenn:

I learned a lot about relationships during my twenties, from compromising to listening and being flexible. But I was tired of the dating scene; it was so exhausting, so I stopped looking for "the one."

The travel club seemed like a good way to stay in the singles' scene while still having some fun and meeting new people. Maybe it was a good compromise for me. At that point, I felt I could simply go out, take part in the excursions, and enjoy myself. Best of all, there were no strings. I was just happy about being free. If "the one" came along it would be okay, but I was in no rush, and I wasn't actively looking for a life partner. Little did I know that my single days were numbered.

I was thirty years old when I met Kathy, and I like to think that's when my life started. I don't remember how I heard about the Going Solo Travel Club. Attending their events was great. No pressure whatsoever.

The organizers would phone me almost every week and tell me they had arranged a walk in one of our city parks or a hike in Banff. If I was interested, I could join. About once a month on a Sunday night, the members would meet in a lounge somewhere in town where everybody could mingle and get to know one another. The organizers showed travel videos of upcoming trips that we could participate in if we chose to do so. I should say this club was not a "meat market." It was just a forum for single people to hang out together, giving us a chance to get out and do some fun stuff in a non-threatening way.

Prior to each of the monthly meetings, the club leaders would ask one or two of the members to act as a host or hostess. When I walked in one evening, a beautiful girl I had never seen before greeted me at the door, introduced herself as the hostess for the night, and found a place for me to sit. This hostess would soon turn out to be my best friend and soulmate … but I'm getting ahead of myself.

I sat down, had a cocktail, and listened to information about the upcoming trips. By this time, everyone had arrived, and the hostess came back and asked if she could sit opposite me in my booth and order dinner. I said, "Sure." I'm not sure, but I probably asked her name—I'm terrible at remembering names—and she told me her name was Kathy. We both ordered steak sandwiches, and we made small talk while we listened to the presentations and looked through the pamphlets on our table. It was an enjoyable evening; the conversation was really good, talking about the day trips the club had available and sharing a few laughs.

The travel club was not really meant for picking up girls. So, with this in mind, I somehow managed to find the courage to ask Kathy to dinner and a movie. I was holding my breath, expecting a metaphorical bullet to hit my forehead, and put me out of my misery. I can remember the hesitation in her response as I waited for an answer. After what seemed like an eternity, which was probably only a couple seconds, Kathy said, "Okay."

My God, I was so pleased and excited to get to see her again. When it was time to leave, I got Kathy's phone number, said I'd call later in the week, and left. On my drive home I was in such a good mood. What a great evening. But moments before I got home, I realized I had walked out and forgotten to pay for dinner! I felt sick. I turned around and hurried back to pay, but everyone had left by the time I got there. I returned home feeling pretty low and stupid.

When I arrived home, I immediately called Kathy to apologize for being a dumb-ass. She said she had paid for me, told me she was happy I had called to apologize and, assured me that, yes, we were still on for the next weekend.

I still remember the dress she was wearing that night: navy blue with flowers on it.

When I was helping tidy up after the function, a server came up to me.

"Where is the guy you were sitting with?" she asked me.

I said he had left. She told me that he skipped out without paying for his meal. I thought, "Okay, here is another dud," and even though I really didn't care about what he had done, I paid his bill. Afterward, I drove home, gave Jamie his daily bath, and didn't give a second thought about the night's events.

Not long after I got home, the phone rang. It was Glenn. He was so very embarrassed. He told me that he was so excited that I had said yes to a date that he drove all the way home before he realized that he hadn't paid his bill. He had returned to the restaurant only to find out that everyone had left. I remember thinking, after hearing his story, "Well, maybe this one *is* okay."

In my mind, we had a fast romance. If we didn't have a chance to meet, we talked on the phone for hours instead. Glenn included Jamie in many of our outings, and the two of them began to bond. When Glenn took Jamie and me to meet his parents, they welcomed us both with open arms.

One time, Glenn was showing us around their beautiful property and took us into the garage. I remember this incident so well. Hans, Glenn's dad, had a riding lawnmower. Glenn was showing it to Jamie and asked if he wanted to sit on the seat. Jamie smiled and said, "Yes." As he ran up to it and was about to jump on, Jamie paused and said to Glenn, "Don't put any money in it!" He thought it was one of the shopping mall rides.

Glenn began spending more time at my house with Jamie and me. Jamie got along great with Glenn, who could see that my son needed a male role model in his life. He was always laughing that Jamie called his own underwear "panties." I guess that was because of my upbringing, being surrounded by girls. I was from a family of all girls, except for my dad, and I never had to use the word "underwear."

Glenn and I continued going on dates and talking on the phone, and before too long, Glenn moved in with Jamie and me. Financially and romantically, it was the best situation for both of us. It was a true test to see if we were compatible.

Glenn:

At the beginning of our relationship, I learned that Kathy had a young son, but this was never a problem for me. Jamie was a great kid, and I loved him from the second I saw him. He had bright blond hair and was so polite; he listened to and obeyed everything his mother said. I am his dad and always will be.

Around two months after meeting Kathy, I moved in. (I told myself I was getting smarter: if it didn't work out, I could move out. I had always had my girlfriends move in with me, and when it didn't work out, they moved out and cleaned me out in the process.) With Kathy and Jamie, I went from me to three. The math worked out, and besides that, we liked being together.

Eight months after meeting Kathy, I started thinking about proposing marriage. On New Year's Eve in 1992, we were sitting in the basement watching John Wayne's *True Grit* on TV. I had always enjoyed watching John Wayne's movies. Kathy had not seen many. There was no planning ahead; I spontaneously and casually took that step of proposing (I know you think that's there's something wrong with this guy, proposing marriage while watching a movie called *True Grit*). And she said, "Yes."

It was New Year's Eve 1992 when Glenn proposed to me. I was elated! I never thought I would find such a soulmate. Glenn and I were so well-connected and knew each other so thoroughly after a short time. Yes, we had differences in our taste in music and other trivial details, but we could finish each other's sentences, say the same phrases at the same time, and pretty much always know what the other was thinking. On top of that, Glenn was accepting of and loving toward Jamie. That was huge for me. The engagement was a new start for Jamie and me, and it couldn't have been a more perfect beginning for us as a family in a new year.

That January, we bought a house in the suburb of Woodbine in Calgary and moved into our new home. Then we began planning a July wedding for 1993.

All of my family travelled to attend. Even Glenn's grandmother came from Denmark. Glenn is of Danish descent and has numerous aunts, uncles, cousins, etc. living in Denmark. My heritage is not Danish, but I was happy to embrace Glenn's traditions. The wedding was at the Danish Lutheran Church and the reception at the Danish Canadian Club. The date, July 10, was also the same date that Glenn's parents as well as his sister were married. We were all married on a Saturday, and now we celebrate the same anniversary date. Jamie was our ring bearer, and we had made our invitations out stating that Jamie was inviting everyone to his mom and dad's wedding. It was a happy day.

A Family of Three

Glenn:

Kathy and I were married on July 10, 1993, with all our family and friends in attendance. I was so happy to be marrying Kathy, and I enjoyed the wedding. The only blemish on the whole event was that I had been so stressed from work and our upcoming marriage, I got a nasty cold sore on my bottom lip. When I got home the night before our wedding, I was filthy and tired. I came in through the garage and into the mud room, where I stripped down and left my dirty work clothes. Kathy came to the door to greet me, as she always does if she is home before I am. I went inside and had a long hot shower to not only get cleaned up but also to rid the stress of the day. I was ready to celebrate with the love of my life.

Our wedding is a wonderful, happy memory for Glenn and me. We hosted a family get-together in our home the night before the wedding. It was great to see our two families mingle and get to know one another before the ceremony and reception.

We were married the next day in the Danish Lutheran Church in front of seventy-six attendees. I remember seeing the pastor without any shoes. Just white socks. I wondered if that was a Danish tradition, but it wasn't. The explanation was simple but strange: for some reason, he had forgotten his dress shoes at home. The pastor was a little bit odd in our eyes and not very flexible when it came to the wedding ceremony. He would only do the service in the traditional Danish style. He read the entire service to us and made sure we were okay with the part that said, "In the beginning, God created man, and decided man needed a helper. So, God created woman to serve man."[1] He paused, looked at the slave (me), then to Glenn. Glenn looked at me. I nodded. Why? Because it's one of those moments when you ask yourself, "If the service has been this way for three hundred years, should I be the one to break the system?"

The pastor was not personable. Nor was he one we could speak to openly. He was set in his ways, and we felt that he was merely going through the motions of being the appointed Danish pastor for the Calgary church. (The pastors are sent by the Danish church in Denmark.) Quite honestly, he was so uninspiring that I don't even remember his name.

On the positive side, the other participants in the ceremony added much more flavour to the service and made up for the stale pastor. My niece Sarah, from Nova Scotia, played a moving flute solo, and two-and-a-half-year-old Jamie was our ring bearer. He wore a white tuxedo, and his hair was slicked back in the same style as Glenn's. The wedding party was dressed in red and white, the Danish colours. My maid of honour was my long-time friend Lauren, who has since passed away from cancer. Lauren and I shared a special bond, both being single moms who would help each other out with our kids. She was the kind of friend who could pick up a conversation where we left off regardless of how much time passed between talking. Having her play a significant role in my wedding was important to me. I was shaking with both excitement and nerves; my nerves took over and produced tears as Glenn and I exchanged our vows.

Our reception at the Danish Canadian Club involved an unending flow of food, drink, and songs. We had a roast beef dinner served with vegetables and potatoes. Glenn's sisters poured wine throughout the evening. Beforehand, I had made from scratch my mother's strawberry shortcake to be served to everyone for dessert. I wanted a piece of my mom there, even though she was gone.

According to Danish custom, friends and family usually write songs for the bride and groom, and so my sisters wrote "An Ode to Kathy," based on a Nova Scotian song. Glenn's parents and his two sisters wrote songs about

---

1   This was the exact wording, taken from the Danish translation that was used in our wedding.

how Glenn and I had met, songs wishing us the best for our future, and songs welcoming me to the family. I wrote a fun one for Glenn, teasingly reminding him and informing all the guests who didn't already know that he had skipped out on our first dinner without paying.

We had a band provide music for a dance after the reception, as well. Glenn and I had the first dance, "Could I Have This Dance" by Anne Murray, and I made a point of dedicating a dance with Jamie. Our son and I danced to Carole King's arrangement of "The Itsy-Bitsy Spider," a song that was special to us.

Everyone stayed until well after midnight, making it a night full of treasured memories for our new family of three.

🐢 🐢 🐢 🐢 🐢

We were enjoying our new family life and Jamie loved having his own room in the new house. Our life became a happy, normal one filled with the typical ups and downs that a married couple with a toddler experience. We were establishing a routine for Jamie, having family over for dinners, making improvements on the house, and so on.

One night, while we were all sleeping, little Jamie woke up screaming, "I am dying! I am dying! Take me to the hospital!" I bolted out of bed and immediately ran into the bathroom adjoining his bedroom. He had the stomach flu and was throwing up in the sink. He had never thrown up before and was terrified; he thought he was dying. He mostly recovered the next day, but I felt so bad for him. It was a short but traumatic experience for Jamie.

There was another incident one morning when Jamie had awakened hungry. He was a fairly picky eater, but Glenn and I had decided that the meals we made were good enough for all of us, and it was fine if Jamie did not want to eat certain meals. We would not make anything special for him. We stuck to the rule that he wouldn't be allowed any snacks if he didn't eat his meals, and as a result, sometimes he would go to bed hungry. So, one morning he woke up famished. He took a toy and ran the toy back and across his bed frame to create some noise while yelling, "I am hungry! I want food!" It was like he was a prisoner rattling his tin cup on the prison cell bars. Jamie soon learned that he needed to eat the food that was put in front of him and not be so quick to reject the meals.

Glenn was working as a bricklayer for his dad's company. I was now teaching full-time, but my job was threatened due to cutbacks and because I was new to the CBE. I had a permanent contract, but I didn't have seniority. A year into our marriage, Glenn suggested that we look into a move to Kelowna, a city nestled in the Rockies of British Columbia (BC), and a fair distance from Calgary. His dad's company had an office there, and if I could get a job, all would be well.

I applied to the Central Okanagan School District, had an interview, and was immediately hired onto a permanent contract. Kelowna is a beautiful city, surrounded by orchards, wide-open landscapes, and water that is so calming. An added bonus to our relocation was the weather in Kelowna being warmer than Calgary's. We put our house up for sale and started planning for the move.

We moved to Kelowna, BC in July 1994. It was a big move, being about a seven-hour drive from Calgary. We found a house in West Kelowna on a half-acre lot with fourteen fruit trees. Jamie had a huge yard to run around in. We all enjoyed much warmer weather, and best of all, the neighbours had a pool, which they invited us to use any time.

Jamie started kindergarten and, since I was teaching, Glenn got to go to Jamie's first day at kindergarten (and grade 1 the following year). He stood with all the mothers outside the classroom and watched as the children went in.

A couple of months after we moved to Kelowna, Glenn's company decided to close down the Kelowna branch. This was a blow to us both. With Glenn pretty much out of a job, he became a stay-at-home dad, and he tried to make my life easier, knowing that I was teaching all day, every day. He even attempted ironing, which I had to redo, but he was trying his best. He was skilled at preparing meals, always experimenting with new recipes. He was quite disappointed, though, one day when I was late getting home from work. It was Valentine's Day, and he had prepared a wonderful celebratory meal. By the time I got home from school, the meal was cold and pretty dried out, but was still a tasty treat after a long day. To this day, we still make the same recipe and call it "Valentine Chicken."

Jamie loved the space, the house, and the weather. When he was in kindergarten, I suggested to him that we sign him up for Beavers, a young scouting program. He didn't want to go. He has never liked change and was almost afraid to try something new, not knowing what to expect. I bartered with him, "Why don't we go, and if you don't like it, you don't have to go back." He agreed, and off we went.

During that first gathering, Jamie looked like he was having a blast taking part in the activities the leaders had planned. After the evening was over, I said, "Well I guess we should tell the leaders that you don't want to come back."

His response? "No, Mom! I want to come again …"

By the time Jamie was in grade 2, we could see that he wasn't as happy as he had been in his earlier days in Kelowna. We'd enrolled him in French immersion starting in kindergarten. However, after a couple of years, something changed. He was acting out. He didn't like school. He didn't like his teacher. We were struggling to help him, but French was not my forte, nor was it Glenn's. I even consulted the French teacher at my school for help, but she had difficulties helping with the homework.

We spoke with the principal and requested that Jamie be moved into the English program. I remember the man telling us Jamie would still have the same problems in the English program as he did in French immersion. I didn't believe that claim. The principal didn't give us a reason, just his opinion that moving Jamie wouldn't make a difference. Jamie had butted heads with the teacher, so I was sure it wasn't the language that was his obstacle, but rather the teaching style. There were a couple of other French teachers at the same grade level, but Jamie didn't like French. He was also having difficulties in his English reading, so we wanted to focus on improving his English skills.

We moved Jamie to the English program in April that year, and he was like a new boy; he returned to being the son we knew and loved. All was well and he began to thrive.

I mention these details to give you an idea about those early days. Every weekend was full, getting together with neighbours and friends for dinners, barbeques, swimming parties, and card games. We loved the more relaxed atmosphere and environment of Kelowna. Life was slower than it had been in Calgary. We were able to actually take in all the joy the environment had to give.

Jamie made so many friends, as well. He had play dates at both our house and his friends' homes. He was a member of the swim and soccer teams and was attending Beavers. Life was good. Glenn was home a lot but was picking up any masonry jobs he could in Kelowna as well as Vernon, Merritt, Revelstoke, and Salmon Arm, small cities all within a couple hours' drive from Kelowna. Sometimes, Glenn would leave at 5:30 in the morning and be home after 6 p.m. Other times, he was away for the weekdays, sleeping in a motel.

It was in the spring of 1995 when I discovered that I was pregnant. After two miscarriages in the first two years of our marriage, Glenn and I hoped this pregnancy would take.

Glenn:

Well, where do I start? There is so much to talk about.

First off, in the beginning of my parenthood, Kathy shared with me her thoughts on raising children. She told me that kids need lots of routine, structure, and consistency. When we said yes, it meant yes, and no meant no. I stayed true to this philosophy over the years. In my opinion, for those of us who have children, the world is in colour with ever-changing variables. I also think for some people who have never had children, the world is black and white or right and wrong.

Watching Jamie and Thomas grow up and become young adults was and remains one of the best parts of my life. Not only did they grow and mature, but so did I. I always had high expectations for them and tried to push them to succeed at everything they did while giving their best. If I thought for one minute they weren't, I would let them know why I thought it was not their best work and ask them why they weren't putting their best effort forward. Teaching them proper etiquette was a challenge sometimes, as kids don't always know right from wrong. I would pull them aside and explain why we do things a certain way. I have, on one or two occasions, been known to be a little anal about this. The boys pulled me aside once and told me so.

🐢 🐢 🐢 🐢 🐢

This pregnancy was both exciting and worrying. Glenn was concerned about birth defects, as I was now an older mom-to-be of thirty-six. We went to Vancouver, about a four-hour drive from Kelowna, for an amniocentesis. That test was very scary for me. With Glenn by my side and holding my hand, the technicians put a *huge* needle in my abdomen to draw some fluid.

The fear of the unknown is always the worst part of any experience, but thankfully the test results came back showing everything was fine. All was well, and after my first trimester, we announced our excitement. Glenn was ecstatic. He was beaming from ear to ear, every day. He was especially good at looking out for me, helping in any way he could: carrying the groceries in, making sure I was getting rest, even doing the housework. It would be his firstborn, even though we considered Jamie as his own.

Little did we know that a check for muscular dystrophy was not part of the testing …

Thomas is Born

Thomas, taken from "Thomas Time"

My middle name is miss-leading [sic] because it's pronounced Foss, not Voss. Voss is my great-grandmother's maiden name. My father and grandfather also share this middle name. My last name is pronounced as it is spelled. In "Sorensen" the last two letters are "en" because of my Danish heritage. Many surnames that end in "son" are usually of Norwegian heritage. My parents came up with my first name through a process of elimination. My mother is a teacher, so when my dad thought of a name, my mom kept comparing it to the students she had already taught. She did not want a name that reminded her of a particular student. The only name my mom and dad came up with, that was not related to a student and one they both loved, was Thomas.

Overall, my pregnancy was great. I was healthy, and the ultrasounds were fine. I wasn't unusually large or small during my pregnancy; in fact, people didn't notice I was pregnant until I turned around to say hi. Funnily enough, people kept asking me if I was having twins, but we knew there was only one baby. We also did not want to know the baby's gender, but my heart told me it was a boy.

We had a huge problem deciding on a name. And yes, being a teacher, the fact that I had taught many children impacted our decision. I wanted a name that was fresh, not the name of a student I had taught. Poor Glenn would constantly throw out a suggestion for a name that I didn't want. We finally agreed on Michella for a girl and Thomas for a boy.

The months rolled past us until the Christmas season was upon us. My doctor said that I was due any day, so in each class, assembly, or Christmas concert event, I wondered if I would make it through without going into labour. Jamie was excited that he had a baby brother or sister arriving. He was sweet and caring, looking after me in his own way while I was pregnant, offering to give me a back rub or asking if there was something he could do to help around the house.

During this time, Glenn was having difficulty finding enough work in Kelowna. He was able to pick up jobs in Revelstoke, Vernon, and other surrounding towns, but that meant Jamie and I were on our own for the week and Glenn was coming home when he could. He also travelled to Calgary now and then for jobs, so in those cases, he would be gone for longer periods. We were managing, but when Christmas came, Glenn was finally able to be home for an extended period of time. The weather was not great for working in Calgary either, as ice and snow are not good conditions for bricklaying, so Glenn was able to be around more often.

Christmas passed with no labour pains, so we thought we'd have a New Year's baby. That wasn't the case. January was rolling by and the wait for Michella or Thomas was long. The doctor finally decided to induce me on January 23. The labour was long. The doctor threatened a C-section because I was so huge and because the baby didn't want to come out; baby was happy where he was! I also remember the doctor asking me if I wanted some laughing gas for the labour pains. Pretty soon, by the fourteenth hour, I desperately needed relief so I gave her the nod. The doctor, however, did warn me that if I had too much, it would make me ill. Glenn was trying to help prevent me from getting sick from too much laughing gas, but he never realized my strength until he tried to pry off my mask through a contraction. And yes, I was throwing up, but oh, it felt so good.

Thomas, taken from "Thomas Time:"

I was born on January 23, 1996, in Kelowna, BC, and I was a long time coming. The doctors thought at the time that I could be a Christmas baby.

Then they thought I'd be a New Year's baby. As time continued, they finally induced my mother, and I was born during a very cold winter. I'm told that the orchard farmers were worried about their fruit trees and vines because they had over four weeks of -30°C below freezing. They went on the assumption that three weeks of that temperature would kill the saplings. Fortunately, the orchards were fine.

As soon as Thomas was born, he was whisked away. All I wanted was to hold him, but they were worried that his lungs were compromised after he had pooped in the womb. The minutes that passed while the staff examined Thomas seemed like hours. The hospital staff returned him soon after his birth, with positive results. They said that Thomas was fine.

There is never a moment in a mother's life that can compared to when she finally gets to hold her newborn child. Thomas was beautiful. He was calm and peaceful, and he felt immediately bonded to me. Yes, it was for me, the second time, but it felt so magical to hold my newborn. God had granted me and Glenn a special gift.

Glenn:

From the moment I knew we were going to have another child I was so excited just watching Kathy carry this new baby to term. It was exhilarating. She had this glow about her. I can't explain it but every once in a while, I see an expectant mother who has the same glow, and it makes me smile and remember when Kathy was pregnant.

Thomas's birth was on January 23, 1996. We'd arranged for the neighbours across the street to care for Jamie for a day or two. Kathy was quite large, and the doctors decided to induce her to speed up the contractions. They hooked her up to monitors, and I could see on those monitors the contractions coming and going, but she could not.

I knew I could never experience the same feelings as Kathy. I just knew that I needed to be there for her and do anything I could to make the birth easier for her.

Then it started; it was time for Thomas's entrance into the world. The contractions were coming pretty fast. I was standing beside Kathy, holding her hand, and she was pushing at the right times. The final moment was getting close, so me being me, I asked Kathy, "Is it too early to talk about the next child?" The doctor and her intern were both between Kathy's legs and looked up at me with plain disgust, but Kathy replied instantly, "Yes, anything for you."

Shortly after that, Thomas came into our world. And then we were four. The doctor was stitching Kathy a little, and as I was standing there watching this happen, I asked, "Is this where the father asks the doctor to throw in a few extra stitches?"

This doctor looked up at me like she was about to open me up with a knife, but the intern said, "That's right, and an extra stitch for Dad."

The doctor looked at the intern, then at me, and said, "Maybe I should stitch my initials."

I asked, "What are your initials?" and she replied, "M.A.D." Margorie Ann Doherty.

I knew it was time for me to bite my tongue. But it was a happy occasion, and I couldn't help it if the doctor had no sense of humour. In any case, from that day, I gained a lot of respect for women and what they go through during childbirth. I always look back on that day fondly and smile about it.

I can't remember how long Kathy was in the hospital, but I went home that first night by myself. It was quite late. I poured a drink to celebrate. There I was, sitting at the kitchen table, looking at this drink, thinking about the day. I stared at the wall for who knows how long, and then I thought about the things a man does, or what he's supposed to do to support his wife during and after childbirth. I wanted to be there for her.

I dumped the drink down the drain and went to bed because I just wanted to get up early, hurry back to the hospital, and not miss a thing.

Life was good.

Thomas is Born

It was January 23, 1996, at 8:31 p.m. when Thomas, at 8 lb. 1 oz., showed up in the world. It was a cold and grey Tuesday. In the hospital, though, it seemed the opposite: a bright and cheery and fabulous day! Our son was born. And he was beautiful. I did the count: ten toes and ten fingers. He had long eyelashes any woman would die for, a wonderfully shaped nose, a curved chin and cheeks, and handsomely dark eyes, the same as his older brother. We were in the hospital for four days to make sure all was well. Thomas was in an incubator off and on for short chunks of time over the four days, but when he wasn't, he was always in my room. I also felt special, receiving the many flowers from family members, and my students gave me enormous cards that covered the entire hospital room wall.

Glenn and Jamie were by our side whenever they could be, and Jamie was so excited to see and hold his new brother. He held Thomas tightly and stroked his hair. Jamie talked to Thomas and was warmed when Thomas made a sound as if to respond. He was very loving and enjoyed every minute of those first few days of being a big brother.

Glenn was a natural new dad, having experienced the birth. He, too, loved holding Thomas and talked to him in his calming voice. Even though Glenn was extremely gentle, I could tell that he was bursting with pride and excitement. Glenn wanted to experience absolutely everything, from the diaper changes to bathing to helping with the feedings. He had little experience in handling a newborn but was a quick learner. He soon learned that changing a boy's diaper meant quick action or else there could be quite a fountain happening when the cold air hit the body. He was cautious in handling Thomas, making sure to hold one hand behind the baby's neck for support. Another of his lessons involved learning how to wrap Thomas tightly in the bath towels after a cleaning to make him feel cozy and warm.

After four days, it was finally time to be discharged from the hospital, but my feet and ankles were so swollen my shoes no longer fit. I managed to put on some extra-big boots over Glenn's work socks. I didn't care about how big and clumsy my feet were because I was so happy to be going home with our new son, Jamie's little brother.

Jamie began playing the role of big brother almost immediately. He helped change diapers and cuddled Thomas. He played with Thomas, talked to him, and tried to entertain him, making googly eyes and funny sounds to try to make him smile. Most of all, he loved to hold Thomas.

Glenn was elated. He had another son. Still, he never faltered in his devotion to Jamie, making sure he spent one-on-one time with him and looking after his needs for both school and home. This included getting Jamie to his swim team practices and his weekly Beaver nights and soccer practices. He also made sure Jamie's homework was completed, and he prepared Jamie's daily school lunches.

Glenn was as wonderful at home as he was in the hospital. He enjoyed snuggling with Thomas, helping with baths, changing his diapers, and taking him for walks in his stroller. He also took charge of both boys to give me time to sleep when I needed it. He was up at night, helping with feedings and cooking meals whenever he could. Glenn was ready to show off his newborn son. Life was great and we were a happy family.

Glenn:

The next year was a tough one for me, work-wise. There were not a lot of jobs in Kelowna and surrounding area. If you're not born there or don't have lots of connections, it's hard to find jobs. The locals were tired of newcomers who came one day and were gone the next, and they tried to protect their own. At one point, during the last year we were in Kelowna, I was doing a job building the new high school in Salmon Arm when one of our employees had a massive heart attack and passed away on the job site.

Finally, after three years of trying to break into the job scene, I was done trying to make it work in BC. I was tired of fighting to get a job, tired of travelling outside of town, tired of having to prove myself in a community that was not accepting of newcomers. Because of this mindset, I started travelling seven hours one-way to Calgary for work stints lasting between one and four weeks.

We had joined the Lutheran church when we moved to Kelowna and attended every Sunday. We very much enjoyed the service, particularly the pastor, a slightly older man who was getting close to retirement. There was something about Pastor Berg that made you feel good just being in his presence. He was the kind of person who set one at ease immediately, with his calming voice and the ability to make you feel he was actually listening to your opinions. He made every effort to get to know each family member in his church.

We held Thomas's christening at the Lutheran church in his first year in Kelowna. My sister and brother-in-law were Thomas's godparents. All of my family came, but we were disappointed that none of Kathy's family made it. Traditions are important in the Sorensen family but less so in Kathy's. The one tradition from Kathy's family that was celebrated was that Thomas was dressed in the McNeil family christening gown. This gown had been worn by not only Kathy and Jamie but her four sisters, four of her nieces, and even her dad. Thomas's christening was something I had been looking forward to.

After the church service, we all went home and celebrated with pictures and a sit-down traditional smorg, which everyone helped cook. (One of my family traditions is to host a huge Danish smorgasbord for big celebrations.) Christenings are definitely great times of gathering and celebration for adults and older kids, but not so much for the little one who the celebration is for. It is not until many years later, through conversations and pictures, that the baby who was christened realizes the event actually happened. But the adults and older kids enjoy the opportunity to get together to celebrate and honour the new family member.

It was April. Lots of family made the trip for this special occasion. Baptism is considered the first official ceremony of a Dane's life. It was the first time we hosted a traditional Danish smorg with the seven courses.

The smorg begins with three different kinds of herring (white pickled herring, red pickled herring, and curried herring), shrimp, hard-boiled eggs, tomatoes, and mackerel in tomato sauce. The second course is a fried fillet of sole served on rye bread with a Danish tartar sauce called *remoulade*. Next is a tasty dish called *tartelette*; creamed chicken and asparagus in a pastry shell. The fourth course may vary; we serve a pork dish with onion, red cabbage, and a Danish sausage called medisterpølse. Next is an array of cold cuts for the Danish open-faced sandwiches along with a Danish-style liver pâté, which is smothered in fried mushrooms and bacon. The second last course is a Danish fruit salad, made of canned fruit, to which you add fresh apple, banana, and sliced grapes, mixed with whipping cream and chocolate. The salad is served along with a variety of cheeses. Finally, a dessert called kransekage, a tree-shaped dessert made from stacked rings of almond paste, sugar, and egg whites, is served with chocolates and coffee.

I was nervous about living up to the Sorensen standard of the smorg. However, all the family pitched in to help prepare the meal. We set up a number of tables to create one long table to seat twenty. It was decorated with a red tablecloth, napkins with Danish flags on them, red and white flowers in vases, and the kransekage as the centrepiece.

It was a fabulous day. Thomas wore the McNeil family baptismal gown. McNeil is my maiden name, and this gown had been originally worn by my dad ninety years before, followed by my sisters and me, their children, and Jamie.

After the baptism, we settled into everyday life, and even our normal days were amazing. Thomas was such a happy baby. He slept a lot, fed well, and was extremely content. He was above his percentile for height, which was no surprise to us with Glenn being so tall. I had no worries, but I do remember a peculiar moment during a routine visit to the doctor for Thomas's checkup. The nurse was giving me grief about turning away for a second as Thomas lay on the examination table. She said he could not be left alone for fear of him rolling off the table. I said that it was okay and assured her it would not happen. I felt I knew what I was doing looking after Thomas. This incident didn't seem like a big deal then, but looking back, I wonder at that sign. For some inexplicable reason, I must have subconsciously known he was not capable of rolling over.

Thomas and I enjoyed eight months together before I returned to work. Those first months of Thomas's life were a special time for all of us, but I, unfortunately, did not have the option of a prolonged maternity leave. We needed the income. In spite of the shortened leave, I did spend many wonderful hours and quality time with our children. We went for lots of walks, had plenty of family come for visits, did some baking, held play dates, and attended Jamie's soccer games. The boys even came to church with me for choir practice.

Glenn had a huge job in Salmon Arm at the time. He was in charge of the masonry part of the new high school being built. He would either leave early in the morning and return late at night or end up staying at a motel during the weekdays. Near the end of the project, sadly, one of his top bricklayers had a massive heart attack at the site and died on the spot. It was a trying and sad time. Glenn and I tried as best as we could to comfort and assist the other bricklayer's family. In the meantime, Glenn had to finish the job.

Glenn began commuting to Calgary for jobs, a seven-to-eight-hour drive one-way. He was staying at his parents' house while working in Calgary and trying to come back to Kelowna whenever he could. The time Glenn was away from home during the weekdays was beginning to increase.

I was managing the two boys on my own. Once my maternity leave was over and I was back at work, I knew my boys were in good hands with a caring nanny, Lisa, who lived next door. It was convenient having her so close by, and the boys loved having her around. I was managing to keep the boys happy, talk with Glenn every day, keep the household running, and continue to do my best in teaching. We knew we had to make sacrifices to make things work. Most importantly, even with Glenn and me apart at times, we were a happy family.

Then, things started to change. We had no idea that the events that followed would be life-changing ones …

The Early Years

Glenn:

Trying to figure out Thomas's needs, and for us to try to have a normal family life, was hard during those first few years. When we were living in Kelowna, our neighbour's daughter would babysit while we worked. When Thomas was eight months old, she thought he should be able to stand at his age, so one time she stood him at the coffee table and said, "You'd better stand or else you are going to fall and get hurt." Thomas was so scared he just stood there, not moving. Over time, with her constant encouragement and his determination, he was able to walk around the table, using it for support, but we started to notice he was slow in developing all motor skills.

On one of Glenn's parents' visits to Kelowna, Alice and Hans commented on the shape of Thomas's head. They gently tried to tell us that his head did not look "normal." They said his forehead looked protruded, his ears were out of place, and the sides of his head were flat. We really didn't think much of their observations as we were around Thomas all the time, and to us, he was our perfect little boy with those ten fingers and toes. But when Glenn and I listened, we looked and we, too, then noticed the differences.

Now that I look back, I recognize that Thomas was not reaching the usual milestones that babies reach. He had difficulty sitting up on his own and supporting his weight. He made no attempts of rolling over or crawling. Yet, at that time, his behaviour didn't seem overly unusual.

Glenn's parents discovered that a doctor in Calgary, Dr. Hamilton, had recently started a special clinic at the Alberta Children's Hospital and they suggested we call for an appointment. Alice and Hans generously offered to pay for a return flight for Thomas and me to Calgary. We certainly could not have afforded the cost, and it was not covered by the medical system, so we were appreciative of their generosity.

In the meantime, we did take Thomas to the Kelowna emergency room to meet with a pediatrician on the advice of our family doctor. Our family doctor was one that I trusted. For two years, he had been the one to clean out Jamie's ear wax, see to our regular checkups, and give us honest feedback on any of our health concerns or questions. Dr. Ervine had no idea what was happening with Thomas's head shape, though.

We went to see the pediatrician at the emergency room, as that was the only way we could get an appointment within the next two months. That pediatrician was furious that we had gone to the ER to see him, believing Thomas's was not an emergency-related case. He agreed to some X-rays only because he thought Thomas should have one, and then came back and suggested that maybe Thomas's skull was not developing the way it should. He was guessing that something was not quite right, that maybe Thomas needed surgery on his skull to readjust the placement of the bones. That definitely did not sit well with us. The doctor looked again at his notes, looked at us, and said maybe nothing was wrong and that we were wasting his time. We never received a follow-up or heard a word from that doctor again.

Glenn and I decided that we should go to Calgary for a second opinion, and in an instant, my in-laws arranged a same-day return flight between Kelowna and Calgary for Thomas and me. We departed for Calgary at seven in the morning. Glenn was working in Calgary at the time and he met us at the Calgary airport and took us to our appointment at the Alberta Children's Hospital.

Oddly enough, one of the things I remember about that hectic day was what I was wearing. Why do we remember our silly clothes on days when our lives seem to change? I recall specifically choosing an outfit to look respectable. Here we were going to the big city, to the well-known Alberta Children's Hospital. I honestly thought we were doing it to go through the motions. I had on navy wool dress pants with a silk navy blouse, and I wore my mom's pearl sunburst brooch pinned between the collar.

The staff there were fabulous. They knew we were on a tight schedule and that I had to get back on the plane to Kelowna by four in the afternoon. I only had one day off work to make the trip, not knowing what the outcome of the appointments would be.

We first met with Dr. Hamilton in his office. From there, Dr. Hamilton's assistant escorted Thomas, Glenn, and me from specialist to specialist, from one department to another. Various technicians did an MRI, took blood work and X-rays, and finally did a casting of Thomas's head. The casting involved literally covering Thomas's head with plaster and tape in order to get a mold of his head. Thomas really didn't like to be held down and confined while the doctors and assistants were doing their work, and it became so messy that both Thomas and I were ultimately covered in white plaster! It was quite a scene.

We really didn't know what any of this process or these tests meant. The specialists told us that they would be in touch to let us know the results. It was a whirlwind of a day, viewing all of the unique departments, from the examination rooms designed cheerfully for kids, to the child-friendly MRI department, and the creative plaster studio. This plaster studio was a brand-new department and the first in Canada, with several plaster heads on dowels placed around the room to show each stage of the construction. At the end of the appointment, Glenn drove Thomas and me back to the airport. To this day, I am not sure we knew the implications of that trip and how much our lives were about to change.

Thomas was diagnosed with *positional plagiocephaly*, better known as *flat head syndrome*. For many children, this diagnosis means that their parents did not know better in laying their children to sleep and shifting the position of their heads from right to left so that the child's head is not in the same position for too long. We found out, however, that Thomas's head didn't form correctly in the womb because of lack of movement. The specialist in Calgary had only recently begun the procedure of reshaping babies' heads at the Alberta Children's Hospital. Just weeks before our visit, this type of correction had only been done in Phoenix, Arizona. For me, it was good knowing that our Canadian doctors could help. Thomas was considered an "old" baby to have this reconstruction done; he was eight months old, but we hoped for the best.

Since we were always with Thomas, we did not see the malformation, at least not until Dr. Hamilton's assistant, Dale, brought out the "headsicle," a mold of our son's head on a stick, minus the hair. It looked like some strange giant Popsicle, but it showed every ill-formed part of Thomas's head. I think both Glenn and I were in shock when we first saw it. I burst into tears. Thomas's head seemed unreal. His ears were probably an inch out of symmetry. The top of his head was triangular, his temples were pushed in and looked sunken, and the top and sides were flat.

Thomas was fitted with a helmet. It was a hard, white, plastic form lined with Styrofoam designed to realign a baby's skull. It wrapped around Thomas's head and was held in place by Velcro. The top of Thomas's head was visible, and the circumference of his head was covered with the white plastic. A chinstrap helped keep the helmet in place. The idea was that each week, the doctor, and his assistant would carve the foam on the inside to resculpt Thomas's head.

They warned us that at eight months of age, Thomas might be a bit too old to have this procedure done. They preferred treating younger babies when their skulls were still much softer.

This helmet would be on Thomas twenty-three out of twenty-four hours a day. We were only to remove it long enough for Thomas to have a daily bath.

The staff at the clinic had said that we were free to decorate the circumference with stickers or paint. Glenn and I looked at each other. We were on the same page. We did not want to draw more attention to Thomas with stickers or colour applied to an already strange-looking headpiece. We declined.

As the weeks progressed, Thomas adjusted to his new headgear. He was able to sleep, his appetite was good, and he didn't seem to notice the extra weight on his head. He was not pulling at the helmet, nor did he seem unhappy. I was leaving it on religiously for twenty-three hours a day, timing how long it took for a bath, checking for any sores, and making sure it was back on within the hour. After a few weeks, we could see that the helmet was working. Thomas was one of the first patients in Calgary to go through this procedure, and we were pleased that it was making a difference.

Airports became familiar to us—part of our routine. The early morning rise, getting Jamie to a sitter, taking the car to the airport, and getting Thomas and me checked in. We got to know the check-in attendants at the airport. They would see us approaching the desk and come running with trollies. They helped with our carry-on bags, let us board early, and at times, would even upgrade our seats free of charge. Thomas mimicked the sound of the airplane as it was taking off. He had perfect pitch and always found the exact note the plane was chiming. Thomas could also precisely imitate the three notification sounds which alerted the flight attendants to prepare for takeoff or landing. As a musician, I was floored at his perfect pitch.

There was one moment at an airport that really struck me. It was on one of our returns to Kelowna, and Glenn had Thomas, helmet on and happy in his stroller in the airport. Remember, this medical device and procedure were new in Calgary and, therefore, completely new to Kelowna as well. When I stopped to go to the washroom, one of the airport staff came up to Glenn and suggested that he take Thomas to a private room so other airport patrons would not be disturbed. I couldn't believe someone would even suggest that. Even to this day, I am puzzled at this kind of reaction to our son. Perhaps the attendant was embarrassed for us, or maybe he thought Thomas would throw a tantrum. I guess this was a new revelation to the staff member, not knowing what the helmet was all about. Although this staff member thought he was being considerate, Glenn declined the invitation.

Nevertheless, throughout the whole "helmet" experience, Thomas was a trouper. He didn't complain, even though there were several times he had pressure points on his head from the weekly adjustments made to the helmet. He had this heavy piece of white plastic stuck on his head, which only came off for an hour a day during bath time, and yet, Thomas smiled. He was alert, happy, and so well tempered. Our son took everything in stride and gave us the strength we needed.

During this time, Thomas was not able to pull himself up to sit or crawl. We were getting worried, but the doctors assured us it was because of the weight of the helmet and told us not to be concerned.

Glenn:

The helmet was lined with Styrofoam, which would be carved out over time to slowly reshape Thomas's head. Kathy and I didn't have much money in those early years. Mom and Dad knew this and said, "He's our grandchild, and we are paying for all your flights for as long as it takes."

Luckily, Thomas was underage and he could fly for free, so the cost was for only one return flight each week even though there were the two of them. The weekly trips went on for eight months. The Alberta Children's Hospital knew Kathy and Thomas were flying in the morning and back out in the afternoon, so we never had to wait. The helmet was effective, and I give many thanks to Mom and Dad.

The weekly trips to Calgary from Kelowna for Thomas's helmet adjustments at the hospital were hectic ones. My Kelowna school board allowed me to take the days off work without penalty. It was tough, but I was willing to do what it took to correct the formation of Thomas's head. Not only did I have to plan weekly for a substitute teacher in my class, but I had to coordinate childcare for six-year-old Jamie for a full day.

Jamie came along to visit Glenn and his grandparents when the appointments happened to be on a Friday or a Monday and we made it a weekend trip. Glenn was able to come to the many appointments while he was working in Calgary. He continued working in Calgary most of the time, and I felt like a single mother during his absence.

Glenn:

There is real generosity out there when you least expect it, but sometimes when you do expect it, it's not there. I am forever grateful to my parents for covering the cost of the plane tickets when Kathy and Thomas needed to commute between Kelowna and Calgary every week.

Being a dad is, and has been, fun for the most part, but when things are out of your control—not so much. As a parent, it's natural to want to dive in and rescue your children from any hardship they experience, but sometimes it's just not possible to do so. Raising a child with special needs has its challenges, and Kathy and I needed to be on the same page. We've been lucky. We get along well, and we never fight or scream at one another. We don't necessarily always agree on everything, but we're always on the same team.

We've always known we don't own our children and that it's a privilege to have them. Getting to nurture and teach them, watching them grow, is incredibly fulfilling.

Thomas's procedure was nearing an end. On the long weekend in May 1997, our niece Janice came for a visit in Kelowna. Glenn, the boys, and I were excited to have her come. I remember the five of us relaxing in our bathing suits in our backyard on a beautiful, hot day. We couldn't have asked for better weather.

Jamie loved racing around the yard playing tag with his cousin. Glenn and I watched Thomas. He was enjoying our visit with his cousin, playing catch, getting tickled, and being smothered with love. We played some board games, had a delicious barbeque, and enjoyed getting to have some downtime to visit. It was a wonderful weekend.

Thomas was getting his helmet off that Tuesday. Glenn was still working in Calgary, and Thomas and I rode back to Calgary with Glenn in his truck for the last appointment. When we arrived in Calgary, it was snowing. I had sandals on, so I trudged into the hospital, sloshing through the wet snow. I didn't care. We were excited to get the helmet off. Celebrating the end of this process was our focus for the day. After eight months, the results were positive. We could see how Thomas's head had reshaped. He looked totally fine, and we were pleased, thinking that was the end of the hospital visits.

We were wrong.

More Questions

Immediately after the helmet came off, we experienced a moment of feeling that things weren't quite as they should be. A half-heard whisper coming from someone behind us, a gut feeling, a wave of uncertainty. Glenn and I were worried that Thomas was not progressing well; he wasn't hitting his developmental milestones. He still didn't sit up on his own. He was eighteen months old, and he hadn't yet crawled.

We took him to another pediatrician in Kelowna. The doctor asked questions about Thomas's motor skills and was curious to learn about the helmet. He asked how much milk Thomas drank. I said he loved milk! He would have six to eight, 8 oz. bottles on any given day. The doctor raised his eyebrows and asked me if I knew that too much milk could cause an iron deficiency. I sank down in the chair. Toddlers who drink a lot of cow's milk can't absorb iron, which can contribute to iron-deficiency anemia. The doctor decided to send us for blood work and would have us return after the results came in.

The next day was a Friday. I took Thomas to the hospital lab during my lunch break. The blood work requisition was in a sealed envelope, which at that time I thought was strange. I handed the envelope to the receptionist, and Thomas and I took a seat to wait our turn. Thomas played with the toys in the children's area as we waited. He knew he was getting another needle for blood work and I was trying to calm and reassure him that the test would be over quickly. The receptionist finally called his name, and we went to the counter, where she handed me back the requisition. She informed me that we would have to come back on Monday as the blood work needed to be sent to Vancouver, and we had missed the cut-off time. I glanced at the paperwork and saw words that were not meant for me to read. I don't think they were meant for anyone to read: *test for muscular dystrophy*.

I was in shock. Somehow, I managed to find my keys, get to the car, and secure Thomas safely into his car seat. I was trying to hold back my emotions, to not show Thomas how upset I was, and to collect my nerves enough to safely drive him home and return to school. I was so distracted by what I had read that I was surprised I managed to drive at all. Here beside me on the passenger seat was a sheet of paper that said "Thomas" and "muscular dystrophy." I was terrified about the unknown. All I knew about MD was that it wasn't good; in fact, I knew nothing else about this disease.

From work, I called the doctor's office. I wanted answers. Most of all, I wanted to be told someone had made a mistake. The doctor's receptionist told me that I could come in, and one of my colleagues drove me to the clinic since I was in no condition to drive.

I sat in the waiting room with so many questions. I wondered what a diagnosis of muscular dystrophy would mean for Thomas. I wondered about his future and what life might hold for him. I wondered if a diagnosis would mean the end of his life, and if so, how soon? How much time would we have with our precious boy, and what would that time entail?

The doctor finally called me in. He told me that he had sealed the requisition because he didn't want me to know his suspicions until they were confirmed, but he was pretty sure Thomas had muscular dystrophy. I called Glenn in Calgary, and he immediately got in his truck at the job site and drove straight to Kelowna. To this day, I'm not sure how he ever managed to arrive home in Kelowna. By the time he did, my eyes were swollen shut from crying. Glenn called his family to let them know the news. It was the first time I ever saw him cry. Jamie was six years old, but he was old enough to know what was going on. He looked up at me and asked if Thomas was going to die.

🐢 🐢 🐢 🐢 🐢

From that day, Thomas started to go through a battery of blood tests. One of the main tests checks for levels of a protein called *creatine kinase*, or CK. CK is an enzyme that muscles release into the bloodstream when they are damaged. The level of CK in the blood is elevated in patients with muscular dystrophy. Each time they took blood, they were checking Thomas's CK levels. With the many blood tests, they were hoping to see a decrease in the CK levels, but the tests confirmed the doctor's suspicions: Thomas had muscular dystrophy. However, we did not know which form of the disease our son had. At that time, there were over forty known types. The worst kind was *Duchenne's*; it was the most crippling type and the one with the shortest life expectancy. At that time, we hoped and prayed Thomas did not have that type, but in the end, we had to wait years to discover the real answer.

We didn't know much about muscular dystrophy, but we learned that it occurs when a child is born missing one particular protein that repairs muscles and makes them stronger. The absence of the protein causes muscles to degenerate and weaken. Developmental growth slows and ultimately stops. It was starting to make sense. Thomas wasn't able to gain any muscle strength to sit up, roll over, or crawl.

At that point, Glenn and I decided to sell the house in Kelowna and move back to Calgary. Not only was Glenn having trouble finding work in Kelowna, but we felt that the medical care Thomas required would be better served at the Alberta Children's Hospital. Kelowna did not have any specialists in the field of muscular dystrophy. I felt confident that I could, with time, re-establish myself in the teaching field in Calgary.

Glenn took on the task of finding us a new house. This was during a time when the housing market was hot; houses listed in the morning sold by evening the same day. It was tough to find a place, but Glenn knew I trusted him. He looked at many houses and finally found one to put an offer on. He sent me a video of our newly purchased house by Xpresspost. It was a small house but had a solid foundation and a private backyard. All of the bedrooms were on the main floor. It was definitely a downgrade from what we were used to. But I proudly shared the video with my school staff in Kelowna, who, in turn, enjoyed my excitement watching the video of our new house.

In June 1997, we sold the house in Kelowna at a loss, I resigned from the job I loved, and we left behind so many close friends. Life was changing and it was a tough time, moving back to Calgary to begin again and facing unknown territory with Thomas's new diagnosis. However, I had Glenn by my side. I knew I was not on my own, and at least we were all living under the same roof again. But I didn't know if I could get back into the school system, and I'd pinned all my hopes on a video of a little house on a busy street, which I had never ever seen.

Now, Thomas was a patient of the neuromuscular clinic at the Alberta Children's Hospital. The specialist there wanted to do more testing to determine the kind of muscular dystrophy he had. The first test was the worst. Glenn and I took turns holding down Thomas and the doctor took a device that looked like a small cattle prod and administered electric shocks to both of Thomas's wrists and ankles. I didn't know what century this test came from, but I was horrified at the process, and I had to trust that the doctor knew what she was doing. The purpose of this test was to determine Thomas's nerve sensitivity. It was a brutal test to conduct on such a little child. Thomas screamed, and both he and I cried. Glenn was our strength, but I knew he was feeling the pain, too.

Thomas endured more blood tests so that the doctors could eliminate one type of muscular dystrophy after another. And they did a muscle biopsy—a day surgery under general anesthesia, during which they removed a piece of muscle from his thigh, which was sent to Toronto for testing. After all that, we went home to wait for the results. Another five months, to be exact.

🐢 🐢 🐢 🐢 🐢

September came, and Jamie started grade 3 in Calgary. His reading and comprehension were low after being in the French program. No parent ever wants to hear that, so I worked with him at home to improve his skills. He would only read *Anamorphs*, a book series about teens who turned into animals to fight the bad people in the world. Not the best reading for kids, but I figured it was better than nothing.

This was at the time when the Harry Potter books were a literary hit. One night, I began reading the first Harry Potter book to both the boys. A few nights later, I had to go out so I couldn't read about Harry Potter to the kids. The following night, when I went to read to the boys and pick up where we had left off, I discovered Jamie had already read the next two chapters on his own. He had finally discovered the love of reading.

Jamie adapted well to Calgary. He loved being close to his grandparents, and he made a few new friends. He started karate, art classes, and soccer. Because Jamie has never been one for change, it always took a couple of sessions in any new event for him to feel comfortable. But he was beginning to excel in school and enjoyed special school projects like science experiments and social studies posters, especially with Mom's help.

While we waited for the results of his biopsy, Thomas went for an initial visit to the Alberta Children's Hospital Pediatric Neuromuscular Clinic, where he had numerous appointments scheduled for an entire day. We had to go for X-rays of his spine, a pulmonary breathing test, both an echocardiogram (an ultrasound of the heart) and electrocardiogram (EKG or ECG—a test using electrodes to look for irregularities in the heart's structure), and more blood work. After the tests, we sat and waited to see each of the specialists: cardiology, orthopedic, physiotherapy, pulmonary, neuromuscular, seating (a seating specialist is someone who designs a wheelchair for kids with special needs). Even a social worker was part of the team. Each specialist had an intern under them, which meant the questions doubled every time we had an appointment. The interns always came in first, then the specialist. This would be the routine for the rest of Thomas's "childhood" life at the hospital until he reached the age of eighteen. It was all so overwhelming.

Even though Thomas endured a multitude of tests done by an army of specialists, we always left the hospitals and clinics with more questions than answers. No one offered any real predictions as to what lay ahead. The uncertainty was frustrating. We felt like we were parts of a car being pushed through a production line in a factory. Every time we went to a hospital, there were more tests with more doctors and interns but no forecasts, no palm readings, no certainty. No answers. Nobody ever gave their opinions about what we were facing. We listened and vowed to do anything to make Thomas's life a better one. We bought shaving cream for Thomas to use to make sketches on the bathtub tiles during bath time. We also provided him with a tall mirror and washable paints so he could make pictures, all to hopefully improve his strength in his upper arms and torso. It was suggested we go for regular visits to the physiotherapist, who taught us stretching exercises that we could practise each day at home. Really, those were the only things we could do to help Thomas.

A couple of months after Thomas's diagnosis, Glenn and I met the with the staff at the General Genetics Clinic, located at the Children's Hospital. We started by filling out pages and pages of questions on our family histories. Then they drew our blood, and it turned out that both Glenn and I were carriers of the gene called Pure Congenital Muscular Dystrophy. The odds of us meeting and having Thomas were off the charts. According to the team, our chances of winning the lottery were higher than holding those cards.

The genetics team also informed us that we should tell them if we were even thinking of having more children. If I were to become pregnant, the odds were one in four of having another child with muscular dystrophy. They did have a prenatal test for muscular dystrophy, but it was a dangerous one, and that test would have to be sent to Paris, France. Results would take months. Glenn and I really wanted to have more kids, but upon hearing those odds, we decided we would not have any more children.

Five months after Thomas's muscle biopsy, we received word that the results were in. Out of the forty different kinds of MD, the test revealed that Thomas had Pure Congenital Muscular Dystrophy, which meant that strictly his muscles were affected and that he'd been born with it. We were relieved to know it was not the worst kind (at least at that time we thought this was the case), but in the back of our minds, we were aware that the heart, too, is a muscle.

Life in Calgary was rough. I was so depressed the first year, longing for our good friends in Kelowna. I didn't have the same support system in Calgary that I had in Kelowna. I really did miss our old home and the environment, the warmer climate, the slower pace of life, the fruit trees, the weekends of barbeques and playing cards. I didn't know anyone in Calgary outside of Glenn and our extended family. In terms of work, I also had to start from the beginning. I had to regain entrance to the CBE and work for at least two years before I could obtain a permanent contract. I had to prove to a new staff that I was capable. It was all too familiar.

On top of my professional demands, there were so many appointments for Thomas and so few answers to our questions. We still had no idea what it meant for Thomas to have muscular dystrophy. This was unknown territory, and we had an encyclopedia of questions. For the doctors, it was all routine.

Glenn began to renovate our new home. The house was dark and dated, so we painted the walls in brighter colours and gave the boys' rooms each a theme. Thomas's was Thomas the Tank Engine, and Jamie wanted the stars and planets. I spent hours in the backyard planting flowers we had brought back from Kelowna. We freshened up the basement to make a play area for the boys, a family room where we could all watch television, and an office with a computer. At this point, Thomas was able to walk short distances. He was also able to go down the stairs to the basement one step at a time on his bum. He couldn't make it back up, but he was happy and confident going down.

I remember my dad coming from Nova Scotia to visit during our early days in that house. Dad loved musicals, and one musical we watched together during his visit was *Brigadoon*. The boys sat and watched it with us. Thomas loved the song "I'll Go Home with Bonnie Jean" and quickly learned the words and melody. He sang the song for weeks after my dad's visit.

We also were able to visit Heritage Park with Dad. The boys loved the old museum displays and the train and other rides. Thomas especially enjoyed the train. He was in his element. He loved sitting in the old seats hearing the wheels go "cha-chunk, cha-chunk, cha-chunk." He even loved the smell of the old leather. The boat ride was just as enjoyable. The boat was an old paddlewheel built in 1898, called the SS *Moyie*. We loved to hear the paddle on the water, feel the wind on our face, and smell the fresh water. Taking the boat ride was as close as we could get to being on the Nova Scotia ocean!

Glenn and I took turns taking Thomas to the many appointments for assessments. I was working part-time and tried to schedule appointments when I was off. When that was not possible, Glenn would go. Most of the day-to-day care was my responsibility—bathing, dressing, driving to daycare, and making meals—but that was okay with me. Glenn and the boys had their time together while I was making meals and doing housework.

Glenn:

Our little house that I had found was temporary. It was small and on a busy street. We knew we would be there short-term. We soon found another house that better suited our needs. We sold the little house in a day and moved to a much larger two-story house with a decent-sized yard. The boys had their own bedrooms, and the new house also had a formal dining room and a finished basement, where the boys had room to play.

A Frustrated Toddler

Thomas had been walking for about six months by the time he turned two. He didn't have any strength in his arms to stop a fall, so his forehead had several bruises from the number of tumbles he took. I am sure he was beginning to get discouraged. We were able to get a special soft helmet made to protect his forehead, but the bruises still appeared.

He was only beginning to talk, and he would point to his forehead and say, "Mommy, owie, owie!" We always thought it was because of the bruises from his falls until we took him to the hospital and discovered the poor guy had a massive sinus infection. He was on a liquid antibiotic for six weeks. Sadly, the use of the antibiotics led to major tooth decay, and so he then had to go in for day surgery for dental work and have a cap placed on his tooth.

Glenn:

There was one exercise I made Thomas do that he never forgave me for. The doctors encouraged Kathy and me to make him practise rolling on the floor. I would put him on the carpet in the family room and tell him he had to do a certain number of rolls before he could stop. At the time, we didn't realize that rolling on the carpet was burning off his eyebrows. For many years, he did not have much for eyebrows. Thomas reminded me often that this was my fault.

Jamie and I loved to exchange back rubs, and Thomas wanted to get in on that, too! He would insist that I sit in front of him on the floor, and he would rub me with his feet. Little did he know that this, too, was making his muscles more flexible.

As we were getting settled in Calgary, I was teaching in the daytime and selling clothes at home parties, part-time. Glenn was not so happy about the sales job. However, it was an outlet, a chance to get away for a couple of hours, and an opportunity to make more of a financial contribution. I'm sure I spent more on the clothes for myself than making any profit, though.

Glenn had, at this point, taken over his father's masonry business. It was a stressful time for him and his dad. Glenn's dad had made the choice to retire and to let Glenn and his partner buy out Hans and Hans, the two owners. Yes, the previous owners were both named Hans. Glenn's partner actually bought out Glenn's dad, and Glenn bought out the other Hans. I am not sure Glenn's dad was ready to retire.

Glenn, wanting to make his dad feel needed and wanting advice, took him to an important meeting one day. He asked his dad to be an observer and to give advice should he need it. Hans ignored all of Glenn's wishes and instead, spoke up at the meeting giving his opinion and pushing Glenn aside as if he was still in charge.

Glenn and his partner even invited the two Hanses and their wives to attend a national masonry conference in Hawaii and paid for the entire trip. In the end, the two Hanses were paid out in full over the years, perks included.

🐢 🐢 🐢 🐢 🐢

In May of 1999, Thomas was three years old. Glenn and I had the opportunity to attend the national masonry convention that month. Certain parts of the conference were offered to spouses, including some excursions, so I was pleased I was able to book off work to attend. We were also happy that the convention was to be held in Halifax, Nova Scotia. This meant that we could sneak in a visit with my dad, who was eighty-nine by this time. He was still living independently in his home and still driving. As luck would have it, Dad needed to go for a driver's test while we were there in order to renew his driver's license. It was convenient for my sister in my hometown

A Frustrated Toddler

that we were there to take Dad for his test. Sue had been caring for Dad over the years, and so taking him for the driving test was the least Glenn and I could do for her.

While Glenn and I drove Dad for his test, I thought back to Dad's checkered driving history. In my view, my dad had never been a great driver. One morning, during my school years when Dad would often drive me to school, he put on his seat belt, put the car in reverse, and stepped on the gas pedal. He plowed the car through our garage door, forgetting he had backed it into the driveway the night before. The garage door was bent in every direction and ripped off its hinges, damaged beyond repair. He also wasn't great at watching for stop signs and would often drive through them without so much as a wave hello. And Dad loved his gas pedal. He had a habit of putting the car into second gear and revving it up before shifting gears. And that was with a manual car. It's amazing that my four sisters and I are alive.

On the day of the test, Glenn and I watched as Dad pulled out of the Department of Vehicles. The examiner had his head down, reading his clipboard. We noticed that Dad didn't have his seat belt on, he didn't signal for the turn, and he drove straight past the stop sign. We waited patiently and nervously for them to return. When they did, Dad was not happy with the report. He had twenty-seven traffic violations during his test. The examiner told my dad that he could no longer drive unless he took a written test along with a new driver's test.

This was a big blow. Here he was at eighty-nine, losing his independence. He could no longer go wherever he wanted whenever he wanted, and it was sad to see my dad at this stage of his life losing those freedoms. Thomas was at the other end of the spectrum fighting to gain independence, one step at a time.

In one afternoon Dad had lost his license. With no warning, he was relegated to sitting at home, relying on anyone who might chauffeur him on his whim. He was rebellious, though, and started to drive without permission. With this being a small town in Nova Scotia, everyone knew everyone, and soon word got back to my sister that our dad was driving without a license. My sister and her husband had one of the local police officers show up at Dad's house to help encourage him not to drive, to remind him that he did not have a license, and to hopefully put a little scare into him. That didn't work. Dad kept sneaking out. Before too long, my sister had to take the car away from my dad's house. It was a devastating blow to my dad.

Glenn:

When we moved to Calgary, Thomas was able to walk a little bit on his own two feet. But after five or six steps, he would fall, sometimes on his face, which really hurt him both physically and emotionally.

After a month in Calgary, Thomas cried out one day, "I don't want to walk anymore. I can't do it." No matter how much we talked to him, he was not to be persuaded. We never saw Thomas walk again. That was really a hard day for me, to never to see one of my boys walk again.

Thomas could be a really stubborn little man, and when he made a decision, nothing you could say or do was going to change his mind. In hindsight, this stubbornness would serve him well in the future and propel him toward great success. Thomas would not take no for an answer, and he would attack problems head-on.

The doctors recommended that we order a wheelchair for Thomas. Choosing a wheelchair definitely was beyond our level of understanding and outside of our comfort zone. When we went for the initial meeting with the supplier, they asked us a million questions. Which brand would we like? What kind of cushion would we like? Which armrests do we think are best? We had no idea what questions to ask or what type of wheelchair to request. They had a few samples of wheelchairs for young children. The chairs all had different features. Short, tall, taller, different seats, different wheels. All we could do was to ask for their expertise and hope for the best.

It took about six months for the wheelchair to arrive. It cost approximately $4,000 to purchase one independently, but thanks to Alberta Aids to Daily Living (AADL), a government program that provides funding for

A Frustrated Toddler

medical equipment and supplies to Albertans with long-term disabilities or chronic or terminal illnesses, we paid $500. The only problem was that the committee members who approved the subsidies looked at files only; they never met clients in person. They decided what was best based on what they saw on paper. Here was little three-year-old Thomas with low muscle tone. The AADL grant committee deemed that Thomas was strong enough to propel himself great distances in this manual chair. However, Thomas only had the strength and endurance to push himself about five hundred feet. As a result, we did receive a push wheelchair in which Thomas was seated comfortably; however, the back handles of the chair for someone else to push fit the height of Jamie, a nine-year-old. We had to spend another $500 for extended handrails, which would fit an adult. It seemed ludicrous to us, as parents, that the committee would not recognize the needs of the client and would also not consider the repercussions for the family.

It was, however, the start of some independence for all of us when Thomas's push wheelchair arrived. Instead of being pushed in an oversized stroller, Thomas could use the chair to move himself around for short distances.

We continued with regular six-month visits to the neuromuscular clinic. Around the time we got Thomas's first wheelchair, he was seizing up. He had started getting *contractures* (permanent tightening of the muscles, tendons, and skin) at the age of three, and they were getting worse. It was becoming more difficult for him to straighten his legs. His tendons were tightening up, and he required "routine surgery" to lengthen his tendons. The thought of the surgery was scary for all of us, but we had to believe that the doctors were right. We planned for him to have the surgery early in the summer after the school year ended so that I was able to be home to care for him.

The surgery was scheduled for the first week of July 2000 when Thomas was four. The doctor told us that it would be a long operation, between four and eight hours. We arrived early at the hospital to get Thomas settled. Glenn, Jamie, and I were able to go into the prep area with him. He was scared but happy we were with him, and he definitely was not looking forward to being put under. Glenn, Jamie, and I finally had to leave him, and we went to the waiting area.

After only a couple of hours, we heard our names over the PA system. We were terrified that something was wrong. The three of us went to the surgical area and found the doctor holding a clipboard. He said Thomas was okay and he had done as much as he could, but the tendons just would not lengthen any further. The doctor explained that it was like a garden hose being stretched—they could only go so far.

Poor Thomas had two heavy casts, one on each leg from his entire foot up to his groin. He was glossy-eyed, and I was scared to move him in any way for fear of causing him pain. Thomas, surprisingly, was in pretty good spirits. He was spoiled with visitors, flowers, stuffed animals, and chocolate. After a few days, the hospital staff tried to wean him off the morphine, but it was too soon. He was in excruciating pain, and they immediately put him back on the morphine. It was at least another twenty-four hours before they could try again.

After his discharge, we were given a standing frame that Thomas was supposed to spend a few of hours in every day to help straighten the tendons and build strength. This was a huge challenge. Thomas really hated the standing frame. He didn't like being strapped in, being forced to stand, and feeling so uncomfortable. He had to stand in the frame as long as he could endure, strapped in at the waist, hips, knees, and feet. These exercises were certainly no fun for a four-year-old. Thomas desperately wanted to go and play and not be in this horrible contraption. We tried to be creative and find toys and activities he could use and play with while doing his time in the frame. The casts were heavy and awkward, even for Glenn and me. It was a challenge to carry his body with two lead legs, without causing him pain, and get him safely from point A to point B.

One of Glenn's friends, Steve, is a finishing carpenter. During this time, Steve built a special table for Thomas that fit a large playing area featuring Thomas the Tank Engine. The table allowed him to play with his trains and village while spending that time in the frame. Steve had gone so far as to make the tabletop reversible so we could also use it as a coffee table in our living room. It was a thoughtful and special gift.

A Frustrated Toddler

At the same time, Glenn decided to give the boys a treat. Without telling me, he took Jamie out to find a new puppy. They came home a few hours later with a Brittany spaniel named Brandy. She was a beautiful dog, energetic and curious, with razor-sharp teeth. She needed constant care, though, as all puppies do. She got into the garbage and needed walks, baths, and training. If we went out for a couple of hours, we would return to the house and find destruction everywhere. She chewed on everything she could get her teeth and jaws on, and she ruined our white living room furniture. We still have the evidence. I certainly didn't have the time for any dog obedience courses. I was at my limit doing my best to keep Thomas happy along with completing all the daily chores of running a house.

After two or three months, Glenn realized how much more work Brandy was and that we were definitely not ready for a puppy. We were relieved to find out that our cousins were willing to take Brandy on. Over the years, every time we went to visit our cousins, Brandy was there to greet us. There was a bond, and fortunately for us, that was enough.

Six weeks after his surgery, Thomas was relieved to get the casts off, but next he had to be fitted for knee-foot orthoses (KFOs). A knee-foot orthosis is a support that spans the entire leg in an effort to stabilize the joints and assist the muscles of the leg. These plastic supports strapped around his shins and feet, and he had to wear them twenty-four hours a day. Since these supports made Thomas's legs and feet bigger, we had to find footwear and clothing that easily slid on and off over those extra apparatus.

For years after the surgery, Thomas complained about the sensitivity around his groin area from the incisions that were needed for the surgery. I always had to be careful around there when washing him. He never did get rid of the scars left by the surgery. There were six scars: two at the groin, two behind his kneecaps, and two on his ankles.

Around the same time that Thomas started to wear the KFOs, his wrists started to seize. His hands were slowly contracting—bending and curling up under his wrists. From the time that he was around six, Thomas had played the piano. In fact, he played until his fingers and wrists started to curl under and into his forearms. It was tough to watch this happen to his hands, especially as a musician myself. I struggled watching him lose the ability to make music. Now, not only did he have the KFOs to wear, but he had to wear splints for his hands at night, all of which made it terribly uncomfortable to sleep.

One of the aids we acquired early on for Thomas was his "arm pillow." His arm pillow is (I still have it) a rectangular, brown, fuzzy pillow, offering him physical but also psychological security and comfort. Tucking the pillow into his side between his chest and arm while he was sleeping or resting ensured his arm didn't press against his body. The pillow made him super comfy and quickly became a part of him. It fit his body well, with his arm resting over top of it. Psychologically, it was like a proverbial security blanket.

For the most part, Thomas seemed to avoid the seasonal colds and flus that were going around, but he had the strangest, most inexplicable ailments now and then. One evening as I was brushing his teeth, I noticed strange white bumps on his tongue. We had no idea what caused these, so off to the Children's Hospital ER we went. Thomas and I sat in the ER for over three hours waiting. When the doctor finally came in and looked at his tongue, he laughed and said, "Oh! That is *geographical tongue*. His tongue will change formations like little white mountains and valleys. Nothing to worry about. It doesn't cause any harm. You can go home!"

Schooling Begins

Since Thomas was born in January, he could begin school when he was four. We believed that an earlier start would do no harm and decided to enroll him in a privately-run preschool program when he was only three. Because of his muscular dystrophy, Thomas qualified for a Program Unit Funding (PUF) grant, a program serving kids in Alberta with severe abilities. PUF grants are available for children ages two years eight months old to six years of age who need educational support. Thomas began working one-on-one with an aide, and this work became a vital source of lifelong additional support outside of his home and family. Fortunately, the preschool was located in the same building as the before-and-after school care program, which he also attended. He was in the before-school daycare, went downstairs to the preschool, and then returned to the daycare later in the day. We were able to drop him off on our way to work and pick him up at the end of our day.

At times, Thomas exhibited peculiar physical symptoms, which were confusing to his caregivers at the daycare. We received many phone calls from the staff during his early years at the preschool telling us that Thomas was running a fever and that we needed to pick him up and take him home. We finally realized that Thomas's ears became red and hot. When the caregivers took his temperature, they utilized an ear thermometer, which would often read 102–104°F. We eventually figured out that there was no fever at all. Thomas simply had hot ears.

All in all, he had a jump-start on schooling and an important early start to socializing. He was able to progress in his reading abilities and took part in drawing, colouring, and crafts. Building trust with each educational assistant became a key factor in Thomas's progress and happiness. A year later, he "graduated" from this early program with pomp and circumstance, proudly wearing his hat and gown.

Glenn:

The annual dentist checkups for Thomas were always an issue. We realized that the regular dentist was not set up to meet his needs, so we had to seek someone who was able to tend to a child with special needs. Thomas couldn't fit comfortably in a regular chair. Beanbag cushions, and other aids were needed to help him settle into a chair in order to get the dental work done. Eventually, we found that the best dentist for Thomas was at the Children's Hospital. There, he had regular checkups every six months.

At one point, Thomas had three cavities, so we made an appointment for the following week. Kathy asked me to take him to the appointment, so I started to work on his mindset, talking to him about the importance of having his teeth fixed, explaining what the procedure would involve, and assuring him that all would be okay. I wanted his head to be in the right place when we got there, and it worked!

We arrived at the dentist's office, and when it was Thomas's turn, he was pretty nervous. But I reassured him I was going to stay with him the whole time, and the less fuss he made, the faster we could get out of there. The dentist started her work, and after about fifteen minutes, she came over and whispered in my ear that Thomas had not three but seven cavities. She told me she would try to fix them all without telling him and see how many she could do before Thomas got too restless. She managed to fill six of the seven.

When it came to Thomas's education, we were up against multiple battles throughout the years: fighting for aide time in his classrooms, getting proper bathroom facilities in his schools, getting access to handicapped buses during school hours, and even dealing with a couple of bullying situations.

Many of the school issues had to be handled carefully. I was an employee of the school board, and I couldn't "cross the line." Glenn constantly reminded me to bite my tongue, use diplomacy, and "make lemonade" out of what we'd been given. I knew the system. I knew the channels to go through, but family came first in my eyes. I have always remembered a speech from one of the chief superintendents of the Calgary school board saying, "Family comes first." Can you imagine a child in a wheelchair who is incapable of managing his personal hygiene having a successful experience in school? I have always felt bad for parents with children with special needs, especially those who don't know where to turn for help and don't know when to not take no for an answer.

In September 2000 Thomas began a regular kindergarten class in the public school system. Consultants gathered to assess his needs. The school system provided occupational therapists, physiotherapists, and speech therapists along with a special-needs strategist. Thomas's cognitive abilities were never an issue, and he definitely had no problems communicating, but he needed help physically. From the beginning, Thomas had difficulty participating in any physical activities. He was unable to walk on his own and, except for the time in a standing frame, spent most of the day in his wheelchair. His fine motor skills were also challenged. The assistants gave him occasional stretching exercises during the school day to keep him limber. We wanted to prevent his limbs from contracting and stiffening.

Thomas tired easily throughout any given day, especially if he was required to raise his arms or move a pencil to paper. His body was incapable of regaining strength throughout his school years, but he learned to listen well. He retained so much information and required little repetition or practice to understand a concept. He remembered the correct spelling of words and quickly learned the multiplication tables. His mental math was extraordinary. Throughout his school years, Thomas missed countless school days because of appointments with doctors and physical therapists, yet he never fell behind.

Gregg, Thomas's Best Friend:

One of my earliest memories of Thomas goes back to when we were in kindergarten. It was pajama day at school so I was wearing my PJs. However, because this was not a kindergarten activity, we were not supposed to participate. I was the only person in class wearing pajamas, and this really embarrassed and upset me. Thomas had brought his pajamas with him but was not wearing them. When he saw how upset I was, he changed into his pajamas so I wasn't the only child wearing them. I will never forget this caring act and his willingness to stand out just to help someone.

🐢 🐢 🐢 🐢 🐢

In the summer of 2000, Glenn and I took the boys to Nova Scotia for a three-week summer holiday. Of course, we had to plan for special seating on the plane and a vehicle in Nova Scotia to handle the wheelchair. We planned to make the trip as convenient as possible for Thomas and his mobility. He was still quite young and, for us, he was easy to pick up and move. But Thomas needed twenty-four-hour care.

Somehow, we managed quite well on the flight from Calgary. Thomas was thrilled to be on a plane. The flight attendants checked regularly to see if we needed anything. They brought crayons and a colouring book with pictures of planes. They gave the boys a model airplane and even arranged for them to see the cockpit with the captain. The washroom was still easily assessable because of Thomas's size. The boys were as excited as we were about getting a change of scenery.

Our home base was the family cottage, which my dad had put in the five sisters' names. Glenn and I were able to book the cottage for the month of July. It was a one-floor cottage on stilts, which made everything easily accessible for us with Thomas. I'd spent my childhood summers there, only twenty minutes away from our home in New Glasgow. The cottage was a totally different world from Uptown, as we called New Glasgow. It was a short drive from home and yet, we enjoyed the smell of the ocean, the low and high tides, and the sandbar, which was a sort of heaven with its untouched sand dunes. The cottage is not insulated, so living there in the winter was, and still is, unheard of. It did have a flat roof, and so when it rained, we could hear the rain as it fell, rattling, giving a feeling of calmness. And the storms ... oh the storms ... To watch them coming in from over the ocean with their power! Seeing the lightning and hearing the thunder, feeling the cottage shake. These were my memories that I hoped to share with Glenn and the boys.

We made the cottage our home for the month and spent most of our time on the beach. We built sandcastles, and we felt the salt from the ocean on our skin. We also took multiple day trips to the surrounding communities, taking in the maritime festivals and celebrations that happen during the summer, checking out antique stores, and gorging on all the seafood we could find.

After exploring Halifax, we made our way along the coast, hitting the colourful small towns along the way: Chester, Mahone Bay, and Lunenburg. Lunenburg was especially beautiful with its houses painted in almost every colour of the rainbow. It is also the home of the famous schooner, the *Bluenose*. Unfortunately, the *Bluenose* was not in Lunenburg while we were there, so we consoled ourselves by picking up souvenirs, stopping for fresh, homemade fish chowder at a quaint restaurant, and window-shopping throughout the town.

One of our favourite stops was a little restaurant on the water along the roadside not far from Chester. They had picnic tables outside where customers could enjoy their lunch. The boys ordered shrimp, scallops (deep fried, of course), and one of Thomas's favourites: fish and chips. It was one of the best meals we had in our three weeks in Nova Scotia. Everything was so fresh, and the servings were plentiful. We all enjoyed watching the greedy seagulls trying to snatch a piece of our lunch. The boys were throwing pieces of French fries in the air for the seagulls to catch. The smell of the ocean and the heat from the sun added to the beauty, and simply enjoying this family time was magical; it was good for the soul.

My sister Sue and brother-in-law Bruce had something they wanted to talk to us about while we were visiting their home. They told me and Glenn that they wanted to look after the boys for us if we wanted to take an overnight trip to Halifax. Glenn and I jumped at the idea. We had twenty-four hours away, holding hands, taking in the sights, walking through some of the places of my childhood, and experiencing the modern changes in the city.

When we returned to my sister's, we were, of course, so happy to see the boys. They had had a wonderful time being spoiled by their aunt and uncle. My sister came to me with a hug and said, "I know it was only twenty-four hours, but I now have an appreciation of what you do every day." To this day, I have never forgotten Sue's words. I was so surprised and touched that someone took the time to acknowledge what Glenn and I were living day-to-day. It is always comforting to know that someone else recognizes how far beyond you go in a day.

When Jamie was in grade 6 and Thomas was in kindergarten, Jamie had to do a science fair project. We had heard about a possible "cure," an improvement of sorts for people with physical disabilities, which involved applying ostrich oil to one's body. We all hoped that this would be beneficial to Thomas, perhaps helping him gain mobility and improve his muscles. Jamie decided to take this topic on as a science fair project. He found a rancher not far outside of the city who raised ostriches, and we made arrangements to visit his ranch. The gentleman was very kind. He gave both Jamie and Thomas a tour of his property and surroundings, showing them his many ostriches, the fields they were kept in, the barns, his supply of ostrich meat packaged for sale, and the jars of oil he had produced. The owner gave Jamie a cracked ostrich egg—an empty shell—for his project and answered the many questions Jamie had at the time. We purchased some of the oil to take home for the experiment.

Jamie made charts, diagrams, and posters depicting facts about the benefits of ostrich oil. He took measurements, made graphs, and took pictures for his project. In the end, his project was not judged as worthy to move on to the provincial science fair, but Jamie wasn't concerned about winning at a higher level. His goal was to help Thomas, hoping that the oil would make a difference.

Jamie had put so much work into his project and we were all hoping the ostrich oil would help Thomas regain some strength. However, the oil stank and, more importantly, did not really seem to make any difference in Thomas's physical well-being. We ended up throwing out a lot of bedding, clothes, and towels, as we could not get rid of the smell of the oil. It had been a stretch to hope that it might work, but we were all willing to try.

There were times when I was able to become a child again; Thomas kept me young. Whenever he was invited to a birthday party, I took him and helped him maneuver through the party. I had so much joy in sharing his fun, whether it was swimming in a wave pool at a recreational centre, playing the party games, or simply enjoying hot dogs.

We went to numerous swimming parties; saw *Fantasia 2000* and *The SpongeBob Squarepants Movie* in 3-D; visited the science centre, the zoo, and community pools; and attended child-friendly plays at a number of centres throughout the city. Everything Thomas did, I did with him. There were several times he was not invited to a classmate's party simply because he was in a wheelchair. I understood the hesitancy of the parents, but I felt so bad for Thomas when he wasn't included. I always tried to be an advocate for him so that he felt included in whatever was happening. Perhaps this was the beginning of our family's larger advocacy efforts over the years.

In spite of Thomas's personal obstacles, his years in elementary school hold a lot of fond memories. They started when Thomas entered grade 1 in a split class, a combination of both grades 1 and 2. He enjoyed being in the split class because it gave him an insight into what was expected in grade 2. I remember that he learned to spell the word "because" after he witnessed a second grader being reprimanded for misspelling it on a test.

Taken from Thomas's grade 1 portfolio, age five:

My goals are to not talk and get my work done. I should listen to my teachers, not argue and become stubborn and refuse to move [sic].

I should not talk and work quietly [sic].

I should pay attention and less talking [sic].

Now I like writing more than colouring!

Challenges with School

When Thomas was in grade 2, he broke down crying one night as I was putting him to bed. I asked him what was wrong. This was one of the occasions when Thomas had kept his feelings bottled up for months. He confessed that there was a little girl that was bullying him. The next morning, I was at his school.

It turned out the little girl who was saying mean things to him about being in the wheelchair had problems of her own. Her mental capacity was low, and she was a special-needs child with major issues. The staff at school explained the situation to me and spoke with the student. Thomas was never bothered again by her, but he felt so bad about getting her into trouble.

Gregg:

Thomas and I were just like any other friends, which included staying up late on sleepovers. This happened more times than can be counted; just ask Kathy, who had to deal with us!

When we were around eight years old, we were having a sleepover. Kathy had already put us to bed, but we decided that we were hungry and needed snacks. It was too late to ask for any because we were supposed to be sleeping. To solve our problem, we decided to get our own snacks. I helped Thomas out of his bed and onto the floor. At this point, Thomas was a tremendous "scooter." It was relatively easy for him to go short distances scootching on the floor. This ability allowed him to move from the bed, down the hall, and to the top of the stairs. These stairs were just another challenge along the way to reaching some snacks. We made our way down the stairs one step at a time, trying to keep the noise of Thomas sliding from one step to the next to a minimum. Thomas made it halfway down the staircase when we decided it would be a good idea if he waited there while I continued on by myself to complete our snack mission. I managed to reach the cupboard containing all the goodies, but that was as far as I got before I was caught red-handed. Kathy must have heard us after all.

It turned out this was a good thing because Thomas and I had failed to think about how we were going to get him back up the stairs. Neither of us had reached the age to fully think things through before putting a plan into action. Luckily, Kathy let us off easy.

For Thomas to succeed in his school life, there were a lot of factors to take into consideration. An adult always had to be available for Thomas during his school day. Outside supervision was difficult, especially on cold, snowy days. His wheelchair would get stuck in the snow. It took at least seven minutes to dress for the weather, and the one-on-one time an educational assistant spent with Thomas would not allow for the supervision schedule to work outside over the recess period. As much as Thomas wanted to be with his friends, he spent many recesses inside at the office.

Lunch was also always an issue. He required assistance not only in getting his lunch out, but over the years, he progressively required more help with feeding. He didn't want to be singled out or isolated. He wanted to be with his friends when they had their lunch. However, the educational assistants often took their lunch break at the same time, and so Thomas would be told he had to leave class early in order for an assistant to help him eat. He understood why he had to eat on his own, but it was tough for a young boy to leave his class early, miss what was happening in the class, and eat with an adult, without the company of his friends.

Field trips also always presented a concern. The research prior to the class trip was a struggle in itself. Was the venue wheelchair friendly? Had a handicapped bus been booked? Would there be a wheelchair-accessible washroom on site? Was the educational assistant allowed to go with Thomas on the entire trip? Many school trips required us to hire a caregiver to accompany Thomas at an additional cost. We did not have a problem with that; we could afford it at the time, and it was more important that Thomas was able to attend the field trip. On occasion, we had the caregiver drive Thomas in our own van to and from a field trip so he could participate, or either Glenn or I would take the day off to attend.

A plethora of paperwork was always needed for Thomas to attend field trips. Filling these forms out was tiresome, even on the best of days, especially when it came to liability. We basically had to sign our child's life away. If outside help was required, there was more paperwork. And more questions. Did our caregiver have security checks approved by the school board? Additional forms needed to be filled out if our van was being driven for medical reasons. More information was required regarding car insurance, and emergency contacts for the caregiver. We had already checked out our personal caregivers. We were comfortable with the people we chose to be with Thomas. The additional security checks for the school board took up to six weeks to be approved, though, sometimes even more. We understood their legal obligations, but at times, it was a bit much.

Thomas wanted to be included in all class activities. In his eyes, he was normal. For one field trip, we were informed that if there was a fire, Thomas would actually be left alone, sitting in his chair on the fifth floor until the fire department arrived to carry him down the stairs. Glenn actually took time off to accompany Thomas on that particular field trip. I couldn't ever imagine leaving a child behind. However, there is a policy in place with the school board: no teacher is ever to pick up a child, especially one with special needs.

Educational assistants came and went. Thomas had ten different assistants in his elementary years, not to mention the substitutes. Some assistants found other jobs. Others moved away. There were those who simply were not meant to be assistants and were either let go or they quit. Thomas would, at times, feel frustrated when his regular assistant was not able to go to work. A substitute meant a difficult day for him, teaching a new person his needs in the classroom or washroom. He spent the day building his trust with the person assigned to work with him.

He was fortunate to be assigned an outstanding educational assistant in grade 3. Crystal, a young, vibrant woman, saw Thomas's potential and pushed him in his schooling. She collaborated with him to publish a guide for teachers and assistants on how to support students with disabilities in gym class. He worked with Crystal to come up with ideas on how he could be a contributing participant in the gym while achieving his personal goals. The booklet they published helped inform others on how students in wheelchairs could become more involved in the gym class activities.

Riding the school bus was a concern from day one. Each September, we didn't know which bus would pick Thomas up or what time it was supposed to arrive until a week before classes began. There were a couple of years when the school board utilized the city HandiBus service. This specialized service is designed to allow those who have wheelchairs or other mobility devices to travel throughout the city. It was not the best service for punctuality. A twenty-minute window could be expected, even on a good day. Throw in the number of drivers assigned to the job, and you have instant chaos every day.

Glenn and I worried how the drivers could manage to help Thomas with him being so young, especially during grades 1, 2, and 3. If the bus was late, we were on the phone trying to find out an estimated time of arrival. I was usually the one to see him off, but I had to get to my school on time, as well. Sometimes we had to phone our neighbours and ask them to hang out with Thomas until the bus arrived. And at the end of the school day, Thomas was often left sitting alone by the school's front door waiting for the bus. The school staff said that they were not responsible for watching him while he waited. Sometimes I would come home expecting Thomas to be there, only to find out he was still at school waiting to be picked up.

Jamie was getting older. He was gaining strength playing soccer and doing other sports at school. He was also growing a greater understanding of and appreciation for his brother and his needs. As Jamie matured, he was getting taller and more muscular, and he reached a point when he was able to pick up Thomas on his own and carry him from point A to B. That was a great help to me.

He truly cared for Thomas. You could see it in his smile and demeanor. Jamie would grab a book that Thomas needed, feed him a snack, or give him a drink of water. Later on, he even assisted with Thomas's washroom needs. Granted, toilet duty was not Jamie's favourite thing to do, but he sucked it up without too much complaining. Thomas would often tease Jamie about his "bum wiping techniques."

Even if they had their squabbles, Jamie also included Thomas in his endeavours with his friends and in choosing what activities to play. The two of them played Xbox together and online with friends. Many hours were spent in battles. They went to hockey games, movies, and concerts.

We decided that the two-story house was too difficult to manage in terms of carrying Thomas up and down the stairs since the bedrooms were all upstairs and the playroom was in the basement. Thomas was growing and was getting heavier to carry. We considered an elevator, but the cost of installing one was going to be over $40,000. Added to that, the logistics of installing an elevator in the house seemed impossible. Since this wasn't a viable option for us, Glenn started doing his own research, and we called our realtor to help in our search for a new house.

One day Glenn saw a for-sale ad on the Internet for a large bungalow on a lake. It seemed, again, so far out of our reach at twice the cost of the house we were currently living in. But we thought that it would be wonderful for us as a family because it was a bungalow. With the main living space on one floor, all rooms would be accessible. Thomas would have lots of space to move around with his wheelchair, and there was added room for Jamie to have some private space as he was getting older. It would also be an investment for our future. Lake property would only grow in value. The house was such a wonderful prospect that we shared our excitement with Glenn's parents, even though it was still a dream.

We thought about the house for a long time and kept crunching the numbers. We had enough for a down payment but not enough to escape additional financing. We needed 25 per cent down to avoid CMHC financing. Glenn's mother Alice called a good week later and said she and Hans felt it was a good purchase for us. She said she would loan us the extra

Challenges with School

money we needed so we could save on the financing. We put an offer in, subject to the sale of our home. In turn, the seller of the lake home sent his agent to see if our present home was actually sellable. In less than twenty-four hours, we managed to make our home a seller's showpiece. We sold it after eight days, confirmed the offer on the new house, and on May 1, 2003, moved into our gorgeous new lakefront home. It still seemed like a dream, and Glenn did not sleep well for the first three months after the move, worried about making the payments. In the end, we managed to pay Glenn's parents back for the loan in just over a year, and we also purchased a travel voucher for Hans and Alice to thank them for all of their help.

Glenn redesigned much of the house to make it work for Thomas. He consulted professional renovators and home builders about handicapped washrooms. They told him that they did those types of renos all the time, but in the end, they did not really know any industry guidelines. They would do whatever they were told to do for a handicapped washroom, and so just as they did for all their other customers, they did what we asked them to do and left it at that. Glenn checked into an overhead rail system to carry Thomas in a sling to the washroom from his bed, and he looked into installing a drive-in shower that allowed Thomas to enter with a shower chair. Glenn pretty much figured out everything on his own. Anything he couldn't do, we hired someone to come and do according to Glenn's specs.

There wasn't much help out there to assist us in the planning of a special-needs home. There were no manuals to consult, no support groups to give us suggestions. Most of the construction was based on Glenn's knowledge and experience of living with Thomas, and we hoped that everything we were doing would work.

The house had two bedrooms off a hallway with a shared Jack and Jill washroom between them. We removed the tub and tore open and moved the walls. The washroom needed the extra space for the wheelchair. One bedroom had a large closet, which became part of the new bathroom. Glenn found a company that custom-made a drive-in shower, large enough to fit both Thomas in a shower wheelchair and a second person, who would do Thomas's scrubbing. The bathroom door was extra wide, floor to ceiling, to accommodate the wheelchair. Above the top of the door, Glenn created a notch in the door frame to allow tracking to run from Thomas's bed into the washroom and over the toilet while still allowing the door to be closed. Thomas now had the sling and overhead rail system to carry him from his bed to the toilet and back again.

An important point we needed to factor in was the height of Thomas's chair so that the vanity was open underneath for the chair to fit. Glenn searched to find just the right faucet for the sink. The faucet came straight up, then out, allowing the water to fall in the centre of the sink. This was a crucial detail, as Thomas required someone to wash his hands for him.

Most of the financial assistance available to renovate for a special-needs child was for families based on one income; there was nothing for a two-income family. That seemed unfair, but we did manage to get some help from the local Shriner's club. They paid for half of the cost of the power lift from the garage to get Thomas into the house. This powered elevation system was placed in the garage to allow Thomas to drive his wheelchair onto a platform, which raised him to the landing in the garage, which led into the house. The only other financial help given was by a drywall company called Elktone Interiors. The owner, Cliff Francis, determined that they would not charge for Thomas's bedroom and bathroom during their part of the renovations. Such generosity from both agencies was very much appreciated.

The entire renovation for Thomas's bathroom and bedroom took about two months. It was a great relief to have it done and it better suited to Thomas's needs.

The summer of 2003 was an eventful one. To begin with, the mosquitoes had discovered Thomas. One afternoon when Hans and Alice were looking after him, Thomas was enjoying blowing bubbles on the deck with Grandma and Grandpa. Unfortunately, Thomas got a mosquito bite on his foot. He reacted so badly to the bite that his foot swelled to three times its size and he had to be put on antibiotics. After that, Thomas always freaked when mosquitoes and bees came along. He was never really able to swat them away, and his anxiety over seeing them only worsened as he got older.

We had just moved into our new home and were busy painting, cleaning, and unpacking. Soon after we moved, Glenn's parents also decided to take the entire Sorensen family, fourteen people, on a tour of their native country, Denmark. The boys and I were so excited to be able to see our

Challenges with School

Danish relatives and take in Denmark's beautiful landscape and architecture. The four of us stayed in a summer house with Glenn's sister and her family. The boys were in their element! We went to Legoland, saw the tall ships in Aarhus, had multiple family dinners with our Danish relatives, and spent time on the beach. Thomas especially loved Danish ice cream. He couldn't get enough. He took every opportunity to indulge. One of his favourites was a Smarties ice cream that was served in a push-up tube on a stick. He would moan with pleasure with every bite.

Glenn:

One day of our vacation was spent at The Old Town, which is similar to Calgary's Heritage Park but much older and much more developed. Thomas was in a push chair, and nothing was wheelchair friendly. I maneuvered Thomas and his chair through the cobblestone streets, lifting him in and out of the chair and carrying him around inside the buildings. It was a long, hot, tiring day. At the end of it, one of the relatives asked, "How are you doing?" I replied that I was tired of pushing, lifting, and carrying Thomas. My back is killing me! "Yes, I know," she said, "I have kids, too." She had no idea.

Through all of this—the move, the vacation, and normal life beyond those events of that summer—Glenn was my better half. We were a team. I took care of the day-to-day tasks like getting Thomas ready for school, making the school lunches, helping Thomas shower, and assisting him with his bedtime routine including toothbrushing. I had a collection of bathing suits for every day of the week, and I always wore one when giving Thomas a shower.

Glenn always appeared the minute I asked for help. He carried Thomas from place to place and took him to the washroom. And that was frequently. I laugh about the hours they spent in the washroom making jokes or talking about life. Thomas would indicate his need to use the toilet by saying, "Dad, I have to drop the kids off at the pool," or "A turtle head is poking out." Thomas was not the fastest in the washroom. He needed time, and he also sometimes needed support to hold him upright while on the toilet. Glenn was patient.

Glenn:

He loved a great debate, and if it was about something he was passionate about, he was like a dog with a bone. When I was home, I was usually the one who took Thomas to the washroom. When I arrived home from work, I would hear, "Thomas needs the washroom," or "Thomas is waiting for you."

When Thomas was on the toilet, he wanted me to stay with him. We had a stool on wheels for the caregivers to use, so I would sit there. Thomas loved to talk. It didn't matter if I had things to do; I was there for him. We often had great discussions in the washroom. At times it smelled so bad, though, I would ask Thomas for a courtesy flush. Thomas had a great sense of humour and could make people laugh in most situations, including when using the bathroom.

Fall 2003 approached and along with it, school. Thomas loved his grade 3 teacher, Mrs. Hannah. She was an older teacher, kind and gentle, and she had total control of her classroom. Mrs. Hannah was understanding and was always looking out for Thomas. She kept in close contact with us to make sure Thomas's needs were being met, and she kept her classroom arranged so that he felt comfortable moving around and had plenty of space to do so.

Mrs. Hannah's comments on Thomas's Grade 3 report card:

Thomas's positive involvement and caring attitude make him well-liked and respected by his peers. Thomas works hard at improving his independent reading skills. After reading a book numerous times, he often seeks out a peer or an adult to listen to him read aloud. Thomas responds [to what he's] reading with examples from his own life and by making connections to other books we or he has read.

Thomas self-selects writing topics and ideas. He engages promptly in writing activities. His narrative writing shows character and theme development. I am scribing some of his most recent picture books, and he is very enthusiastic about the results so far.

Thomas looks forward to Physical Education classes. He participates with enthusiasm and joy. He has a well-developed sense of fair play.

It was in Thomas's grade 3 year that the "powers that be" (doctors at the neuromuscular clinic in consultation with the people at AADL) decided he was ready to receive a power wheelchair. Thomas, Glenn, and I went to a local vendor to review the options and order a chair for him. The gentleman had so many questions, which we were once again unprepared for. He asked which model of chair we wanted, what kind of cushion was needed, what kind of headrest and armrests were required, and so on. We had no idea what to look for in a power wheelchair.

Then he told us that it would take up to six months to get the chair, which would cost approximately $10,000. Fortunately, the Alberta government helped us with the cost. We paid $500, and the rest was covered through funding supports.

We sat with the vendor for a few hours trying to answer his questions and posing our own. Thomas, of course, was excited at the possibility of having something that he could work on his own. We answered the questions to the best of our ability and could only hope that the chair was going to make Thomas feel more independent.

Thomas's Character Builds, His Advocacy Begins

In May of 2004, Thomas was eight years old. On one of our routine clinic days, he and I were approached by a social worker named Sharon, who was connected to the neuromuscular clinic at the Children's Hospital. She was looking to recommend a child who could get their wish granted through the Children's Wish Foundation of Canada. She asked me if it would be okay to speak with Thomas to see if he had a wish. I assured her, "Of course, you may ask," although I was a little taken aback by her question. I had always thought that wishes were granted to children who were terminally ill. She informed me that wishes were also granted to children who lived with a disease that created daily challenges for them.

She turned to Thomas and asked him if he had a specific wish. He promptly replied, "I would like to go to Denmark, to see Legoland." Sharon asked why he didn't want to go to the California Legoland. Thomas immediately responded that he wanted to go to Denmark to the original Legoland, and to also see his Danish relatives, especially his Aunt Lena. I thought that that was an awfully big wish, but Sharon didn't seem worried in the least.

Later that week, the Children's Wish Foundation in Calgary contacted us to say that Thomas's wish had been granted. They pulled out all the stops for the four of us to travel to Denmark, including arranging for our transportation—what seemed like a small bus—to accommodate Thomas and his wheelchair! He was given spending money, and the food and accommodations were arranged for us, including a stay at Hotel Legoland. We were to leave a few weeks later.

🐢 🐢 🐢 🐢 🐢

That same summer, we discovered an amazing camp that catered to children with disabilities. Easter Seals Camp Horizon was only twenty-five minutes from our house, situated in the beautiful area called Kananaskis, an expansive provincial park system in the eastern slopes and foothills of the Rocky Mountains between Calgary and Banff. Camp Horizon has rustic log cabins, where the participants sleep. It has a main hall with a huge fireplace, where campers meet for meals and activities. There are pathways made to be accessible for wheelchairs, an outdoor pool, high rope activities, and a giant forty-foot swing. Glenn and I were apprehensive about letting Thomas attend camp for a full week, not knowing if his needs would be met. We were assured that the counsellors were trained to care for kids with disabilities. There was also a full-time nurse on hand to meet any emergencies, and we knew it was only twenty-five minutes away.

Thomas totally wanted to go. He was ready for a new adventure and a chance to experience a week away on his own without his parents. He had already attended many sleepovers at friends' homes and therefore didn't have any worries about being homesick. We relented and drove out to Camp Horizon to drop him off.

It was the beginning of a wonderful ten-year tradition for Thomas. He loved camp! He always said that Camp Horizon was his favourite place on Earth. There, he could not only be himself without his parents, but more importantly, make his lifetime memories, meet friends, and contribute in his own way by giving back to others. Thomas was able to relate to so many of the campers. He was always a good listener and quite often was the one who could calm down an anxious camper. He would make many suggestions to the counsellors on games everyone could participate in. Others at the camp saw him as an inspiration.

Twice a year starting when he was eight, Thomas was able to attend weekend sleepovers at the Easter Seals Camp Horizon. An added bonus on the weekend camps was that siblings or friends could also attend. Gregg was able to participate in many of the weekend sleepovers.

Gregg:

Thomas had a mischievous side—a prankster personality. He loved to play tricks on people. One particular prank stands out to me.

While he and I were attending a sleepover at Camp Horizon, we participated in a muffin-making contest. The counsellors were the judges.

Of course, Thomas knew these counsellors well from all the camps he attended, so he decided this would be an optimal opportunity for some shenanigans. We agreed that instead of competing for first place with the best-tasting muffins, we were going to bake the most disgusting muffins we could just to see how the counsellors would react when they were completing the taste test. While the other groups made tasty banana or chocolate chip muffins, Thomas and I threw ingredients like pepper, peas, carrots, and mustard into ours.

As much as Thomas loved pranking people, though, he was never good at keeping a straight face while following through with the joke. This meant that many of the pranks we played on people didn't go as planned, including this one. Unfortunately, the counsellors clued in to our suspicious activities. Even though our muffins were baked and disguised to look like a tasty treat, none of the judges were willing to taste them. But at least we had a ton of fun making them.

Thomas, promotional video, Camp Horizon 2013:

She came and said, "Thomas? Your name is Thomas?"

"Ya."

"Well, you must be new here, 'cause I don't recognize you. I'll show you around."

And instantly, everyone ... it was such a connection. Everyone at camp was just so friendly.

I may seem to a lot of people that I need a lot of help. But at the camp, I'm sometimes, I'm even able to help people. Now that I'm older, it's become, I don't know, it's just really rewarding. Just that I'm not constantly needing help, but that I can also give back a little bit.[2]

---

2   Easter Seals Camp Horizon, "Easter Seals Camp Horizon," YouTube video, 2:19, June 5, 2013, youtube.com/watch?v=w9u6cVB5wbo

The week after Thomas returned from camp, we were off to Denmark. Glenn's parents wanted to join us on our Children's Wish adventure and decided to pay their own way to come along. We were all up early getting ready for the flight, which did not leave until the evening. The boys were so excited about the adventures ahead; the excitement had been building for a few weeks. We had everything packed, and our relatives in Denmark were lining up to take turns hosting us in their homes.

Thomas was so excited. He had gotten up early, been awake all day, and stayed awake during the entire flight to Frankfurt and then the one to Denmark. During our layover in Frankfurt, we were treated royally, having a family room to hang out in before our next flight took off. Glenn, Jamie, Thomas, and I explored the airport in Germany. We found a mannequin riding a bike, chocolate displays, and especially to Thomas's liking, the Smarties section.

When we arrived in Denmark, Glenn went to pick up the van that had been arranged for us, which was more like a small bus. We tried to get Thomas to nap in the van but he was too wired, taking in all the sights. There was plenty of room in the van for the six of us and room, too, for Thomas's push chair. (We were still waiting for the power chair.) The minivan was so tall on the inside that we could stand up in it. We drove to the Sorensen hometown of Jorløse and went straight to Glenn's aunt's house, which is still the family farm now. It was built in the 1800s. Glenn had to bend down through each of the doors in the house so as not to hit his head. Gertrude, Glenn's aunt, had prepared a feast and had invited all of the Danish family to welcome us back.

We visited family and historic Danish sites, and, of course, we spent two days at Legoland. Our whole family was given Children's Wish Foundation T-shirts to wear to Legoland. Even Grandma and Grandpa had one on. (I truly believe that is the only time I ever saw either one of them in a T-shirt.) Thomas appreciated the fact that because he was in a wheelchair, the staff at Legoland not only allowed us to get to the front of the lineups for the rides but also allowed him a double ride without getting off. We have great pictures of us going down the rollercoaster, and the Legoland photographers captured our elated expressions as we went down the biggest run on the log ride. Thomas was thrilled to eat French fries in the shape of

Lego pieces. He even had his picture taken with the king of Legoland as we enjoyed breakfast.

Breakfasts in Denmark are always a feast containing everything anyone would care to eat. Our breakfasts, which were included with our hotel room, consisted of bacon, ham, sausage, eggs, cereal, and fruit. The Danish also include their special *morning breads*, an assortment of buns and sliced breads including white, whole wheat, and rye. There were also platters full of cheeses, cold cuts, smoked salmon, and, of course, the famous Danishes—sweet breads with jams or creams. Quite often after a Danish breakfast, there is no need to eat until supper time.

Glenn's Aunt Lena was a major reason Thomas wanted to have his Danish wish granted. She is petite, with short blonde hair and beautiful blue eyes. Her English is not great, but she is able to speak much more English than I can Danish. She is able to communicate sufficiently, and when she questions how to say something, Glenn is always able to translate. Lena is a kind and gentle woman who commands a room with her presence without trying to draw attention to herself. Her smile is genuine.

Thomas had first met Lena a few years earlier, when Lena and her partner, Abbe, visited Calgary. Thomas was only three, but he saw something in her, and they immediately struck up a special connection.

I remember Lena and Abbe visiting our home for dinner one evening on their trip. It was a pleasant summer evening, and we were able to sit on our deck after supper. We had finished a wonderful dinner, the evening air was warm, and we could smell the flowers that were hanging in the baskets surrounding our deck. Thomas was sitting on Lena's lap, and she told us of this incredible feeling she was experiencing with him. An aura, she described, with colours all around Thomas, and the waves of energy she was receiving. She said that Thomas had a special place on this earth. She felt a strong bond with him. We will never forget that evening and all the colours she described.

Lena went out of her way to welcome our family on our visit to Denmark. She made us delicious meals, gave us some beautiful Danish

Christmas plates, which hang in our dining room, and even presented me with a beautiful amber heart pendant.

Lena specializes in what she calls "healing hands" but what is formally known as Healing Touch:

> Healing Touch is an "energy therapy" that uses gentle hand techniques thought to help re-pattern the patient's energy field and accelerate healing of the body, mind, and spirit.
>
> Healing Touch is based on the belief that human beings are fields of energy that are in constant interaction with others and the environment. The goal of Healing Touch is to purposefully use the energetic interaction between the Healing Touch practitioner and the patient to restore harmony to the patient's energy system.
>
> Healing Touch complements other healing techniques a patient may already be using, including conventional medical practice in hospitals, clinics, and in-home care, or other body-mind oriented therapies such as massage, guided imagery, music therapy, acupressure, biofeedback, and psychotherapy. It is not intended as a cure.[3]

With her touch, she is able to pinpoint a patient's pain, help relieve the pain, and more. Thomas wanted to have a session with Lena, but in the end, he had several. The local newspaper in Kalundborg, the small city west of Copenhagen where Lena lived, did a full-page article on Thomas's visit, and included pictures of Thomas wearing his Children's Wish Foundation T-shirt with Lena working on him. I was amazed to watch Lena work on Thomas's legs. At this point of his life, his legs were already seizing up and he wasn't able to straighten them. Lena gently touched his legs, running her hands up and down his calves, and I could see his legs begin to straighten. It was unbelievable. I kept thinking that I wished we could take Lena home with us so she could do this every day.

---

3   University of Minnesota, "Healing Touch," accessed November 24, 2021, takingcharge.csh.umn.edu/explore-healing-practices/healing-touch.

Glenn:

Yes, my Aunt Lena has "healing hands." If she lays her hands on someone, she can feel what is wrong with a person's functions and relieve their pain. (I'm not sure if I'm a believer, but she has a lot of followers, and people from all over make appointments and come to see her.)

When we arrived on our Legoland trip, Thomas had been quite constipated for a while. Kathy suggested that maybe Lena could help Thomas with this problem. We asked Lena for some help on this matter, and she said she'd try.

She doesn't like a big audience when she uses her healing hands, so we left her alone with Thomas for maybe a half an hour. After we left Lena's place, Thomas said he needed the bathroom, and he had a great bowel movement. Kathy and I were happy for him, and a little while later Thomas needed the bathroom again. Kathy was convinced that Aunt Lena had helped! Again, Thomas needed the bathroom. Thomas used the washroom *eight times* that evening. I remember how often it was since I was the one that usually took Thomas to the washroom.

Thomas was feeling much, much better after seeing Lena, and after the eighth trip to the bathroom, I asked Kathy, "Do you think Lena overdid it with Thomas? If this keeps up, we might have to go back and see if she can dial it back a bit!"

It was tough to leave Denmark. Our relatives had treated us to many enjoyable family dinners, and Thomas had had the special sessions with Lena. The four of us had also learned so much about Danish history. We'd gone to Skagen, the most northern point of Denmark, where two seas, Skagerrak and Kattegat, converge. On our visits to antique stores and the markets, and after spending time in the Danish grocery stores, we were envious of all the items we could not get back in Canada. Thomas wanted to bring home tubs of Danish ice cream, which we obviously couldn't do. We all wanted to bring home the cheeses and dishes made with *crème frâiche* and the delicious morning breads.

When we returned, we wrote thank-you cards and sent pictures to the staff at the Alberta and Northwest Territories chapter of the Children's Wish Foundation. (Their office is in Calgary.) In response, they asked if Thomas was interested in helping out as a spokesperson for events they were having in the future. Thomas eagerly accepted, and for him, this marked the beginning of new, meaningful experiences instead of the end of a single trip.

Thomas's Advocacy Begins

After the trip to Denmark, Thomas started doing charity work and advocacy for people with disabilities, and this work continued for the rest of his life. He found it most gratifying to give something back by participating in these activities. This is when we most clearly saw his passion and talent for helping others.

Thomas's involvement in charity events was a beginning for Glenn and me, too. We didn't realize the impact Thomas's advocacy would have on all of our lives, and we couldn't have predicted what and how much we would learn about the importance of giving back. The three of us began this work by sitting at a table in a mall selling tickets for a fundraiser.

Next up, in June of 2009, Thomas was invited to a golf tournament to support the Children's Wish Foundation. At the golf course, Thomas buzzed around in his chair, convincing people to buy raffle tickets for draws. He was speaking to as many individuals as he could, convincing them to open up their wallets for such a great cause. There was also a silent auction during the tournament. One of the items was a day of fishing on the Bow River with a guide. The Bow River is world famous for large trout with an estimated 2,500 trout per mile. Thomas thought this would be a great gift for his dad. He and I started to bid on the item, but it quickly went too high for our budget. The owner of the fishing company could see that we were trying to win the bid. He was so impressed with Thomas that he presented Thomas with his own day of fishing on the Bow.

The owner also went out of his way to accommodate a boat that would make Thomas as comfortable as possible. As a result of this man's generosity, Glenn, and Thomas, along with Glenn's friend Steve, were able to have a memorable day together on the Bow River. They shared in their excitement of catching a few fish and releasing them back to the river, and they experienced the thrill of seeing a natural side of Calgary along the banks of the river. They returned home at the end of an extraordinary day with official Bow River fishing hats to keep as souvenirs along with wonderful memories to cherish.

The Children's Wish Foundation continued to invite Thomas to events. He was the parade marshal for their annual fundraising walk two years in a row. We always decorated a refrigerator box with the Foundation's logo and placed it on top of Thomas's wheelchair so it actually looked like a float. Thomas's head could be seen at the top of the "float," and he was able to maneuver the box with his wheelchair's joystick.

He was a guest at another mall fundraising event for the Children's Wish Foundation's anniversary. At this event, Thomas scurried around asking passersby for donations. In addition, he was a guest speaker for an organization that supported the Children's Wish Foundation, and he spoke at the grand opening of a restaurant. Thomas also talked my friend and me into co-chairing a women's gala at the Danish Canadian Club, where the funds raised would go to the Children's Wish Foundation. We raised over $24,000 that night, the most ever raised by that event in several years, and it has not been met since!

After his experience at Camp Horizon, Thomas started volunteering for Easter Seals Alberta, an organization that provides respite for parents, and more importantly, provides incredible experiences for kids with disabilities. Easter Seals' mission is to provide services that foster inclusion, independence, and recreation for individuals with disabilities and medical conditions. At the beginning of his volunteer work, Thomas spent a few hours every now and then at our community Safeway store raising awareness and asking for donations. Soon, Easter Seals asked Thomas to come out to the camp to give tours to potential supporters. He loved showing visitors around and sharing his experiences of camp. Safeway's head office also invited Thomas to attend national video conferences with their employees across Canada. At the time, Safeway was a huge contributor to Easter Seals Alberta.

Not everything in Thomas's life was about the logistics of preparing for events and activities. There were times when his life was just about him and his classmates being kids. Thomas had just received his power chair and was returning to the school from the appointment where he'd been taught how to use it. He was excited to show his new transportation off to his friends and teachers. The room was abuzz with the students, teachers, and support staff, who were busy inspecting, asking questions, and taking in the new motorized wheels. This was the first time the school had a child in a motorized wheelchair. This chair meant a whole new life for Thomas. New independence, new responsibility, and a new way for all of us to get him from point A to point B. We all learned how the chair worked, when to plug in its battery, how to put it in push mode, and when not to. For such a young boy who had no mobility, driving a vehicle seemed like a fearsome responsibility.

The other children were anxious to know if they could climb on the back and go for a spin. They wondered if they could help move the joystick to maneuver the wheels, and they wanted to know how fast the chair could go and if Thomas could do wheelies on it.

The teachers were busy adjusting the legs of his desk to allow the chair to move freely under the desk and enable Thomas to place his books comfortably on the desk. They, too, were wanting to know about the joystick, the batteries, and how fast the chair could go.

Suddenly, Thomas's chair began to propel forward rapidly, plowing everything in its path out of the way. Amidst a sudden throng of shrieks, the crash from tumbling books, and Thomas grinding against a bookshelf, he suddenly came to a stop. Apparently, someone's sleeve had become caught on the joystick, jamming it in the forward position. Once the sleeve was untangled, everyone gave a sigh of relief with a nervous laugh. The staff learned quickly that there was an on/off button they could use to put an end to the mayhem.

Over time, Thomas had to earn the right to have the speed increased on his chair. The staff watched closely as he maneuvered through the hallway to see if he was looking ahead, turning corners slowly, and watching out for any toes that he might run over. They also kept an eye on his movements on the playground during recess and lunch. They made it clear to him that he had to use his common sense while on the playground. He wasn't allowed to go too fast or plow through any holes or bumps in the field, and he had to be conscious of other children playing in any area he was in. There were four speed settings, and each level could be increased to 100 per cent. Like a typical boy, he looked forward to doing wheelies and bombing down the corridors. He also enjoyed going full speed on the playground. The assistants were quick to inform us if he was misusing his power. It only took one or two mishaps before he understood that I, Glenn, and the school staff were communicating with each other. He was able to quickly grasp his chair's potential power, and he held true to his word to be responsible, honouring and respecting the power of the chair.

Ryan (Thomas's friend from school):[4]

He taught me all the tricks there were to know for *Halo Kart* and *Mario Kart*, and I swear I beat him at *Super Smash Bros.* every time. We would stay up as late as we possibly could at every sleepover and wake up as early as possible so we could start hanging out again, clearly trying to annoy Kathy, Glenn, and Jamie as much as possible. We spent many hours out at the lake playing hockey, soccer, and any other silly games we could think up. I was lucky enough to sit in on a lot of family dinners, when I got to know his absolutely amazing family, and he got to know mine as well.

When I moved to Ontario for two years, Thomas remained my only friend back in Calgary. I would call him sometimes and he would call me other times, even though we were only nine years old. We wanted to call and check in on the other's life. Thomas and I made sure to see each other almost every time my family would visit Calgary. And when I finally moved back after two years, we picked up our friendship as if I had never left.

---

4   Ryan and Thomas met in grade 2. Ryan had moved away to Ontario and always kept in contact by phone and when he came to visit in Calgary. Ryan moved back to Calgary while in junior high and picked up the friendship right away.

During his elementary years, quite often Thomas was off from school on Professional Development (PD) days while my school had regular days with kids. My principal at the time was okay with their teachers' children attending our school on those days, so I brought Thomas along. The students at my school absolutely loved Thomas's visits. They weren't used to seeing a kid in a wheelchair, and they were curious about a teacher who had a child with a disability. The questions began. And Thomas totally engaged my students. He made lasting impressions on hundreds of my students over the years.

Natalie Bauer, former student of mine:

Even though it's been several years since I was in Canyon Meadows School, memories of Thomas are still clear as day. Some of my favourites include the Hop-a-Thon that he hosted the year he was the child representative for Easter Seals, and all the times he came to visit us in music class.

Everybody I knew in Canyon Meadows School thought he was the coolest thing since sliced bread. As for me, Thomas was (and continues to be) an inspirational figure who never let his illness get in the way of what he wanted to do.

There were many years when we had to fight for Thomas to have an aide at school. Each September, the school administration would assess Thomas's needs, and one year, when he was in grade 5, the strategist informed us that Thomas would not receive any help at all. We shook ourselves awake. Thomas was in a wheelchair and had such weak muscles. Seriously. He couldn't use the washroom on his own let alone get his books and pencils for class. Thomas went to school with a bag packed with books, a computer, which we supplied, and his lunch. He couldn't get these items out of his bag, and he had to have help physically to use them. How could they expect him to perform these seemingly easy tasks without help?

I spent hours making phone calls and sending emails to both the principal and the strategist listing our concerns. I outlined for them a long list of his physical abilities, or lack thereof. The communication went back and forth, back, and forth. It seemed like we were waiting for the paint to peel. Ultimately, the strategist had the final decision as to whether Thomas would qualify for an aide. I had to convince her that having an aide was necessary for our son to be successful in school. Finally, we got the call at the end of September saying they would provide Thomas with a full-time aide.

As it turned out, that strategist ultimately became the chief superintendent of the CBE and hired me the following year (the year after our fight to get Thomas an aide) to be an assistant principal.

In January 2006, Thomas turned ten. He had only one request: a "backwards" birthday dinner. Thomas felt that every time we had a dinner, people weren't hungry by the time they got to dessert, so he wanted to start his birthday dinner with dessert. Each course after that was in reverse of what was normally served.

We began his celebration with his birthday cake—a traditional Danish three-layer cake that I'd made the day before. I used the recipe Glenn's mother gave me that had been translated into English. Once the cake cooled, I topped each layer with almond pudding, strawberries, and fresh whipped cream. When no one was looking, I sprinkled some cherry or strawberry liqueur on each layer, too. After I completed the final layer, I covered the entire cake with more whipped cream, chocolate slivers, Canadian and Danish flags, and ten birthday candles.

Next, we had his favourite meal—KFC chicken and fries with all the fixings: gravy, coleslaw, and macaroni salad. Thomas didn't bother with either the coleslaw or the macaroni. He went straight for the fries. We ended with what would have been the appetizer: cocktail wieners with ketchup. Thomas loved ketchup on his ketchup. He even had a T-shirt with the same saying. The family we had invited for dinner thought the whole idea was great fun. It was certainly unconventional for a birthday celebration, but in our household, a birthday wish is always granted.

The next month, I became the acting assistant principal at my school. Our principal had taken leave, and because I was working toward my master's degree, the school board assigned me the position of principal for six months. I was at school on February 28 when one of my sisters called to let me know that our dad was on his last days.

He was ninety-six and had led a full life. He always wore a suit and tie topped off with a fedora. The hat may have changed with the weather, but he mowed the lawn or painted the house dressed in his suit. Dad was always proud of his five daughters. I was the baby, and he and I were always close. He still has a special place in my heart. I often have dreams about him that make me smile.

Of course, I wanted to fly home to Nova Scotia to be with Dad. I knew that Glenn could manage the boys. My sister Marj and I took the red-eye home. After the long flight, the layover in Toronto, the time change, and the two-hour drive home to New Glasgow from the Halifax airport, we arrived late afternoon the next day. We went to our sister Sue's home for a hot shower and a change of clothes, and after having some supper, we left for the hospital. Marj and I decided that we would take the first shift to be by Dad's bedside. He was not conscious. I was so sad to see him lying quietly in the bed. He had failed so much since the last time I had seen him. Being so far away had always been so difficult.

It was midnight on March 2, my birthday, and four hours after Marj and I arrived at the hospital, when Dad opened his eyes briefly. Another sister, Liz, was there with us. We told Dad how much we loved him and assured him that we were there. Dad took a couple of breaths, and then he was gone.

In Nova Scotia, funeral homes post visitation hours indicating when people can come to pay their respects to those who have passed and to the family. The visitation was overwhelming. So many people I had not seen for years came to honour Dad: many of my high school friends, former neighbours, and people in the community who respected our father. Elmer McKay and his son Peter came, too. Elmer was my guardian while growing up, should anything have happened to Mom and Dad when I was a kid, and Peter was a fixture in the political world.[5] Peter and I use to play together as children.

My sisters and I planned the most wonderful funeral with lots of music. The church was packed. The organ in my hometown was regarded as the best pipe organ east of Montreal. There are six huge panels of pipes in the church that range in size up to twelve feet. The organ also has many stops, which refers to the different sounds like flutes, trumpets, and strings. In my high school years, I played this six-manual organ on many occasions, so I certainly knew the capability of its sound. We asked the organist to "open it up," and let it blast, and she did not disappoint. That would have been Dad's wish. My sisters and I sang our hearts out and teared up with the powerful sound of the organ. We felt the vibrations in our bodies, and our ears were blessed with the volume. I looked at my sisters, smiling at the tremendous sound, and thought only one thought: Dad would have loved it.

Glenn:

When Kathy was away for a few days to attend her father's funeral, I gave the boys whatever they wanted for supper, but on one condition: when Mom calls, tell her we ate fish, rice, and corn. Over the years, this became our standard answer whenever she called while she was away. We ate pizza, burgers, chicken fingers, chips, and tons of other junk food, but she was hoping to hear we'd been having fish, rice, and corn.

Thomas would say, "Now that Mom's away I think we should drink some beers!" (Root beer, that is.) And so we did, and we would have belching contests.

The rules were more relaxed when Kathy was away. It was just us three boys. They loved it, but they also knew when proper etiquette was called for.

---

5   Peter MacKay was a member of the Canadian Parliament between 1997 and 2015. He is most known for as serving as Minister of National Defense, Minister of Foreign Affairs, and Minister of Justice and Attorney General in his time as a Member of Parliament.

🐢 🐢 🐢 🐢 🐢

Glenn was always there for the boys. Always. He gave more in the way of gifts to each of them to compensate for their needs, spoiling them with the newest versions of Xbox, big screens to play on, and other treats when what they already had was sufficient. He had always told Jamie that he would never help buy him a car, so what did he do? He helped Jamie buy his first car. He was also often worried that Jamie was losing out in some way because of the extra time we gave Thomas.

Pets, computers, games, and junk food. Glenn was always there to provide for their wants. I knew they were watching movies, eating popcorn, and drinking root beer when I wasn't around, and that was just fine with me.

🐢 🐢 🐢 🐢 🐢

Glenn:

Kathy is an excellent and creative cook. We know children can be picky when it comes to food, so we never forced the boys to eat what we had prepared. We told them, "You don't have to eat it, but that's all there is, and you get nothing later." We all ate the same food; no one got anything special.

Once, when Thomas was in elementary school, in the middle of dinner one night, he was looking around and noticed Jamie wasn't eating. The meal was not one of Jamie's favourites. Thomas spoke up and said, "If nobody eats anything more, there's just enough food leftover for Jamie's lunch tomorrow!"

Family and Friends

It's hard to talk about a child with special needs; this a touchy subject for family and friends. I know so many families with children with disabilities, and the parents often complain how their family and/or friends don't understand what it's like to care for such a child all day, every day. You can't stop and relax at any time. You can't find a babysitter who can roll a teenager over in his bed or attend to his bathroom needs. You are on call twenty-four hours a day.

All of the family loved Thomas. He had such a bright spirit—a zest and passion for life. He loved people and engaged with everyone he met. The family spoiled him, loved attending his birthday parties, loved hearing his accomplishments, and fully accepted him as a member of the family. But when it came to offering help in the way of Thomas's personal care or covering duties during a night off for Glenn and me, it didn't always happen. There were many times when Glenn and I wished we could have an evening out, but neither of our families living in Calgary ever called to offer to babysit. Glenn once made a comment to his dad saying, "It sure would be nice if someone reached out to cover one night so Kathy and I could go out." His dad's response: "No one ever asks to watch our house while we go out."

Our family was happy to come to our house for dinner and leave without any obligation. They came, ate, and left. Sometimes, but not always, they would offer to help with dishes or care for Thomas. They would offer their opinions on Thomas's upbringing without understanding the daily reality we faced. Whenever we had issues with the HandiBus or other services we needed, they would offer up suggestions and not believe us or understand if we told them we had already tried what they were suggesting or if we explained why their suggestion wouldn't work. Raising a child with a disability is something people cannot understand unless they are living it. At least we found it to be that way. Yes, family may ask how they can help and people will say they understand, but truly, they don't. When out-of-town relatives came to Calgary, Thomas wanted them to come to our house to visit or have a sleepover. He didn't always get his wish.

There were many times when we needed immediate help, and yet, some family member had made plans for the day they felt they could not change, so they couldn't assist us when we most needed it. They couldn't rush over when our son was home sick even if they were not working and we had to go to work. They were not around while we scrambled to find someone to care for Thomas. We needed someone who could take him to the washroom, care for him if he woke up from a sleep, entertain him, keep him company when he was awake, or feed him when he was hungry.

I believe when our family reads this, they will have much to say. I don't want to hurt anyone, but I want to tell our story in hopes of increasing people's understanding and awareness of what it's like to raise a child with special needs. We often had other families ask how they could make their family understand what their day to day lives were like. It is a difficult subject for many, and we don't, sadly, have any helpful suggestions on this.

As for friends, they have come and gone, and we have learned to accept this reality. We always tried to make people feel welcomed in our home. I think we did that, but over time, the reciprocation wasn't always there. And after a while, we would give up.

🐢 🐢 🐢 🐢 🐢

Thomas's love for family was evident in the way he anticipated seeing them, vibrating in his seat, smiling, and showing excitement in his conversations with everyone. He loved Danish celebrations. And he loved the big birthday parties. His favourite celebration was Christmas: the Danish Christmas Eve dinner with both turkey and pork roast, red cabbage, potatoes, and the surprise gift for the person finding the almond in the pudding dessert. This dessert, risalamande, is a mixture of milk, pearl rice, chopped almonds, and whipped cream. The pudding is topped with hot or cold cherries. The fun part is that there are one or two whole almonds hidden in the dessert.

Whoever finds the whole almond(s) gets a prize. While they were growing up, all the children under the age of fifteen always had their own serving with an almond in it, so each child always ended up with a present.

The family singing around the Christmas tree, waiting for the special visit from Santa. Thomas loved it all, and even when he was old enough to realize that Santa was Kim, a dear family friend, he still played along.

Glenn, Jamie, and I took turns pushing him around the tree in his chair during the carolling. This is another Danish tradition—circling the tree while singing. The last song gets faster and faster every time you sing it, and you have to keep turning to the opposite direction every time you sing a verse, so it gets a little dizzying by the time the final song comes. Thomas loved every circle he made.

Glenn:

PLEASE, PLEASE don't take this the wrong way—I love all of my family and would do almost anything for them. It's hard writing from the heart. I have no intentions of hurting anyone's feelings. If I do, I'm sorry.

But when it comes to having a special-needs child, family dynamics come into play—the full range of the relationships. From compassion to awkwardness to ignorance to love. I guess our family thought they were helping, but we often felt they were not. They never offered to give us a night out by caring for Thomas. They never offered to take him to the washroom or give him a bath. Even when we were desperate for someone to stay at home with him when he had a PD day or was not feeling great, we would have to scramble to find a babysitter because our family members had other plans those days.

I have often heard other parents with special-needs kids ask how they can make their family understand what they are going through on a daily basis. Many parents of children with disabilities have approached both Kathy and me at special-needs conferences, and Kathy at school, asking for advice. They, like us, wanted answers on where to go for help and support, for suggestions for activities for their child, and for help with their extended families, getting them to understanding their daily home life and challenges.

I hope other families with handicapped children can read our book and see that from midnight to seven in the morning, from bed to toilet, the hours don't matter. Not really. Life is good, regardless. I wouldn't change a thing.

Susanne (Glenn's sister) and her husband, Bill—Thomas's godparents:

As Thomas's godparents, we always held a special place in our hearts for him. Thomas wore a constant smile. His positive attitude is something we will always remember, along with his competitive spirit in hockey and soccer, loving the connection with his teammates as much as the games, his caring personality, and how he put others' worries before his own. Susanne has fond memories of playing games with him online. He was always challenging his aunt.

If Christmas or my birthday was coming, Susanne would take Thomas out to buy presents for me. He loved the attention, but he especially loved his Aunt Susanne and the special time he got to share with her. He was grateful that she took the time to go from store to store looking for the right gift. He loved the treats in between, and he was appreciative that he could purchase something for his loved ones with Susanne's help and expertise. Thomas would save up his money to pay for presents on his own, but at the same time, Susanne never spared any expense when it came to buying treats for both of our boys. She always spoiled them rotten.

She was the only aunt who ever took Thomas out by herself. Anytime she came to Calgary, she made a point of phoning and asking what movies he wanted to go see, and she would take him and Gregg to the theatre.

She didn't hesitate to buy them popcorn, pop, candies, etc. No was not in her vocabulary.

Glenn's dad commanded any room he walked into. Hans would always make a point of letting everyone know he had arrived. He would make the rounds, shaking everyone's hands, cracking a few jokes along the way in his booming voice.

But Glenn and his dad are different that way. Glenn has always been less boisterous. I'd like to believe that the shy, generous guy that I fell in love with has learned to come out of his shell since meeting me. He certainly has become more open to sharing his viewpoint, and he's more comfortable in any social situation, but it has never been Glenn's manner to stand out or make a scene. Hans, however, would speak his mind, be direct, and give no consideration to whom he might be offending. Quite often Glenn and I would blush after Hans had made a comment about something while in our presence.

Glenn is Hans and Alice's only son. He has worked hard to be a good son, father, and husband. One Hallowe'en is a good example of the stark differences between Glen and his dad:

Glenn:

Mom and Dad would always come for an early dinner on Hallowe'en at our house, and then Dad and I would take Thomas trick-or-treating. Jamie always came, too, until he was thirteen and didn't want to go out anymore. Kathy and my mom would stay at the house to hand out candy to the trick-or-treaters.

When we got to a house, I would ring the doorbell because Thomas was in his wheelchair, and he would holler "trick or treat" when the people opened their doors. My dad would immediately bellow out, "He can't come to the door because HE HAS A DISEASE!"

I said, "Dad, why are you saying that? Thomas has muscular dystrophy, and it does not sound good when you say that. Thomas is right here with us, and it's hurtful for him to hear you screaming at every door about his disease."

Dad got mad at me and told me that Thomas did have a disease and the sooner I understood that the better. Obviously, I knew the reality of Thomas's condition; I was more worried about his feelings. I hated that my dad kept saying those words, especially in front of Thomas. So, the last few years before Thomas got too old to go trick-or-treating, Kathy and Dad took him out while I stayed home with Mom to hand out candy.

My dad was accepting of Thomas; he loved him with all his heart. But he didn't understand Thomas's daily challenges or know what Kathy and I did every day for our son. His loud proclamation to complete strangers about Thomas's condition, and his reminding me of Thomas's condition, were unnecessary reminders of what we were all too familiar with in our everyday lives.

Thomas on Facebook, October 19, 2009:

Mama-mia! A Mario hat just came in the mail today! Hmm. Wonder what I'll be for Hallowe'en?

Gregg:

Thomas was always creative. Me, not so much. His imagination appeared each Hallowe'en when he transformed his chair into something unbelievable. One year he had a Thomas the Tank Engine with the train laminated on the front, the numbers on the side, and the coal at the back. He was the conductor. The next year he transformed a fridge box into a firetruck that had flashing lights and a siren. Another Hallowe'en, Thomas was Mario and transformed his wheelchair into Yoshi, Mario's dinosaur, who served as Mario's transportation.

With my less-than-inspirational costume ideas, I usually ended up going out with a mixture of whatever costume pieces I could find in the basement. Of course, this wasn't satisfactory for Thomas, or for me. So, the year Thomas dressed as Yoshi, I rode on the back of his wheelchair dressed as Mario. This turned out to be a popular costume when we stopped at houses along the candy route. People passing us along the street yelled, clapped, and cheered. It was definitely the best costume we ever had, and it was the most fun, too.

Glenn, Jamie, Thomas, and I were a family. Together, we found solutions to every problem and created a happy household. Thank goodness we had each other.

Glenn's parents were amazing in their own way. Their financial support when Thomas needed medical treatment to reshape his head and when we bought the bungalow was hugely helpful. They came and spent time with the boys when they could, assisting with Thomas before he became too heavy for them to pick him up. While both boys were growing up, Glenn and I had his parents over for meals regularly, and our family of four also attended Sunday dinners at their house.

Hans and Alice lived in the same house for more than forty years, and their house had an indoor pool. The pool, in particular, ended up being another significant way for them to contribute to supporting Thomas's needs. Thomas loved to swim, and although one of us always had to be in the pool with him, swimming was something he could do independently, going from one end of the pool to the other. As part of Thomas's physical therapy, I took him (and often Jamie, as well), to their house on average three times a week so he could enjoy the pool and exercise his muscles. Sunday dinners at their home were often preceded or followed by a dip in the pool. The grandparents loved having the boys over for swim dates, and Alice always treated the boys to apple slices or other snacks after their swims.

Hans and Alice were always supportive of any events the boys were in and usually slipped them a "bill" as a way to say congratulations. Neither

Jamie nor Thomas expected to receive anything; they were simply happy that their grandparents came out to watch a game.

Hans and Alice also came out to any fundraiser that Thomas was involved in. They were there to not only support Thomas's participation in the event, but they also usually contributed to the cause. Any time they had an anniversary or big birthday, they always asked their friends for a donation to Muscular Dystrophy Canada, Easter Seals (the Alberta chapter), or Camp Horizon in lieu of gifts.

Alice always made a point of making food that Jamie and Thomas liked. If the main meal didn't pass, she prepared a side dish for them. She knew what they liked and always catered to their whims. Both boys always appreciated that and knew how much their grandparents loved them.

🐢 🐢 🐢 🐢 🐢

When Jamie was in high school, Glenn and I pushed him to get a part-time job. We wanted him to learn the responsibility of working with others, getting to work on time, and saving money. It took a while to convince him to take this step, but he finally applied to our local Co-op grocery store and was hired. He began as a bag boy and was packing groceries for customers. He quickly became quite bored with the job, though.

He did receive an award at one point—a certificate and a lapel pin. One day, he caught someone walking out the door without paying for hundreds of dollars of meat, and that prompted a promotion to the bakery department, which he quite enjoyed. Shortly after that, he was promoted again, this time to the produce department, which apparently was the best section to work in. The guys in the produce department initiated him into the department by making him eat the hottest pepper they had in stock.

Jamie enjoyed his time at the grocery store, but he soon found a part-time job with a security company, Back Stage Support, doing security at concerts and other performance events. This was an awesome job for a young adult in school. Not only could he pick and choose his shifts, but he also got to choose the jobs. He was able to see so many talented artists, such as Robin Williams, Marilyn Manson, (who listened to Chopin and Debussy in his green room), The Cat Empire, The Red-Hot Chili Peppers, The Doobie Brothers, Sarah McLachlan, (who was, according to Jamie, very short), and Cypress Hill, just to name a few. He saw hundreds of concerts along with hockey and football games. Jamie worked the concert for Paul McCartney, and Paul actually patted Jamie on the back. I *was* envious of him seeing Paul McCartney in concert but also so proud of Jamie. I loved to hear his stories of the behind-the-scenes action, and I was delighted to hear Jamie say that my kids' choirs at school could have accompanied Paul in his songs.

Jamie continued this job through university and even after graduation. He certainly made an impression with the company and with the venue organizers as one of the best security guards they had. Jamie was even put in charge of a long-term Cirque de Soleil appearance in Calgary. Cirque actually offered him a long-term contract which Jaime, in the end, declined. It would have meant being on the road for months, overseeing security in multiple cities. We were proud of his accomplishments and also proud that so many others could also see his innate abilities.

Glenn and I were conscious of Jamie's needs. We often worried about how equal the boys were in terms of care and attention. Sometimes we worried that Jamie was losing out on opportunities because of all the additional time we spent caring for Thomas. We worried that we weren't a "normal" family that went skiing, snowboarding, or tobogganing. There are so many activities a family does that are not inclusive for children in power chairs. We only hoped that we were compensating in the right ways, trying to make Jamie's childhood as normal as possible.

Increasing Demands, Increased Awareness

Thomas's teen years saw more and more demands being placed on me and Glenn. He was getting older and heavier, and we needed some help. There is no manual for life's obstacles, so after many phone calls and asking everyone we could think of, we found Family Support for Children with Disabilities. This organization gave us limited funding to find caregivers for a couple of hours per week for respite.

Thomas's attending Easter Seals Camp Horizon for a week each summer, and gradually four weeks or more as he got older, gave Glenn and me a much-needed break, and it was also a great opportunity for Thomas. He made a lot of friends and got to know all the camp counsellors. Most of our caregivers were counsellors we hired, and it was a win-win for them and for our family. They were young and needed to make extra cash through fall and winter while going to university. The fact that Thomas knew them from camp and liked them was an added benefit. Their interactions with him at camp also meant they were already in tune with his needs before they began to work for us directly. There were some fantastic ones that really helped him to grow and become independent, thus giving him more confidence.

Glenn:

There was one caregiver, however, whom Thomas did not like at all. She was an older lady who never gave him an inch. The way she demanded a routine reminded me of a drill sergeant, but at that time, she was all we had. She took Thomas to the washroom as needed, did his stretches, and saw to his personal needs when she was in the house. She did do some housework and complained to Kathy about what parts of the house needed any additional work. This woman was confident and competent; she just didn't have a personality our family connected with or warmed to.

Generally, most of our caregivers were in their late teens or early twenties and didn't have two cents to rub together. They were finished by 5 p.m. but we always welcomed them for dinner. Most stayed, which was an excellent way to get to know them better. We learned to trust them. My God, how some of them could make groceries disappear down their throats, as if it were their last meal before a long voyage.

Some of our caregivers moved on to become doctors or teachers, and others later gained employment with organizations helping people with disabilities. We became good friends with many of them. Some still call and come and see us on a regular basis. Thomas left a lasting impression, and their continued presence in our lives feels good. (It might just be Kathy's great cooking that left the fond memories … who knows?)

Thomas enjoyed his Grade 6 year. Mrs. Nichol, an experienced teacher with silver hair, was his homeroom teacher, and she was team teaching with a male teacher that year. She worked closely with Thomas and kept in regular contact with us regarding his progress and needs. She wanted Thomas to succeed in his learning and be accepted by his classmates.

All of Thomas's Grade 6 teachers worked hard to allow the children to explore and achieve their creative abilities. Thomas created several artistic projects that year, including a turtle he created from plaster of Paris. He sketched pictures for social studies and science classes, and he painted a self-portrait in the style of Picasso. Along with the painting, Thomas had to do a written assignment:

My inner dragon is that I have many fears. Things like spiders, snakes, bees, wasps, and geckos scare me. If I'm touching the floor and I hear any of the bugs or reptiles I'm afraid of, I seize up. I think this happens because I am unable to get to them; my fear is having any one of these insects bite me or touch me. If I see a spider or any of these at home, I will scream loudly as if I'm in a lot of pain because I know I won't catch it. At school, I become very cold inside and my heart really starts pounding. Just thinking about these gives me a creepy, skin-crawling feeling I can't control. This feeling to me is like nails on a chalkboard. At night before bed, I sometimes worry when I awake a big, hairy, wolf spider will be staring me right in the face. I try to hold in these fears, but I find it impossible to keep [them] in.

Thomas also met the mayor of Calgary during a "study of the city council" class trip and had his photo taken with him. This was an important year because Thomas was preparing for junior high school, which would be a huge transition. He was saddened to learn that his school aide was not allowed to follow him into junior high. He was extremely anxious not knowing who would be helping him the following year.

That same year, the doctors were concerned about Thomas's hands and wrists. His hands were completely bent under his wrists, making it difficult for him to write. He was pretty good at utilizing two fingers on the keyboard of a computer, so he wasn't concerned and didn't want to take any action to correct his wrists. But this time, Thomas couldn't win the battle; he was overruled by the doctors. They decided he needed *serial casting*. Each hand, one at a time, was cast for six-to-eight weeks. Every week during the two six-to-eight week periods, the cast would be replaced with another, each of them forcing his hand to straighten out. The casts covered all but the tips of his fingers, right up to the elbows. The result? Well, yes, the casts did straighten his hands, but only for a short period of time, and then they were bent again. The worse result was, because of the weight of the casts, Thomas permanently lost the ability to raise his arms or even feed himself. Thomas never forgave the doctors for this decision.

🐢 🐢 🐢 🐢 🐢

Another wonderful assistant was assigned to Thomas during Grade 6. Jane was a classy lady. She was always well-dressed, well-spoken, and extremely caring. She was one of those people who always took initiative. Fortunately for us, Jane accepted an offer to become Thomas's personal assistant in our home after school for the next two years. She knew Thomas well and was able to help him with homework and personal needs. She went above and beyond her duties and also helped me out with household chores, preparing meals, laundry, and cleaning. I was extremely happy to have Jane in our lives.

Glenn:

Kathy and the boys adored Jane, and I have to agree. She was fantastic with Thomas and helped above and beyond with household duties. But she created extra work for me. I will always remember her for knocking the toilet out of place whenever she helped Thomas with his bathroom visits. I don't know if she did it to irritate me or if it was accidental, but having to constantly fix the toilet was a pain in the ass! Her habit of knocking the toilet out of place is still something our family laughs about.

🐢 🐢 🐢 🐢 🐢

In the spring of 2007 Thomas was selected as a participant for the Air Canada's Dreams Take Flight. This non-profit organization is dedicated to providing a trip of a lifetime to Disneyland for children in challenging circumstances. Their mission is "Making Magical Memories for Special Kids."

We had not heard about this program before. We definitely looked into the organization's background and the details of the trip. We were hesitant to allow Thomas to take part, but also thought that this was, indeed, a trip of a lifetime.

As parents, we were not allowed to accompany Thomas on the trip. However, after looking into their plans to take care of Thomas, we were assured that he would be just fine and knew that it would be an incredible experience for him. Of course, Thomas was pumped. He so wanted to go and was feeling great about his independence.

We answered all the questions on the paperwork and gave our permission for Thomas to attend.

When the day arrived, departure made for a very early morning. Thomas maybe slept two hours; he was hardly able to sleep due to the excitement ahead. I had to rouse him at 3 a.m. to get him to the airport by 4 a.m. It was a weekday, so Thomas was missing school, and I still had to get to work. The morning was cool, and Thomas had been given a T-shirt and shorts with the Dreams Take Flight logo on them. He was up and dressed and ready to go by 3:30 a.m. I wrapped him in a coat and blankets to keep him warm on the drive to the airport.

Upon arrival, we were directed to a secure area. There, we saw many excited kids, enthusiastic volunteers from the program, and a lot of nervous parents!

Thomas and I were introduced to two gentlemen who would be his personal volunteers. If I remember correctly, they were both firefighters. Both were also well-built, meaning they could pick Thomas up easily, and they were excited to be part of the program. These two men were personable and asked a lot of questions, open to suggestions as to how they could help Thomas enjoy his experience. Thomas barely saw me saying goodbye as he waited to board the plane.

I left, hoping all would be fine. It was a long day at work for me, being tired and wondering how things were going for Thomas.

We had been told to return to the airport at 11 p.m. I was there in plenty of time.

When I saw Thomas and his two volunteers, they were all smiles! The volunteers had fallen in love with Thomas and went on and on about what an incredible day it was. Thomas had not slept a wink from when we left home that morning.

He had had his picture taken with Mickey and Minnie Mouse, gotten on several rides at the park, was treated with any food he wished for, and received a backpack full of gifts. He returned home toting Mickey ears, a fanny pack, a key chain, a cowboy hat, several knick-knacks with the Dreams Take Flight logos, and even a gift for his mom: a necklace.

It took several hours after we got home for Thomas to unwind after being awake for more than twenty-four hours.

What an experience! Thank you to Air Canada and all the volunteers with Dreams Take Flight! Our words cannot express our appreciation for making such a memory that Thomas cherished for years!

🐢 🐢 🐢 🐢 🐢

As Thomas got older, he got wiser about his condition. He began reading up about muscular dystrophy, and he understood the terminology much better than Glenn or I did. During any hospital visits, Thomas was the one asking the tough questions and then, at home, he would explain the answers to us.

On one occasion, when Thomas was around ten, he and I were home alone in the kitchen. He had the idea that he wanted to write a book and was working on it that day. He wrote all the way to the third chapter, which was about his muscular dystrophy, and he was asking me questions. Suddenly, he looked up at me from his laptop and asked, "Mom, my kind of muscular dystrophy affects my muscles, right?"

I replied, "Yes."

Then he inquired, "But, Mom, isn't the heart a muscle?" Well, that realization hit him like a ton of bricks, and so we talked about this revelation for a while that day. That was the point he stopped writing his book.

After this realization, Thomas began secretly researching the Internet, looking for more information and answers. He learned that vitamins might boost his immune system. We asked the doctors if he was old enough to try certain supplements like Q10 and what kind of dosage he would be allowed. (Q10 is a nutrient that is found in the body as well as in many foods. It's most commonly used for conditions affecting the heart and fluid build-up in the body.) Thomas hated taking pills of any kind, but he wanted to try whatever he could to help himself. Many times, he would gag and the vitamin would come right back up. Sometimes it would take up to twenty minutes before he eventually swallowed it.

I have to admit, when it came to Thomas taking a pill, Glenn had no patience. Whether it was a vitamin, Imodium, or eventually meds for his heart, it all took a lot of time and energy to administer Thomas's drugs.

He would have to say he was ready to take the pills. Otherwise, if he tried to swallow them too soon or as quickly as possible, as many of us may do, Thomas would end up vomiting them back up. He was highly irritated when Glenn was there to administer the pills because Glenn just wanted this task done and over with.

Thomas applied the same conscientiousness as he displayed researching his illness to taking care of his beloved pet fish, Flamin' Thunder. He would spend time daily talking to his fish, giving the fish the required amount of food, and putting a mirror against the bowl to give Flamin' Thunder exercise, making the fish think he had another pal to play with. This was definitely an easy pet for Thomas, and he took his fish's care very seriously.

Thomas, taken from "Thomas Time:"

In my house, we are a family of four: my mother, my father, my brother, and of course, me ... The only other one left in my family is my pet fish, Flamin' Thunder, a red-blue bi-colour-Betta male, who I haul around my house with me. I tend to observe him to the point where I can diagnose his health problems. Just after I got him, he developed fin rot. I was able to find a medicine to reverse the damage.

Together, our family enjoys just sitting after dinner in front of the television and watching movies or interesting shows together. We enjoy getting together with other relatives, especially for celebrations. We also support each other in events that are important to each of us individually, like concerts, fundraisers, and sports.

Sometimes, Jamie was maybe a little rough on Thomas. There were moments when Thomas complained that Jamie plopped him down on the bed or in the chair a little too forcefully for his liking. On the other hand, Jamie put up with Thomas's personal care issues, duties that most siblings or saints would never even consider, like the bum wiping. Jamie bit his tongue many times while helping out his little brother.

All in all, his role as caregiver made Jamie stronger. He understood Thomas. He knew that Thomas needed help with everything from getting schoolwork out of his bag, to eating, or having his nose scratched regularly. Now, as a young man in his thirties, Jamie has a deep understanding of people with disabilities. He can see beyond the wheelchair and empathize with the daily challenges someone in a chair experiences. He's not quick to judge and will help without hesitating.

Junior High School

Not only was Thomas learning more about himself, but he was also facing big changes as he entered grade 7: a new school, new educational assistants, a larger student population, less help, a different teacher for each subject, and of course, a heavier workload for every subject. Thomas was assigned an Individualized Personal Plan, which teachers create for students who have special or additional needs. The goals written by the teachers focused on giving him more independence. Thomas was excited to do more on his own. He always saw himself as a normal kid. However, he still required assistants in each class to organize his books and computer, help with the washroom, and feed him lunch. There were new friends for him to meet, new people for him to teach about his disabilities, and new teachers who had to figure out how to get him where he needed to go.

We had the usual battles securing an educational assistant, and more issues with bussing. Also, Thomas was now part of a leadership program within the school. This required him to go to a seniors' home once a week during school time. The school board refused to pay for a wheelchair-accessible bus to transport him to the seniors' home. They told us to talk to the city. When we called the city, they informed us that HandiBus was only for transporting clients to medical appointments. They said they were going to charge $27 for each one-way, ten-minute trip.

So, we fought. We called our school trustee, our city counsellor, the city office, our Member of Legislature (MLA), the school board, and HandiBus. After spending hours on the phone and sending multiple emails, we were finally able to get HandiBus to agree to book the trips for $2.50 one-way. We were happy that Thomas could fulfill his leadership responsibilities without the cost being too onerous. As an added bonus, we had paved the way for future students in the same situation.

As he got older, Thomas came to better understand the logistics of school field trips and was able to admit that sometimes they were not a realistic option for him. One science trip included a boat ride in a dinghy down the Bow River. As much as he wanted to be able to do that, he agreed that he would meet up with the group at the end of the ride.

Perhaps one of Thomas's biggest thrills was speaking at the galas, particularly those in support of Easter Seals. He also spoke at functions for Calgary's Between Friends club, Calgary Cerebral Palsy, Janus Academy, The PREP Program, and the Children's Wish Foundation.

On October 20, 2007's Giddy Up Gala, "Back to the Saloon," not only did he write and deliver a speech to over seven hundred in attendance, but he sang a solo called "When You Have a Dream." I accompanied him on the ukulele. Calgary TV news anchor, Gord Gillies, was the MC. He interviewed Thomas prior to his speech and held the microphone for Thomas as he spoke. I was holding his script. Gord continued to hold the microphone as Thomas sang his song. I had a difficult time holding back my tears. I was so proud of him for his courage to speak in front of so many, and I was beginning to realize the impact he was having on the crowd. He was growing up in a way I could not have imagined.

Thomas's speech:

Good evening ladies and gentlemen, special guests, and Stampede Queens' Alumni.[6] *Or in cowboy talk maybe I should say, "Howdy, partners!" My name is Thomas Sorensen and I am both honoured and privileged to be invited to*

---

6   "The Calgary Stampede Queen's Alumni Committee is a diverse and dynamic group of past Calgary Stampede Queens, Ladies in waiting, and Princesses. While celebrating the amazing sisterhood that the Stampede has created, they work tirelessly to bring authentic and fun Western events to children with special needs throughout the year." Source: The Calgary Stampede, accessed November 27, 2021, csroyalty.com/queens-alumni.html

speak at tonight's Giddy Up Gala. I am eleven years old, and I attend MidSun Junior High School in grade 7.

When I was two years old, I was diagnosed with a rare form of muscular dystrophy. The specialists told my family that I am one of twenty in the world with my disease. My Pure Congenital Muscular Dystrophy basically means that I have extremely low muscle tone.

Every day is a challenge for me. I need help with the simplest things like scratching my nose, getting a drink of milk, or rolling over in my bed during the night. My mom, my dad, or my brother help me get dressed, carry me from place to place, and get me whatever I need to do homework, play a game, or watch TV.

When I learned about tonight's gala, I did a little research. I found out that the Stampede Queens' Alumni continue each year to raise monies to support children with special needs. You have no idea what this means to kids like me!

I'm sure the Alumni Queens dreamt about becoming a Stampede Queen!

All of us need dreams to look forward to. I know that my friends and I continue to dream about the next time we are able to attend camp! I have been fortunate to be able to attend two camps [because of] the Stampede Queens' support. I have attended the Light Up A Life camp at the Easter Seals Camp Horizon and Camp Bonaventure with the Between Friends club of Calgary.

Camp Horizon is awesome! It is a week-long, overnight camp full of incredible activities. The Light Up A Life camp is specialized for kids with physical disabilities. Camp Horizon also holds camps for other kids with special needs for the remainder of the summer.

Each year we go to No Ka Oi Ranch. At the ranch, they have special gear that allows kids like me to be able to ride a horse. We also get to go on hay bale rides. They have a ramp built so that we can simply ride up onto the wagon in our wheelchairs to go for the ride. I love the evenings when we gather round the campfire and sing camp songs like "Your Momma Don't Wear No Socks!" The cooks at camp are the best. They prepare gourmet meals every day for us. My favourite is curly fries with lots of ketchup!

At Camp Bonaventure, we attend a two-week-long day camp. We have a different theme every day. We get to go rock climbing, swimming, horseback riding, sailing, and many other things. Camp Bonaventure has kids with all kinds of disabilities.

Both of the camps provide me opportunities to do things that I would not normally be able to try. The counsellors are awesome and I have met many new friends. Camp always goes too fast, and I can hardly wait for the year to go by so that I may go again.

Camp is a learning experience for me, too. It is interesting to make so many friends who are similar, but at the same time different from me. What I've learned is that even though we all had a disability and couldn't do everything, there were things that we could do to help each other. We definitely gave support when someone was struggling to overcome a fear of trying something new.

I am very glad that Camp Horizon and the Between Friends club exist. They offer things for me to do that I perhaps would not be able to do otherwise. They give opportunities for so many kids to get out, make new friends, be themselves, and have a sense of belonging. I also know kids with cerebral palsy and kids who attend the Janus Academy. All of these organizations are crucial in our lives.

So, in closing, I just want to say thank you to the Stampede Queens' Alumni for continuing to support kids with special needs, and also a thank you to all of you for being here tonight and supporting such a wonderful cause.

I know that I am not alone when I say how awesome these organizations are. Many of my friends feel the same way. We all dream about the adventures we have had and hold wonderful memories until we get to go again. I have a song to sing that kind of sums it all up. "When You Have a Dream."

When you have a dream, you can make them come true, if you believe you can.

Set your goals, make your plans, don't let anything stand in your way 'til your dreams come true.

Dream, dream, follow your dream, without dreams how can wishes come true?
Dream, dream, follow your dream, without dreams how can wishes come true?
Each day starts a new, full of promise and hope, take a step toward that goal.
Put your fears on a shelf, just believe in yourself and you'll see that dream come true.[7]

---

7   Used with permission from Denise Gagne.

Thomas received a standing ovation! Many of the attendees came up to both Thomas and me to let us know how much he inspired everyone. If my memory serves me correctly, well over $200,000 was raised that evening. I would like to think that Thomas had a big part of that success.

More and more opportunities came along. Another non-profit organization, Between Friends of Calgary, which offers programming for people with disabilities, asked Thomas to speak at their gala. He had been a participant at some of their summer camps and took part in some weekend activities throughout the years. My sister Sue was in town from Nova Scotia, so she was able to attend the dinner with us.

In 2008, when Thomas was twelve, he was appointed the Easter Seals Youth Ambassador for Southern Alberta. What an honour! Easter Seals held an official presentation of his appointment at our local Sobeys grocery store, and then the fun really began.

Thomas was invited to so many events and accepted donations from various organizations on behalf of Easter Seals. He spoke to Safeway stores nationwide via video conferences about Easter Seals. Safeway was a huge supporter of Easter Seals for many years, and this role was a perfect fit for Thomas to work with both organizations to raise awareness about people with disabilities.

Thomas continued to spend time at grocery stores, working to get donations from customers. Overall it was a positive experience, but one particular grocery store was not his favourite. The community seemed oblivious and could not even acknowledge Thomas's voice. They just walked by as if he was invisible. Thomas was not impressed and did not readily volunteer to go back to that particular store.

He also gave tours of Camp Horizon to organizations supporting the camp.

Makrina, Thomas's friend from Camp Horizon, Youth Ambassador for 2019:

I was thrilled when I found out that Thomas was going to be named the 2008 Easter Seals Youth Ambassador. He was able to share his experience at all of the Easter Seals events throughout the year. He talked about his unique experience at camp and was able to relate with anyone who he spoke to.

The Giddy Up Gala invited Thomas back the following year. On October 25, 2008, the gala was called "A Night in Hollywood."

At the gala, Thomas was psyched up and ready to pose for a picture with the royal party of the Calgary Stampede (the Stampede queen and princesses). I was fortunate to have found an almost brand-new tuxedo at a second-hand store. It fit Thomas well, and I had paid little for the suit. He wore the traditional black jacket, pants, and white dress shirt that made the bow tie fit perfectly. With his hair slicked back, he looked so handsome. He was thrilled when someone paid $450 in the auction to dance with him. It was an exceptional evening.

The Easter Seals gala in 2009 premiered the video for country singer Gord Bamford's song "Things Go Better with Love." Another highlight for Thomas was that he had been invited to a full-day taping to be in the video with Gord and other kids connected with Easter Seals. It was a long day, but he was excited to see what went into the making a music video. My principal at the time was by-the-book so I had to take a day off without pay to accompany Thomas. I did enjoy meeting and getting to know the other participants in the video. Some we'd already met and were able to get to know better while others were new friends, children with Down syndrome. All of the participants were so loveable. I could see the excitement in their eyes. Both Thomas and I thoroughly enjoyed the day. I even got my own cameo appearance in the video!

He continued with many fundraisers at my schools: the Give a Buck for Luck fundraiser, several Hop-a-Thons (being the number one fundraiser in Canada for three years in a row) for Muscular Dystrophy Canada, and multiple Paper Egg campaigns for Easter Seals.

With Thomas involved in so many events for the Children's Wish Foundation, Easter Seals, Between Friends, and Muscular Dystrophy Canada, we were suddenly extremely busy.

Jamie took a long time deciding to get his driver's licence. Again, he has never been big on change. In 2008, when he was eighteen, we convinced him to sign up for a driver's education program. Thomas was twelve and in grade 7. We needed Jamie to take this step, not only for his own independence, but selfishly, as parents, we wanted some help with Thomas's transports.

The presence of one extra driver in the house gave all of us some freedom. Jamie began volunteering with the organizations Thomas was involved in. He helped Thomas with the Easter Seals and Muscular Dystrophy campaigns, spending long hours at grocery stores drumming up support for Thomas's cause. He helped get Thomas to events during the weekday hours when Glenn and I were at work and couldn't get away. Jamie and Thomas were loving these moments that enabled them to become closer brothers and friends, and Jamie also grew a greater appreciation for who Thomas was. This newly found source of independence enabled both of them to grow and discover themselves.

Glenn:

Being a family with a handicapped person has its challenges. The average family is able to go out whenever and wherever they decide to. We, on the other hand, needed to talk about where we were going: Was it handicapped accessible? Were there handicapped parking spots and washrooms? Was it snowing? Or raining? Would we need to carry Thomas any great distances? And so on.

Once, we took Thomas and Jamie to Banff in the Rocky Mountains for the weekend. Banff is a tourist town, but it's not very accessible for people in wheelchairs. There were so many stores that Thomas couldn't enter. A step or two at the door barred us from entry. These entryways were designed for *uprights,* a term Thomas used for people who can walk. If Thomas couldn't get in the store, we avoided it and pretended for his sake that we were just window shopping.

Whenever we went out, I told Thomas to let us know in advance, if he could, when he needed a washroom so we could keep an eye out for one. Sometimes it was really hard taking Thomas to pee. When Jamie was along, it was easier. If Jamie and I worked together, one of us could lift and carry Thomas from his chair, and the other could work on getting his pants down and then back up. When it was just me, it was difficult. I needed to hold him up with one arm and pull his pants down with the other, and this was made more difficult by being in a small cubicle. The reverse order is harder: pick Thomas up, hold him with one arm, pull up his pants with the other, and get him back in his chair. But through all this, Thomas never complained. He always said sorry and thank you.

I'm sure we could have taken more holidays than we did, but as Thomas grew older and heavier, I was always worried about transportation and accessibility. Kathy and the kids would have liked more holidays; I was just too scared. However, one of the trips Thomas really enjoyed was to the Royal Tyrrell Dinosaur Museum in Drumheller, about one-and-a-half hours away from home by car. Thomas and I went there every summer for years, just the two of us. We both enjoyed exploring the exhibits, reading about the incredible history, and looking forward to new displays. Kathy was not a big fan of going and preferred to have the day to do the household chores uninterrupted or just to have a day to herself. Thomas's tradition was when we finished exploring the museum, we would sit and have ice cream before heading home.

Thomas thrived in junior high. He enjoyed meeting new kids and staff and was not at all worried about the curriculum. He participated in group projects in his many different classes and enjoyed getting together with other classmates after school to do homework. There were times when Thomas would invite his classmates to our home to work on assignments. It was easier access for Thomas, and other students' parents weren't comfortable inviting him to their homes. They felt inadequate having to deal with a child with special needs, so our house became the place to meet.

Every year, Thomas, challenged his teachers. If the assignment was a poster, a construction that Thomas could not physically create, he would come up with another suggestion and suggest it to his teacher as an option. One project that will always be a cherished memory was a chemistry project on the periodic table. Thomas asked his teacher if he could do a video, showing his understanding of the periodic table. He took a familiar tune at the time, the theme song from a Mario Bros. game, and rewrote the lyrics to fit his understanding of the elements on the periodic table. He did this all on his own. To date, this is one of my favourite videos of Thomas. He was creative, imaginative, on key, and totally effective in getting across his understanding of the periodic table. As I recall, his teacher gave him 100 per cent on his project.

As the end of the first year in junior high neared, Glenn and I received a call from the school extending a special invitation to the school's awards ceremony. We had no idea why we were invited. Much to our surprise, Thomas received The Spirit, Heart, and Legacy Award. This award recognized Thomas for personal development, citizenship, character, and academic performance. It was voted on by the staff of the school and was based on his grades and achievements. He was the only one to receive the award that year.

Gregg:

Likely the most well-known story about Thomas and me occurred while we were in junior high school, but before I get into the story, you will need some background information.

Thomas and I used to travel around the community with him driving his wheelchair while I caught a ride on the back. We thought this was hilarious, and we often received some very odd looks from people passing by. Watching people's reactions as we drove by never got old. This led Thomas to get the bright idea that we should go through a fast-food drive-through using his chair, with me on the back, instead of using a vehicle.

One evening, while Glenn and Kathy were away, Jamie was driving us home and we stopped at a Tim Horton's to accomplish this plan. After Jamie and I unloaded Thomas from the van, I hopped onto the back of his chair. We drove up to the microphone to place our order, which we had decided would be two chocolate Timbits. As we sat there driving back and forth on the pad to try to set off the sensor, Jamie realized we didn't weigh enough to set it off, so he drove the van up behind us. This set the sensor off and allowed Thomas to attempt to place our order.

I never saw Thomas laugh as hard as he did throughout this adventure. Due to his laughter, he couldn't talk to the man taking our order, so after some delay, I placed our order, which came to a total of $0.34. The man taking our order didn't even question us; he simply followed regular procedure, telling us to head to the window—so we did just that. As Thomas continued to struggle to function because of laughter, we drove up to the window with our two quarters to pay. We got to the window, and the man who had received our order had a huge smile on his face, as he thought this was hilarious. While Thomas and I received the two Timbits, I tried to hand over our change to pay. The Tim Horton's worker denied our money and simply said, "Don't worry about it." It was one of the funniest, weirdest, and happiest moments of my life.

Up until 2009, our family vehicle was a green Dodge Grand Caravan with bucket seats in the back along with a bench seat in the rear, which could be folded to create more storage. Thomas was still small enough for me to lift him from his chair to the seat behind the driver's seat, but I knew those days were coming to an end. I was beginning to have problems lifting him high enough to get him into the van. Actually, I was worried that I might drop him. I always said my left arm was my "Thomas arm." It was muscular and much stronger than my right.

His chair was also an issue. I had to somehow find the strength to get the chair on its hind wheels, hoist it up and over the back bumper, and then lift it into the van. This was a 250-lb chair, and I was not getting any younger. I had been managing getting the chair in the van but now, at age forty-nine, I was having a tough time. I remember one day as a young guy saw me wrestling to get the chair into the van, he just walked past, saying, "Wow, that looks heavy." That was the day we decided we needed to get a handicapped van.

Thomas's dental growth mimicked mine, with each tooth appearing at an early age. I was thirteen when all four of my wisdom teeth were removed, and Thomas followed suit. My sister Sue, a now-retired dental hygienist, taught me to brush the boys' teeth properly from their birth. She told me that it's common for kids to have the same experience with their teeth as their parents.

We decided to remove Thomas's wisdom teeth in 2009, but at the same time, his specialist at the hospital wanted another muscle biopsy done to confirm his kind of muscular dystrophy. She wasn't convinced of his earlier diagnosis of Pure Congenital Muscular Dystrophy. She didn't say much beyond that—only that she wanted to use this opportunity for further investigation. We were a little surprised but felt she knew what she was doing. We wanted to know, too, if there was a more definite diagnosis that could somehow help him. We agreed and booked yet another muscle biopsy to be done at the same time as the removal of his wisdom teeth. Thomas would be under and would therefore not feel the incision.

Within hours, his wisdom teeth gone and his mouth filled up with cotton balls, there he was, recuperating from the dental surgery as well as the incision on the right side of his thigh. The entire procedure meant several days at the hospital. I spent the nights with Thomas. Glenn, at my side for the surgery, relieved me through the daytime so I could go to work. The Children's Hospital had video games and movies for the kids to help pass the time.

The biopsy came back giving us the same information we'd heard before.

Thomas on Facebook, November 12, 2009:

Thomas Sorensen is going for his swine flu shot today! Don't worry, it's fine, all the stories are just what the government want you to believe …

Starting in junior high school and for the rest of his life, Thomas was prone to nosebleeds. They came in spurts; when he got one, he got many. We made several trips to the emergency room to have his nose cauterized, which was always an unpleasant experience, but we also became proficient in stopping the nosebleeds. We were told the many ways of stopping nosebleeds such as cold compresses on the neck or holding the head in a particular way. These myths did not work for him. With Thomas, we found he needed to blow his nose. Yes, the clots came out, but for some strange reason, blowing them out would also slow the flow. His worst nosebleed lasted fifty minutes.

Finally, an ear, nose, and throat specialist performed an extremely unpleasant test to help determine why he kept having these nosebleeds. So, at the age of twelve, poor Thomas had a scope put up his nose to examine what was going on. It was painful, and the results were inconclusive.

We continued our known practice: to hold his nose for the first ten minutes, and if the nosebleed didn't stop, another twenty. Watching the clock was usually our guide. Every day we applied a nasal solvent or Vaseline in Thomas's nose and set a humidifier to run in his room twenty-four hours a day year-round.

A New Passion

Thomas had a great love for sports. He particularly loved soccer, and when he was growing up, he only wished he could be on a "real" team.

Thomas would politely ask me to move the car out of the garage so he could have room to practise his soccer skills. He spent hours moving a regular soccer ball around the garage in his wheelchair and with his footrests up so he could use his feet and legs. This was excellent exercise for maintaining his feet and leg muscles while improving his soccer skills.

We wanted to see more sports for people in power chairs, especially in Calgary. Luckily, we found out about a form of soccer for people with disabilities called power soccer. One family had started the soccer group, but they were forced to give up due to commitments with their own child, so I took it over. Thomas wanted this program to happen for himself but also for others who wanted to play.

The players had large grates—specialized metal or plastic frames made to attach to a wheelchair and to maneuver a large, custom soccer ball. At this time, the organizers were trying to find indoor facilities for the players. Power soccer was expensive, not only for the equipment required for the chairs but also to pay for the facilities. Thomas and I made some phone calls to potential donors to ask for help with the costs. Some individuals and a community club decided to contribute to the cause.

Once we were able to order the frames, those who wanted to play on the power soccer team began to get excited. It took some time to figure out just how to attach the frames not only to Thomas's chair but to his friends' chairs as well, as every chair was different and needed various adjustments to get the frame to fit. Many of the players' parents committed to helping with the first few practices.

Thomas was having a blast experiencing a new sport. Powerchair Football Canada plays by international rules, including the size of the ball. This ball is three times the size of a regular soccer ball. Learning how to move his chair to allow the ball to navigate was a skill in itself. Learning how to get the ball into the net to score a goal was yet another skill. Working together with the other players as a team was an extraordinary feat for him and the others.

There were participants of all ages from age eight to seventy, each with a customized wheelchair. Every participant had a different way of maneuvering their chair: either with a joystick, their chin, or even their mouth, depending on their chair and their physical abilities. They each had to learn how to move the ball and work together as a team without running into each other. It was a small group of participants; however, all of them totally enjoyed the experience.

Thomas was featured on the local TV sports news. They did a five-minute story on his starting up the soccer team for people with disabilities:

Thomas on Facebook, June 8, 2009:

Thomas Sorensen says to watch Global TV—Calgary at 5:30–6:00 on Wednesday!

Jamie got involved in Thomas's sports around this time by volunteering as a coach for the power soccer team. He took Thomas to the practices and also helped the teammates set up their bumpers. He was there to help Thomas with the washroom and feed him snacks and water when needed. Jamie enjoyed the sport and understood the participants' passion.

These guys and girls flew! It was fair game on the court with everyone learning how to maneuver the ball in a power chair. The gym was open, and no one knew where anyone might drive. It was a great opportunity, though, for the kids to perfect their driving skills as they rode with the ball, barely missing each other in the process. When watching a game, your heart would skip a few beats just watching the speed and skills they had and seeing the near misses. Jamie knew how important this was not only for Thomas but for the many participants in the sport. He felt satisfied helping out.

The sport was growing. Four months after establishing the group, Thomas, Jamie, and I arranged for a weekend workshop for power soccer in the Calgary area. Twenty-six participants came out for the workshop.

We later managed to have the Alberta Soccer Association oversee the league for people with disabilities. Establishing the league and bringing it to the level where it received provincial recognition and support was a proud achievement for all of us.

Thomas on Facebook, September 10, 2009:

Soccer season starts tomorrow! By next summer, I think we will be ready for the California tourny!!! Woot!!! Go Blizzards!!!

After such a positive experience with power soccer, Thomas found The Calgary Powerhockey League (CPHL), an organization created for people in wheelchairs to actively participate in hockey. The game was played on a gymnasium floor with bumpers around all four sides of the room. A plastic ball served as the puck. Here, too, there were participants of all ages and abilities.

We learned that there were three levels of stick-holding skills. The top level was when a player could physically hold a stick and had the strength to maneuver it. At the second level, the player could hold the stick without having the muscle to move it. The third level included players who did not have any upper body strength. Third level participants had a stick creatively attached to their chair.

Thomas was ecstatic to learn about the possibilities. We signed him up after going to watch some games in action. It was in December of 2009 when Thomas found out that he would be on one of the four teams. This was the beginning of his greatest passion.

Thomas on Facebook, January 9, 2010:

First game today!!!! Got myself an assist in hockey! Broke a kid's stick when he lunged for my tires! End score only losing 4–2! The game was epic!!!! GO VIPERS!!!! WOOT!!!

Sometimes, life throws curveballs. This time the ball came out of the left field: in January 2009, Glenn's dad was diagnosed with lung cancer, and he was given six months to live.

Hans had not let on to anyone that he was feeling unwell. It came as a shock to the family, and Alice was simply a wreck. This was her love, her life, and she and Hans were being told his life was about to end. It was the beginning of a very trying time for everyone. Glenn had one sister who lived in Vancouver and one in Texas, so the onus was on us to care for his parents. We avoided trips and outings, especially during this rough period.

Christmas that year was a break from tradition. Glenn's parents decided it would be okay if Glenn and I hosted the family Christmas celebration. This was a big decision. Hans and Alice had always run the festivities and kept a tight hold on the big dinner, especially. That year we had several family members—Glenn's two nieces, one with her husband and two kids—staying with us. Thomas, now thirteen years old, was so excited! We made sure the house was appropriately decorated for all to enjoy and took charge of all the decorations and planning. It was a busy yet reflective time for us. We all thought this would be Grandpa's last Christmas since Hans had already outlived the doctors' predictions by six months, so we wanted to ensure that everyone would remember this as a special holiday.

We served the traditional Christmas Eve dinner: a giant turkey stuffed with ground pork, onion, and allspice; candied potatoes; small, canned potatoes sautéed in butter and sugar; red cabbage; vegetables; gravy; and risalamande, the traditional rice pudding dessert with the almond(s) hidden in it.

After dinner, Santa Kim made his annual visit. Kim was a long-time family friend who played Santa every Christmas Eve at the Sorensen house. He had been doing this tradition for close to forty years, so he had his visit timed perfectly, just before the Danish tradition of singing around the tree and followed by the gift opening. Christmas Eve always ended up with a late-night snack of turkey sandwiches served with fresh white bread and lots of mayonnaise.

The following March, in 2010, I was turning fifty. Glenn and I decided to host a party at the Danish Canadian Club. We went the night before to decorate the room and invited several guests for a traditional Danish smorg. Thomas was a little worried about timing on that day. He had hockey that afternoon and didn't want to miss it because of the party. He lobbied and eventually convinced us to help him make it to both events. He would wear his tux underneath his hockey jersey, play his game, and be able to make it to the Danish Canadian Club in time. Jamie only had to pull Thomas's jersey off and put on his suit jacket.

The plan worked. He had an awesome game and made it in time to join in the festivities. His best friend, Gregg, came to the party, too. Great food was had, and many of the guests had prepared a song for me, including one from Glenn to the tune of "The Old Grey Mare," and another from our boys.

Thomas on Facebook, March 16, 2010:

Leaving soon for Billy Talent with Jamie! Woot!

Jamie and Thomas had a chance to go together to hear one of their favourite bands, Billy Talent. Thomas was so ecstatic! He looked forward to the evening, spending it with Jamie, and feeling grown up enough to attend such a concert. He was hoping to share some mini doughnuts with his brother. I was thankful that I didn't have to attend as, I have to admit, Billy Talent's music is not the type of music I enjoy. It was a great memory the boys made together, loving every song performed.

Confirmation and a New Pet

When Thomas was fourteen, he decided that he wanted to be confirmed through the Danish Lutheran Church. This was important to him, as confirmation is the second major milestone in a Dane's life after baptism. He attended weekly sessions with our pastor, learning the Lutheran teachings, and he was confirmed in April 2010. We held a family celebration for him with the traditional seven-course Danish smorg. Many relatives travelled to Calgary to help us celebrate. Grandpa was a little sad when Thomas refused to try the Danish akvavit during his celebration, but he understood Thomas's reluctance. With a 45 per cent alcohol level, Aalborg Akvavit is a powerful shot.

Jamie had come to me a couple of weeks prior to the confirmation and asked if he could give Thomas a real turtle as a confirmation gift. Thomas loved turtles and had a vast collection of them from stuffies, to pictures, and carvings. He also had turtles made of glass and metal. I gave in to Jamie's wish, knowing that yes, I would probably be the one who would have to do the feeding and caring for the turtle, but for Jamie to give his brother such a pet seemed like a thoughtful gesture.

Thomas named his turtle Frank. Don't ask me why; I have no idea.

Thomas on Facebook April 24, 2010:

I just got a new pet turtle! His name is Frank. I think he is a four-toed "three-toed box turtle."[8]

You know you have the best pet ever when it's a turtle and it winks at you most times you enter the room.

Frank, you're such a charmer ...

---

8   Yet another example of Thomas's sense of humour, describing Frank. It seemed his three-toed box turtle (the official name for this type of turtle) had four toes!

Thomas received lots of other gifts as well: a watch, a gold chain, a camera, an original framed picture, a cross, lots of money, and more. These gifts were not only from family but from many friends at the church. We were surprised that so many of the congregation recognized Thomas's special day with gifts.

Glenn and I felt that we needed to say thank you to each person who had been so thoughtful. I helped Thomas write thank-you cards to each, and we invited them to our home for afternoon coffee. In keeping with Danish tradition, "afternoon coffee" meant coffee, sandwiches with an assortment of meats and cheeses on bread, pastries, chocolate, and shots of akvavit. More than twenty people came. We had the long table set up to seat everyone comfortably and decorated it with red tablecloths and Danish flags.

Ryan

Right after I was confirmed through my church, my parents organized a confirmation party at our house. I would have been around fourteen at the time. Although I was grateful to have so many around for my sake, I was excited to leave all of the relatives at the table and go hang out with my friends.

Thomas was really good at ball hockey, and it just so happened that Thomas, Gregg, me, and a few others ended up playing ball hockey out on my driveway on confirmation day. All of the grown-ups were inside having a nice, peaceful time eating and enjoying small talk while the kids were outside wreaking absolute havoc—yelling, laughing, and running all over the neighbourhood. There were even some neighbours checking to see what all the noise was about.

There was a point when Thomas had the ball and was headed straight for the curb in an attempt to create some room off the driveway and onto the road. Just as my mom came out to check on us, she saw Thomas go full speed off the curb in his wheelchair. I looked at her, then back at Thomas, unsure of what was about to happen. What kind of trouble we were all about to get in? Suddenly, maniacal laughter emanated from Thomas, as he had successfully evaded the people chasing him, nearly causing his chair to flip over. Thomas continued off, happy as ever, and I looked back at my mom as she turned around without saying a word. I can only imagine that her stress levels were insurmountable. She was left at a loss of words for how bad the situation could have turned out.

Grade 9 was a busy year. Thomas had so many school projects and a lot of homework. When we didn't have a personal assistant, I had great difficulty in transcribing the work Thomas needed to do, such as writing out mathematical equations. He was very patient with me. He knew I was trying my best and never complained.

In the spring of 2010, when the end of grade 9 was fast approaching, we received another call from the school asking Glenn and me to attend the awards ceremony. Again, none of us had any inkling as to why, but we all attended.

We enjoyed the ceremony, but the end was approaching and all but the last award had been announced. Glenn and I were still wondering why we had been invited to attend. Then, we heard Thomas's name announced. He received the MidSun Faculty Award. This award was chosen by the teachers for a student who had achieved honours standing in each term of grades 7, 8, and 9 in all subject areas. We'd had no idea this was coming. Even with all his daily challenges and days he had missed for appointments, Thomas was the top student. We were so very proud. We took photos and Thomas's teachers shook our hands in congratulations. They didn't want to say goodbye to Thomas as he headed off to high school.

High School Approaches

The choice of which high school Thomas would attend opened up a whole new can of worms. Thomas didn't want to follow the direction of the school board and go to the school in our district. He really wanted to go to the high school his best friends from elementary school would attend. Gregg, in particular, had remained a true friend since kindergarten not only in Thomas's eyes but ours as well. We understood why Thomas wanted to spend his high school years with his best friend.

In order for Thomas to be accepted to this particular school, he had to argue as to why he wanted to attend and why the designated school in our district couldn't meet his needs. At the school of his choice, Thomas could apply for Advanced Placement (AP) courses that are offered for advanced education and which lead to first-year university courses. The designated school didn't offer AP courses. Thomas loved science, and he believed he could achieve a good standing in the advanced sciences. He applied, writing a letter from his own point of view explaining why he should be accepted. His application also required references from previous teachers.

It was a joyous day when Thomas received his letter of acceptance. We had many meetings with the administration at his new high school, talking with educational assistants about Thomas's specific needs, his capabilities, and his courses. To our surprise, they had a good understanding of his needs. They requested that we purchase a cell phone for Thomas, as he would have to text the assistants when he required the washroom. The educational assistants were in place, and his new chapter began.

Gregg on Facebook, to Thomas, May 20, 2010:

WOOOOOOOOOOOT YOU ARE GOING TO SCARLETT!!!!!!!!!!!!!!!

Thomas on Facebook, May 20, 2010:

Thomas Sorensen is officially going to E.P. Scarlett next year!!! WOOT! Met with the assistant principal, the AP guy, the class schedule guy, the ed. assistant person, the occupational therapists, the physical therapists, and three other people whose job title I can't remember, and now I'm totally prepared for high school! Will be in all the same classes as Gregg Hamilton, too! Can't wait!

It was the end of power hockey season, and Thomas was both excited and sad. Excited for the banquet and possible awards, and sad because he would have to wait until fall to play again. The awards banquet was being held in June, and Jamie and I attended the dinner with him.

Thomas was dressed in a blue dress shirt and tie. He could barely contain himself. He wanted to leave for the banquet sooner than later. He was bouncing in his chair and had a smile from ear to ear. His cheeks were flushed with excitement. All of his buddies from power hockey were there. The kids were all competitive but at the same time supportive of each other.

Thomas was thrilled to receive the award for Most Outstanding Rookie of the Year for 2010. His hockey career had begun. He also received a trophy with the actual ball in a case commemorating his first-ever goal.

Thomas on Facebook, June 2010:

I GOT OUTSTANDING ROOKIE OF THE YEAR IN HOCKEY! It's all thanks to my team for support! THANKS, VIPERS!

Jeff Barrett, Thomas's friend from power hockey:

Thomas had an unbelievable passion for hockey. He was the kind of player you would definitely want on your team. He was a hard worker, putting hours and hours into practising to be a better player, and he always asked me what I thought he could do to be a better player. Thomas never saw his disability, only his ability to get better. He was like a sculptor, perfecting his craft.

Although he asked for it, Thomas never needed my advice, as he was such a smart hockey player. He knew how to use his stick and wheelchair to give his team an advantage in any situation. I think a lot of the younger players looked up to Thomas because of the confidence he had and for not settling for the skills he had. Every year, he would set goals for himself and work as hard as he could to accomplish them.

He could always bring a smile to your face, whether from his sense of humour, advice, or words of encouragement. As great of a teammate he was, he was also a respectful and humble opponent.

Jamie and Thomas also shared a love for NHL hockey. They participated in hockey draft pools and enjoyed going to our local Calgary Flames games whenever they could. Jamie was completely supportive of Thomas, especially when it came to sports.

Thomas was thrilled to be chosen that June to play in a special hockey game against the Calgary Police Service. It was fun to watch the police officers try to maneuver the manual wheelchairs against the "pros." The police had no chance of winning. Their members had no idea how to push their chairs while trying to move a hockey stick with a puck to score a goal, how to gain speed, or how to watch where they were going while trying to move their wheels. I believe the police went in hoping to boost the spirits of their opponents knowing they wouldn't have a chance. It was a great community builder, and both teams had a great day.

It had hit me within seconds. Literally. I had H1N1 influenza.

It was a hot, sunny Friday afternoon in June 2010. I came home from work, opened a bottle of beer, and started mowing the lawn. The birds were chirping, the flowers were blooming, and the fresh-cut grass smelled wonderful. I was feeling great, physically and emotionally, knowing I only had a couple of days left of the school year.

I came in the house from mowing the lawn, and that was it. Suddenly I felt so ill. My body ached, and I had absolutely no energy. I immediately laid down on the couch feeling totally incapacitated. I was worried, too. Thomas was home, and I wouldn't be able help him if he needed anything. Thirty minutes passed while I waited for Glenn to get home. It seemed like hours. I have never experienced anything like that before or since.

The next morning I did manage to go to a clinic. I put on a mask as I entered, and after examining me, the doctor confirmed I had H1N1. For the next five days, I was flat out in bed, only managing to get up for the washroom. I was cautious, wearing a mask and staying in our bedroom away from everyone. The only thing I wanted to do was sleep. Glenn was amazing, bringing me ginger ale or soup. I was so scared that my boys would catch the horrible virus.

Since the school year was over, it was almost time for Thomas to again head to Camp Horizon. He was excited that the school year had ended and that camp was starting; he always called it the best place on Earth. Within a few days, I was thankfully well enough to get out of bed to see Thomas off to camp.

Thomas on Facebook, July 1, 2010:

Birds are stupid. One of them crapped on me today!

Thomas's high school had fifteen hundred students and only three assistants. We felt he was still too young at fourteen to have a cell phone, but we understood why the school wanted him to have one. Thomas was pretty excited to get his hands on his new gadget!

Thomas on Facebook, July 6, 2010:

Parents + iPhone = BAD

He was bouncing with excitement as Glenn and I drove him out to camp. He never looked back at us as he greeted his summer friends. At Camp Horizon, Thomas could enjoy himself, feeling completely "normal." He could be free from the constraints and struggles of the outside world and help his fellow campers.

But that year, Thomas was only at camp for three days when we received a call to come and pick him up. He was sick. I felt deflated that his week was interrupted. Knowing that I had had H1N1, we feared that he had the same. Off to the Children's Hospital we went. They felt that Thomas had perhaps indeed caught the horrible bug only because I had to tell them that I had had it the week before. They decided, sadly, to do the same test Thomas had previously had with the scope down the nose. He was not at all impressed and Thomas was not happy with me.

Thankfully, he didn't catch H1N1. It was just a cold, and he was able to return to camp for the last day.

Much to everyone's surprise, Grandpa Hans bounced back. Something was working. Within only a few months of refusing any more treatment, being only on painkillers, and eating what his wife thought were healing foods, he was feeling better. We all believed his improved health was because of

Alice, Glenn's mom. She was forever researching and trying out different kinds of food—anything known to fight cancer. Alice concocted a special daily drink with their Danish akvavit and garlic, combined with other ingredients. She made sure Hans had a daily dose of blueberries and broccoli. The cancer was still there, but Hans seemed to be holding his own. When he went to the cancer clinic for a checkup, the doctors asked, "Hans, how are you still here? What are you doing?"

Since Hans was currently able to live a relatively normal life, he announced that he wanted to take his three children to Denmark one last time. No spouses, no grandchildren. Just his kids. Glenn was not happy about this announcement. Firstly, he wanted me to go as well, and secondly, he was dreading three weeks with his two sisters. Glenn sometimes felt he was pushed around by his two sisters, especially when the three of them were together. Both Glenn and I understood that this was Hans's wish, however, so we went along with the plan.

Before Glenn left, he told me that he felt that I needed a break before returning to school in September. Even now, he won't admit this, but he suggested that I plan a trip with my friend, Kathy. (This is one of the many points where the two of us agree to disagree, as our memories are different.) Kathy and I were to go somewhere exciting after his return so that I could have some fun and relaxation. In August 2010, Glenn left for Denmark for three weeks.

Glenn has always wanted to share experiences with me. He told me that while in Denmark, his family was at an incredible historic site and one of his sisters asked why he wasn't taking pictures. He explained that I was not there to share it with him and that it would mean nothing to show the pictures to me unless I had been there with him.

He ended up having to sleep on the floor in their accommodations because one sister wouldn't share her room with the other. The three siblings also had their own thoughts as to who would drive the car, who would be in the front seat, and who would be in the back.

In spite of the arguments, and on a positive note, he did have many opportunities to enjoy time with their Danish relatives. They shared multiple traditional meals and reminisced about the old days. They took in the antique shops and saw the various beautiful landscapes of Denmark. We all knew that Hans was thinking this would be his last visit to his homeland.

It was at this time when I found out that my dear friend Lauren, who had been maid of honour at our wedding, was diagnosed with cancer. Hearing about her diagnosis was such a blow. She lived in Saskatchewan, a province away, and I hadn't seen her for quite some time.

We'd been through a lot together over several decades. Years ago, when I was alone raising Jamie in Lumsden, Lauren was single with three kids of her own. She and I helped each other out, babysitting for one another, taking the four kids to play events, and enjoying so many evenings together sharing meals and watching our kids play together. When we were lucky, we found a babysitter for all four kids so we could go out on the town in Lumsden. Lumsden had a pub which was famous for their "Steak Pit" meal, which was a steak with a baked potato for $5. You had to cook your own steak on the grill, but that was never a problem. Add a beer for a buck, and the night was cheap, but the memories are priceless. Jamie doesn't remember Lauren, sadly, but in his early age, he adored her and called her Yen Yen. When she called to tell me about her diagnosis I felt I needed to go and see her.

The day after Glenn left, I arranged for childcare and took a road trip to see Lauren. Jamie was old enough to look after himself and care for Thomas, but I knew he needed some extra help while I was away. I knew Glenn would be upset and worried about me driving eight hours to see Lauren, so the rebel in me came out; I didn't tell him.

In the end, I had an awesome three-day visit with Lauren. I certainly didn't regret going. I saw the life Lauren had with her new husband and the incredible flower garden she had created. I sat with her for hours and reminisced, and I was able to reconnect with one of her kids. Lauren and I went swimming in their pool when she was well enough, and I helped to prepare a few meals. She gathered the strength to take me out to her garden, where she dug up some of her perennials for me to plant in mine: purple coneflowers, delphiniums, lilyleaf, and ladybells. These plants still remain in our garden.

I had a difficult time saying goodbye. I feared the cancer had taken over and I wouldn't have another opportunity to see her again. Sadly, it was the last time I saw her alive. She passed away that December. The perennials came up the next year and every year since.

My friend Kathy and I had planned an all-inclusive trip to Mexico for one week, so upon my return from Saskatchewan, that was next on my list. The first hotel we stayed at in Mexico was depressing. It was dirty and crowded, the food was terrible, and our room was infested with cockroaches. Through WestJet, we managed to get moved to an adult-only resort. There, we had a blast: lots of downtime, swimming, eating, laughing, and adventures. We enjoyed the nightly shows and the water games in the pool. We even got to witness the release of baby turtles into the ocean.

Glenn arrived home from Denmark two days after Kathy and I left for Mexico and was in charge of the boys for the remainder of the week. I Skyped Glenn, Jamie, and Thomas from Mexico to try to keep in touch. Of course, Thomas especially loved the video and pictures I shared showing the release of baby turtles. I knew he was wishing he could have been there on the beach, given his love for turtles.

Glenn picked Kathy and me up at the airport when we arrived home. He was quiet on the ride home and didn't really want to hear about our trip. Once I was home and getting ready for bed, I noticed a single white rose with a beautiful card lying on my pillow. The card described his love for me and how important I was in his life. I think he realized, with our four weeks apart (the longest we've ever been part), how much I meant to him. He didn't enjoy his time away without me and was not happy that I had had a vacation without him. We seldom bring up the two separate vacations, but I know his thoughts. It won't happen again.

About a month later, we were reading the Saturday paper and having our morning coffee while the boys were both still asleep. Glenn looked at me and said, "Don't move. I'll be right back." A few minutes later he returned with a small box. He placed it in front of me and said, "I have wanted to do this for a long time. You mean so much to me, and I want you to have this so that every time you see it, it shines, and you think of me. I never, ever want to be away from you again."

It was a beautiful new diamond solitaire ring. I am embarrassed by its size, but I look at it every day just to remember how much Glenn loves me. Since then, we have never taken separate vacations. Glenn said, and I have to agree, that seeing something on your own does not create the same memories as seeing it with your loved one does. Had we not had those weeks apart, I think we may not have realized how much we love each other and miss being together when we're apart.

High School Days

Thomas started high school in the fall of 2010. He was exhilarated to be attending this school with his best friend. A whole new chapter was beginning, and Thomas had his dreams in check. As an added bonus and fortunately for me, his high school was a short distance up the street from the school where I was teaching. He was attending Dr. E.P. Scarlett High School and I was five minutes away at Canyon Meadows School, an elementary school. Knowing I was close to him, should he need any kind of support, was reassuring.

I honestly don't know why Thomas posted his next post ... He must have done something to deserve this response! It makes me wonder ...

Thomas on Facebook, September 9, 2010:

I try to be responsible and all I get is grief ...

That fall, Thomas and I went again to the neuromuscular clinic at the Children's Hospital. His checkups there were once every six months for all of Thomas's life, and the appointments often consisted of a long, tedious day. On this particular visit, the clinicians did their regular pulmonary breathing test, checking his lung capacity. In previous appointments, they hadn't really shared their findings on this test, but this time they did. Thomas, by now, had enough knowledge to understand the statistics, much more than Glenn and I ever could.

After we got home, I went to sit out on the deck, as I was exhausted after the long day of questions. The fall weather was pleasant, and I was trying to calm down after the routine visit at the hospital. I was taking in the warmth of the sun, listening to the birds, and watching the calmness of the water. I just wanted to breathe it all in and enjoy some Kathy time.

Thomas wheeled out to the deck where I was sitting and calmly stated, "Mom, I have done the math."

I asked, "What are you talking about?"

"Well, they told me today that my lung capacity is sitting at 45 per cent. I figure that at the rate I am going, I will be lucky to live to be twenty-one."

I had been thinking the same but hadn't shared my thoughts. As the tears welled up in my eyes, I tried desperately not show my emotions and my realization that Thomas knew the reality of his situation. He was a bright kid, and he knew more than anyone else exactly what was going on. I tried to change the subject, hoping he wouldn't see my reaction, but I often wonder if he knew I knew.

Thomas on Facebook, November 5, 2010:

First day of hockey tomorrow. Am I ready? Yes!

The power hockey season was beginning again. The hockey sticks were ready with new tape, the Wiffle balls were out, and Thomas was pumped. He couldn't wait for the first game and to find out which team he would be on or who his teammates would be. He spent a lot of time talking to potential teammates planning out their strategies, getting ready for the first game.

Thomas on Facebook, December 24, 2010:

Merry (Danish) Christmas today!

Christmas this year was spent in Calgary. Hans and Alice wanted to host again. We had the traditional Christmas Eve dinner, danced around the tree, and received our annual visit from Santa Kim. Thomas was thrilled celebrating the traditions with the family.

Growing up, the boys received their own personalized Danish Advent calendar, which included small gifts like chocolate, licorice, toothbrushes, silly putty, etc. The calendar is a traditional embroidered Danish wall-hanging, which has twenty-four rings representing each of the days of December prior to Christmas. Small gifts are tied to each ring with ribbon. The boys each received twelve gifts, as they shared the calendar.

Thomas on Facebook, January 18, 2011:

HOW COME IN EVERY PAIR OF SOCKS I HAVE, THEY ALL GET MASSIVE HOLES ON THE RIGHT FOOT AT THE BIG TOE!!!!!!!!!!!!! I DON'T EVEN WALK!!!!!!! REGGREEWFGLEEFGGGGG!!!!!!!!!!!!

Thomas on Facebook, January 22, 2011:

1 hour, 34 minutes till hockey. 11 hours, 36 minutes till my birthday. 7979 hours, 34 minutes till Christmas!

Thomas on Facebook, February 3, 2011:

What's the point of socks with holes in them if you can't rip them down the middle and yell THIS IS SPARTAAAAAAAAAAAAAAAAAAAAA AAAAAA!!!!!!!!!!!!!!!!!!!!!!!?

In February 2011, Thomas received a special invitation from the Starlight Foundation. Both Thomas and Jamie were invited to a Flames game and received the VIP treatment. They donned their Flames jerseys and were off for a night of adventure! After enjoying the game from box seats, the boys were invited to the dressing room to meet the players. Many of the players signed their jerseys, and the boys also received a package of treasured goodies with the Flames logos. The mini doughnuts were fantastic, but most of all, Thomas loved sharing the whole experience with his big brother.

Thomas had a particular view of procrastination:

Thomas on Facebook, April 12, 2011:

I am not leaving work for later. I am merely working on other things (games, updating pointless Facebook statuses about procrastination, etc.) that will just get done later. I am not being irresponsible; nor am I being short-sighted by not thinking about future work. I am in fact taking care of the future Thomas Sorensen by eliminating future distractions from future work. By not playing games or updating useless Facebook statuses about procrastination, I am in fact being irresponsible most of all. THERFORE [sic], I AM RESPONSIBLE BY DOING NOTHING AT ALL!!! THAT'S HOW GOOD A STUDENT I AM.

Thomas on Facebook, April 30, 2011:

Two assists today out of two goals! Also, I was made permanent assistant captain! Woot!

In the spring of 2011, Thomas was finishing his grade 10 year and looking forward to the summer. He planned to return to Camp Horizon and was also writing applications for jobs. He updated his resumé in hopes that someone would hire him. Coming to the realization that his abilities were limited to having an aide by his side was difficult. How could he hold down a job while needing someone to take him to the washroom? How would he be able to get out the supplies needed for a particular job? I think he was facing a tough reality that summer.

It was also around this time that Thomas realized that he would never be able to apply for a driver's license. I explained to Thomas that with his disability, he couldn't turn his head to shoulder check and that his arms wouldn't allow him to brake or do turns. Even with help, he wouldn't be able to get behind the wheel of a car or van. The day we had that conversation was another tough one for Thomas, Glenn, and me. It took everything in me to try to explain in a kind way that he could never reach that goal. Thomas was understandably sad and disappointed, but when he heard the words from my mouth, he had to admit defeat. I believe he knew already; I think he just needed confirmation from someone else.

Soon after that conversation, Thomas's friend Tegan passed away. He had met her at Camp Horizon. Tegan had cerebral palsy and was witty, kind, and humorous. She enjoyed Thomas's company. This young girl had gone through so much in her few years, including back surgery to implant rods into her spine to keep it straight. Thomas and I visited her at the Children's Hospital many times during her recovery. When Thomas had appeared in Gord Bamford's music video, he was honoured that Tegan was part of the video, as well. They would talk on the phone and message each other regularly to keep in touch. They had much in common, and their friendship was important to both of them.

On top of everything that Tegan was going through, she had recently found out that she had cancer. We visited her at the hospital whenever it was permitted. Sometimes her immune system had to be protected, so she wasn't always allowed visitors. She spent many months in the Children's Hospital fighting the disease.

Tegan did get a Children's Wish granted. Glenn and I were able to attend a fundraiser in the spring of 2011 to help support Tegan's trip, and she then travelled to Vegas to see her favourite magician, Criss Angel. Tegan was obsessed with Criss; he was all she talked about. Thomas and Tegan had many conversations about her idol. On her Wish trip, she met Criss Angel in person, saw his show, and received autographs and souvenirs, along with pictures. It was a magical experience; it was her dream. Shortly after her return, Tegan passed away.

Tegan's passing was the first time Thomas experienced the death of someone close to him. He and I attended Tegan's funeral, which she had planned herself. Tegan wanted her funeral outdoors, in a field. She had painted her own cremation container—a pig (I believe it was ceramic)—with lots of colour. During a simple ceremony, her mom spoke of Tegan's spirit and love for life, about her courage and bravery through her illnesses, and how she would be remembered. Some of Tegan's favourite music was played at her request while her mom and friends had a chance to reflect. That day left a meaningful and lasting mark on Thomas.

By this time, we were in the final month of the school year. Exams and year-end activities were approaching, and everyone was looking forward to the summer. Thomas had another hockey banquet to attend. He was euphoric. He had played hard that season, and he wasn't sure what awards he might qualify for, but his hopes were high. We purchased tickets for the banquet and hoped he would have a great night. Not surprisingly, he won several awards to add to his collection. He laughed when the league gave him yet another ball encased in a trophy, saying his "first career goal." Thomas had already received one! It was another celebratory evening. All was good as we entered into another summer.

Thomas on Facebook, June 25, 2011:

Got my second "First Career Goal" award last night!

In August 2011, Glenn turned fifty. Along with food, another Danish tradition is when someone turns a significant age, loved ones write songs to celebrate their birthday. This was a song that Thomas wrote on his own in celebration of his dad's birthday.

To the tune of "Teddy Bears' Picnic:"

If you go in our house today, you're sure to be in surprise!
Make sure your tummies are empty, for some tasty Flaeskestegs!
For every Dane that ever there was, will gather here together because.
Today's the day that Dad officially becomes old!
Speaking of turning old, we really are just kidding, Flaeskestegs!
I really like to talk to you When I am _____ [pooping!]
Thankfully there are many more years, for you and I to talk like peers.
Today's the day that Dad officially becomes old!

Love, Thomas

The birthday was lots of fun, especially with the many songs written for Glenn. Thomas's song is now probably the most special one for me. When I was going through some pictures and files a while ago, I found the song. I laughed and I cried. Mostly I was saddened by Thomas's words about having more "years to talk as peers."

Also that summer, we had decided to do major renovations on the house. Glenn's birthday was as fancy as we could have it; the walls were torn down and bare floorboards were exposed. We did our best to decorate around this mess. Happily, our kitchen was still functional.

Up to that point, our house had a sunken living room with a huge ramp for Thomas, and the flooring throughout the house was not adequate for all the rocks his wheelchair brought in. Our kitchen also needed a major upgrade. We decided to raise the sunken family room so Thomas could easily access the entire main floor. This meant we had to replace all the windows. We also moved our kitchen, eliminated a bathroom, moved the laundry room, and got rid of a bedroom. The whole renovation was a major job, but we were looking forward to the main floor becoming more functional, especially for Thomas.

The birthday dinner was great. Our Vancouver family members were able to attend, along with Glenn's parents, and everyone pitched in to clean up and put everything in its place for the renovations. I believe Glenn was happy over our effort, despite the renovations. It was not glamorous, but he appreciated it under the circumstances.

The day after Glenn's party, we packed up our boys to travel to Seattle, where we boarded a cruise ship bound for Alaska. We were able to drive the handicapped van to Seattle, see our niece and her family, and leave our van at their house during the cruise. We brought Jenn, Thomas's personal caregiver at the time, Glenn's parents, and his sister and brother-in-law with us on the cruise.

Thomas and Jamie in particular had such a great time. Jamie talked the cruise line staff into allowing Thomas special admittance to the spa area, which was only available to paying cruise ship members. Jamie, Thomas, and Jenn took full advantage of that minor privilege. There was a hot tub, steam room, and a relaxation room, and robes were available to wear after their "treatments." Jamie and Jenn also took Thomas to daily events: video game tournaments, trivia tournaments, and, of course, the twenty-four-hour meals available all over the ship. There was one restaurant that had delicious chicken wings at all hours of the night. We all took advantage of that one. The ships' servers were kind to Thomas, providing him with straws so he could indulge in the many exotic non-alcoholic beverages.

We gave Jenn time to enjoy herself during the cruise. Jamie and Jenn, being close in age, enjoyed the bar-hopping events and the hot dog eating contests. They also had time to enjoy the evening dance events meant for the younger generation.

There was one day when Thomas was tired and not feeling so great due to the motion on the boat. He came to our room and melted into the comfort of our bed. Glenn and I had a premium room with upgraded sheets and mattresses. The bed was so comfortable; it felt like we were sleeping on clouds. The sheets and comforter were crisp and fresh, and the luxurious pillows helped relax every muscle in our bodies. Thomas had a peaceful sleep that day. I wish I could see that sleep again.

Glenn's parents also enjoyed the trip. Probably the most breathtaking moment was when our whole family was out on the deck, wrapped in warm clothing and blankets, looking at a glacier in the rain. Glenn's dad turned to the rest of us and said, "Now I get it. Now I understand why everyone says why the Alaska cruise is the best." Quietly standing and observing that glacier was a magical, peaceful moment. Words simply cannot describe the scenery and serenity of the icebergs, the blues and greens of the water, the outstanding waterfalls, and the glacier itself. This, too, was an important moment for Glenn and his dad. They were on the same page that day, agreeing on such an important memory being made.

We took excursions to the Alaskan towns. The weather was cold, grey, and wet, but we loved exploring the history and meeting the people in the towns. We could break for a cold drink, check out the many stores, and stop to hear entertainment.

It was our last family holiday.

A New School Year

When we returned from our trip, and as the new school year started, half of our house was still under construction. We persevered through the challenges of having no kitchen, no laundry room, and no room to navigate Thomas's wheelchair. I had made several dishes to freeze prior to the renovations, and we had the barbeque, as well, to make ends meet. Our master bathroom was our temporary kitchen, with the sink to do dishes and a microwave to heat up our frozen dinners.

Regular trips to the laundromat were in order. Often, Thomas would come with me to help pass the time. With him offering as much help as he could, which was mostly verbal, we would load several washers at the same time. Thomas kept an eye on which machines finished and which dryers were available. In between the loads, we played games together on the iPad, listened to our favourite songs, or worked on his homework. The trip usually took us at least four hours each weekend.

It was also quite fun, now that I look back on it, how the four of us would enjoy our family dinner in our bedroom. Not having a dinner table was a new experience for us, and it was definitely cozy. Even under those circumstances, we tried to eat our dinners together. It always took a little maneuvering to get Thomas in with his chair, but we made it work.

I was actually surprised when the contractors finished the renos by the end of October. I had heard so many nightmares about people waiting for six months or more. At last, Thomas could go anywhere on the main floor. He was so excited to be able to access the whole house in his chair. We did, however, have to remind him several times about taking the corners too tightly. We no longer live in this house but we had several nicks and scratches around the house until the day we moved. They always made me smile and reminded us that "Thomas was here."

The school year had begun in September with our house in shambles. In theory, everything previously discussed with the administration seemed perfect for Thomas, yet his biggest frustration during his first year of high school was the assignment of the educational assistants. Three assistants were available to a number of students, and each student needed support in a variety of ways. Thomas's needs were mostly for scribing notes and equations, going to the washroom, and eating. Many times in classes, his fellow students were willing to help get out any books or his computer for him. As an added benefit, Gregg was in most of his classes and was always there ready to help.

Thomas was studying chemistry, math, social studies, leadership, and AP art and biology. He was brought to tears when the school didn't have one assistant consistently assigned to one course. That is to say, Thomas would train one assistant to write equations for his math course. Then all of a sudden, another assistant would show up for his class. He'd have to train the new assistant all over again, losing valuable time. He was most upset when an exam assistant was assigned to him, then changed at the last minute. Thomas had accommodations attached for his needs during exams, which mainly granted him extra time, scribes, and time for washroom breaks. We spoke to the administration on several occasions trying to ensure all of his supports were in place, but in Thomas's eyes, this issue was never resolved.

Thomas on Facebook, September 21, 2011:

You know you have a good pair of headphones when they break before you run them over ...

Once he began high school, Thomas had three weeks off each January during the exam period. I didn't want him sitting at home with his caregiver playing video games, so I brought him with me to my school during these breaks. He was used to coming to my school on his days off, and he knew my students well. I was lucky that my administration allowed me to bring Thomas to school. My students adored him and were always excited to see him.

Thomas loved seeing my interaction with my classes. He enjoyed answering the many questions the kids had, and he even participated in the music, singing the familiar tunes he had grown up with: "The Bluenose," "The Friday Song," "The Tailor and the Mouse." I always knew when Thomas arrived in the school with his caregiver—I could hear the kids down the hall gleefully saying, "Thomas is here! Thomas is here!" The kids from kindergarten to grade 4 were full of questions, as children are. Why was he in a wheelchair? Why did his legs not work? How he was able to write with his wrists so bent? Thomas took every opportunity to answer the questions and teach them about disabilities.

Thomas always said that I was the most awesome music teacher a school could have! I remember being on the last ambulance ride with Thomas, hearing him tell the EMS worker that I was "famous." I laughed, as it was such a sweet comment. He was referring to me just being me, taking my students to perform around Calgary for special events. We performed with the Calgary Philharmonic, on the field with Fred Penner for a Grey Cup game, and at the Southern Alberta Jubilee Auditorium singing in front of thousands.

Once, Thomas volunteered at my school and gave some art lessons with different classes. I arranged to have an overview camera, which was connected to a smart board, project Thomas's hand while he was drawing so the children could see his every move. When the teachers saw the impact Thomas was having, not only through his ability to draw and teach but also the positive influence he was having on the students, more and more teachers asked Thomas to visit their classes. He became a community teacher and a fixture in my school. Thomas came to me after thirteen teachers requested that he be in their class, and exclaimed, "Thirteen classes are enough, Mom! I want to have some downtime, too." He volunteered for three straight weeks every January during all three years of high school.

When he entered high school, Thomas had joined the leadership program. We were in the kitchen one day and he said, "Mom, our leadership class needs more to do." I suggested that he ask if his class could come and volunteer at my school, read with kids, help out in the classroom, or help with whatever teachers needed. So, Thomas approached his leadership teacher with this idea. Thanks to Thomas, my school had close to one hundred high school students visiting our school each week. The high school students helped the younger kids read, taught them social manners, and supported those kids who needed friendship and additional companionship. It was a growing program, which gave much-needed support to our young students while providing a meaningful experience to the high school students. Not many people know how this came about, and I still keep it quiet, knowing in my heart that it was Thomas who started this enriching program.

I think Thomas built his own positivity and spread it to others through his passion for sports. He knew that he couldn't physically participate in his high school's athletics, so instead, he gave his time in his own way. He volunteered to stay after school or attend games in the evenings to help keep score, fill out stats cards, or do whatever else he could for the school teams. He could manage a lot of these tasks on his laptop, and he felt he was making a positive contribution.

Overall, Thomas loved high school. The staff gave him freedom, much to his liking. He was able to take off for lunch with his buddy, Gregg, and other friends. Thomas loved to check out the fast-food restaurants at the local strip mall, visit the Rexall store, and simply hang out. He was at the age when Glenn and I had to let go; we had to trust Thomas to know his limitations. The homework in high school was heavier, and like anyone, he could procrastinate, but with the help from his daily caregivers, he was doing well.

Thomas's advanced art course was a bit of a stretch for us, though. He had such low muscle tone, and his wrists were bent inward. He could barely write his name. We were shocked when we saw his first art project. His assignment was to draw three different apples, all with different techniques. His drawings were simply beautiful. The colouring, detail, and shading were all beyond belief. Glenn and I really had no idea that Thomas had such artistic ability. Up to this point, he had not shared his artistic talent or even his desire to pursue art, but somehow the talent and passion had grown inside of him and was launched squarely at an advanced program in high school. We learned to trust his judgement and support his dream, no matter what his hands could do.

His art teacher, Mr. McCrae, totally understood Thomas's limitations and made every attempt to accommodate Thomas and his abilities. Mr. McCrae thought through the assignments and made the criteria appropriate for Thomas, working on his strengths and challenging him to try new techniques. Thomas produced so many amazing projects. Mostly they were drawings, beginning with the drawings of the three apples from different viewpoints. There were a few projects after that, which included a theme with a castle and the blue Smurfs.

There was a period of time when Thomas came home day after day telling me that he was not happy with a particular project. He said he just could not "get his hand right." I didn't understand what he meant. About two weeks later, Thomas came home all smiles, saying that he finally got it. He told me his drawing was right, and he explained.

He had been assigned a project to draw his hand holding a soup ladle and the reflection he saw in the ladle. What we saw was a most extraordinary drawing of his hand holding a pencil and the soup ladle with the soup ladle reflecting the windows behind him. It was magnificent. It has to be my favourite drawing. When you look at it, you feel as if you can actually reach out and grab the pencil. The drawing of his hand, with the cuff from the sleeve of his hoodie, had so much detail that it, too, looked real.

Thomas on Facebook, October 10, 2011:

So, really bad foot infection ... hurts so bad I can't even walk. Oh, wait ... Hooked to an IV in my good hand and can't really move it. Going back to the emergency at ten tonight for round two of extreme antibiotics. Nine a.m. tomorrow at Children's for possibly a twenty-four-hour pump into the blood.

I'm all IV'ed up, with loads of antibiotics in my blood. Did two bags of meds right into my blood and maybe only two more.

I was relieved to see they brought me meds and not a pair of hedge clippers.

Thomas on Facebook, October 11, 2011:

Foot's getting better ... but very slowly. At the earliest I will be at school on Friday! Woot! Seven-day long weekend! Not really. ☹ *"Should" be good for hockey on Saturday ... but I won't be perfect. Two more days of IV and my hand hurts bad already. Just feel gross from so much [sic] antibiotics.*

Thomas on Facebook, October 12, 2011:

Hopefully the last IV for a long time tonight at nine. I've enjoyed (lie) my time at the infectious disease ward, but I hope to be assessed to resume regular treatments tomorrow. I might need a few more days of IV though [sic] they tried nuking me with meds today, so fingers crossed.

Thomas on Facebook, October 14, 2011:

Feeling good. IV out last night. My vein collapsed, so they couldn't do my last infusion and just doubled my oral meds [sic] strength and duration instead. The collapse hurts a bit, but it's better from yesterday. Most importantly I'm approved for hockey tomorrow. The doctor said if I feel ready, then I'm ready. If my hand still hurts, I might play with my stick attached to my chair. Glad I'm better for the weekend. Time off school isn't as awesome when you are going to the hospital three times a day.

🐢 🐢 🐢 🐢 🐢

The latest problem began with a blister on Thomas's foot. For some reason, his foot had become infected. It was Thanksgiving weekend 2011, and he was sixteen years old. His foot ballooned so much we couldn't get a shoe on or even a sock to cover it. We went to an urgent care facility, where they decided to get Thomas on an IV. Urgent Care was extremely busy, so we took Thomas home with the IV in his hand.

By this time, his veins were known to collapse, which was always a concern. Because Urgent Care had been so busy, we worried about the wait to go back for another IV dose. I had to take the day off work to take him for the next treatment. Glenn and I were so concerned that Thomas's vein wouldn't hold up for the next round of medication, and on the second day his foot wasn't much better, so we went to the Children's Hospital instead of Urgent Care. For unexplained reasons, the hospital team decided to continue the IV treatments, but they didn't want to admit him. We were told that we had to come back three times a day for treatment until further notice.

Looking back, I should have spoken my mind and my concerns. I knew his weaknesses and the condition of his veins. I knew the shape of his hands and the worry that Thomas had that he might need additional needles. He should have been admitted. It's hard to communicate that stress when driving through the city with a sick boy and his wheelchair behind me was stressful in itself.

I was teaching full-time, so I booked off time from work to get Thomas to the hospital three times a day. The hospital was twenty-five kilometres away from our house. Every time we went, we had to wait for our appointment, and we were all worried that the IV was not going to hold up.

In the meantime, my principal was not very understanding of the situation. She texted and called me, leaving messages. She accused me of taking time off to attend "regular" appointments. After four days of travelling three times a day to the Children's Hospital, worrying about that vein and Thomas's health, caring for him through the night, agonizing about the IV, and feeling guilty about missing work, I was exhausted. I returned to work that Friday, after arranging for a caregiver to be at home with Thomas. When my principal saw me, she sarcastically said, "Gee, you could have taken today off, too, after the week you had!"

It wasn't just the physical needs that warranted care, but also Thomas's emotional well-being. He tended to keep things bottled up inside. If something upset him, he would hold it for months at a time. At times, I would go to him and find him in tears, only to learn that he was upset about something that had happened weeks earlier. We would talk about it, and I would make him promise to let me know the next time something happened. Otherwise, I might not be able to help him.

As he got older, he became more selective as to what he told me, as is typical of any teenager. Many times, he wanted to handle his own battles. Thomas knew, though, that if he told me, I would do something about whatever struggle he was facing. I believe that worried him, both because he didn't want me to worry but also because he knew I would confront the situation no matter who was in the way. His mom had his back, and he knew it. Finding the middle ground between supporting him and letting him find his way fighting his own battles was a bit of a tug-of-war in those teenager years.

One of the courses both the boys had to take in high school, was called Career and Life Management (CALM). They each questioned the course. Thomas's answer was, "I'll be waiting …" (waiting to understand why he had to take CALM, as he felt it was a waste of time).

Thomas on Facebook, February 5, 2012:

Why is CALM a required course? Think of CALM as building blocks for your future.

CALM will:

- *ensure you have a practical plan to make your transition beyond high school*
- *give you opportunities to access resources to manage your career*
- *give you an awareness of budgeting your money*
- *allow you to explore healthy living choices*

🐢 🐢 🐢 🐢 🐢

We received a call from the school administration at the beginning of Thomas's grade 11 year expressing their concern that Thomas was stressed out and could not handle the workload of AP Biology. Glenn and I were angry because we had confidence in Thomas's knowledge of science. Thomas was not at all concerned, and Glenn and I always followed his conviction that he was capable. We pushed our kids to be their best, we wanted the best for them, and we always treated them respectfully.

But we went to the meeting, as requested by the administration. We put on our Sunday best and entered the room with a positive mindset, hoping for the best. The setting was ominous. The school's entire team of administrators were lined up on one side of the table and just two chairs for us were on the other. Their unanimous position was that the school load was too much for Thomas. Thomas remained silent, but he was definitely not in agreement. We supported him, trusting his beliefs and feelings. It took an hour, but we convinced the administration to allow Thomas to continue in the advanced biology course. We assured them that we would do everything in our power to give him the support he needed to succeed. We would hire a tutor, if needed.

🐢 🐢 🐢 🐢 🐢

His obstacles were everywhere and seemed to come from any place. During Thomas's grade 11 year, the elevator at the school was not working so well and needed regular maintenance and repairs. He needed to use the elevator to access the second floor for classes. One day, the custodian came to Thomas and said, "So today, I'm really busy, so if you could please, TRY not to get stuck in the elevator. That would be great!"

A New School Year

🐢 🐢 🐢 🐢 🐢

At the end of his grade 11 year, Thomas was thrilled to learn that he was placed on the Selects team for power hockey. This meant that he would travel to Ottawa to participate in the national power hockey tournament. Jamie agreed to go with Thomas to support him, not only with his physical needs but also with his game. And the boys had an absolute blast. They shared the excitement of the games, explored a new city, and were able to hang out with the other team members and their caregivers. Thomas's team unfortunately didn't win the tournament, but he was already making plans on how to win the next time. He spent his off time chatting with his teammates, replaying the games, and making suggestions for new plays to score more goals.

🐢 🐢 🐢 🐢 🐢

One evening, after Thomas returned from his hockey tournament, he turned to me from his laptop and said, "Mom, can I have your Visa card? If I have your Visa number, I can call and get my mark for AP Biology."

So I pulled my credit card out of my wallet and we called the number. We were put on hold.

While we were waiting on hold, I asked Thomas, "What's a good mark?"

"Mom, our teacher said that if you get 3/5, you've done really well. If you get 4/5, you've done super good. And he said nobody gets 5/5."

All of a sudden, the voice on the other end of the call came on and said, "Thomas Sorensen, you got 5/5."

We laughed, and I cried.

🐢 🐢 🐢 🐢 🐢

On Thomas's return from Ottawa, he headed off to Camp Horizon on July 17 for a three-week leadership program. We arranged for his caregiver, Layne (Gregg's brother), to accompany him to the camp. Layne loved the outdoors and appreciated his time with Thomas. He had been Thomas's caregiver throughout Thomas's grade 11 school year, so he knew Thomas's needs for personal hygiene and considered Thomas a good friend. We knew Thomas was in good hands.

Thomas experienced new adventures during this camp session. He spent an entire day in his wheelchair in the woods on his own (Layne was on call should he be needed). Later, he gave up his power chair for a makeshift wagon, and the team pulled him over the rough terrain for a four-night, five-day hike. Thomas loved every minute. He was in a wagon, completely out of his comfort zone, out of his element, and he was fully dependent on others, yet he experienced the adventure of a lifetime. He knew that outside of Camp Horizon, he wasn't able to experience anything like the adventures he was having there. To this day, many of the participants have many special memories of Thomas during this amazing trip.

The camp staff shared a funny story with us that summer: Thomas was being pulled in the makeshift wagon. This was a huge compromise. He was out of his power chair for five days and he had to rely on everyone on the hike to see to his needs. He had no way of scooting around on his own. At the same time, he was feeling a bit guilty that all the staff and fellow campers were carrying food and camp supplies that were fairly heavy, especially at the beginning of the trip. Apparently, the group had been given several cans of baked beans to take on the trip. Nobody in the group liked baked beans, except Thomas. So, Thomas, being Thomas, said, "You know, if it helps out, I'll eat all the cans of beans. That will lighten the load."

Continued Struggles and Triumphs

Scoliosis is a common occurrence in children with muscular dystrophy. Every time we went to the neuromuscular clinic, the technicians took an X-ray of Thomas's spine. His curvature was continually getting worse. The orthotic doctors would remind us during each visit that Thomas would be a candidate sooner or later for surgery to correct his posture. They wanted to insert steel rods in his back.

Thomas never liked the idea. As he got older, he did his own research, not only on the Internet but also by having discussions with friends who had had the procedure done. In Thomas's mind, the surgery would not improve his quality of life and it would take away six months to a year of his life due to recovery periods. He continually argued with the doctors about this operation, always clearly stating his mind and backing it up with solid reasons not to proceed. The doctors admitted that if they did the back surgery, his knees would end up against his chin due to a chain reaction within his body, requiring yet another surgery to break his hips and put in more rods. Finally, Thomas won his fight. The doctors agreed that his quality of life would drastically decrease. In hindsight, it was a good decision not to have the procedure.

Nights with Thomas were always a guessing game. Nine times out of ten, he would be tucked in the way he wanted, and by the time I brushed my teeth and crawled into bed, he was calling on the baby monitor Glenn and I kept in our room. On a good night, Thomas would call once. On a not-so-good night, which was more often than not, he called anywhere from three to eighteen times. There were many mornings that I dragged myself into work with a forced smile on my face and tried to function professionally. Frequent disruptions in my sleep caused me to come up with some sort of formula—my own personal gauge—for how often I should get out of bed to help Thomas. I went with the first three calls, and then I would wake Glenn for his turn. I tried not to wake Glenn any more than necessary because I knew he needed a clear head and a good night's sleep to do his job the next day.

Thomas was always terrified that a spider would crawl into his bed. Living beside the lake, we had spiders year-round. I was told that this was a sign of a clean house. However, this didn't relieve Thomas of his fears. He wanted to be tucked in so tightly with his bed covers that a spider had no chance of sneaking in. This always took vast amounts of patience from both Glenn and me.

I guess I felt it was a mother's duty to take care of her child. Sometimes, I was just so tired that I didn't hear the first call, but Glenn would hear it and get up to help Thomas. When I missed these calls, I would most likely hear about it the next morning from either Glenn or Thomas. I guess there is nothing like a mom's tuck-in.

🐢 🐢 🐢 🐢 🐢

For most of his schooling, the usual school bus arrived to take Thomas to school. This was a bit more reliable than the HandiBus as they had regular drivers assigned for the routes, but there were still complications with snowfalls, buses breaking down, and substitute drivers. There were many years when Thomas was either the first to be picked up or the last to be dropped off, so he often spent up to two hours, one-way, on the bus.

When he reached high school, we decided to have his personal care providers pick him up at the end of the day. His school was only a twelve-minute drive away, but riding the bus could take over an hour, so on many mornings, I drove Thomas to school, retuning the van to the house so his caregiver could pick him up when he was done school. I usually did the return at my lunch hour. We were fortunate to have another vehicle so I could make the exchange.

We always tried to make a point of ensuring our bus drivers felt appreciated by giving them small gifts, especially at Christmas and end of the school year. We considered ourselves lucky to get the same driver two years in a row. George, one of the drivers, enjoyed Thomas's sense of humour and intelligence. He was always kind to Thomas and treated him with respect, greeting Thomas every morning with a friendly, "Good morning, Thomas." He took the time to ask Thomas how his night before had been and how his morning was going. He was always pleasant loading Thomas on the bus and asked Thomas if he was ready to go before starting to load him. At the end of the day, George always asked how Thomas's day went and wished him a good evening.

This ease and pleasantry we could rely on from George was not always the case. There was one driver who scared Thomas on a daily basis with her racing skills. Thomas was hesitant to tell us because he didn't want to get his driver in trouble, but he finally started telling us about some of his trips to and from school. We began recording dates, times, and infractions. Finally, we made a phone call to the dispatch office, and fortunately, they took us seriously and had someone follow the driver on a few occasions. I can only imagine what happened one particular day in traffic when they were observing her, but she was immediately fired.

Many of the students who took that bus had wheelchairs and were unable to communicate verbally. Thomas looked out for them and spoke up immediately if he felt they were being treated unfairly. He was such a strong advocate not only for himself but for others.

Glenn:

During Thomas's last couple of years in high school, we were fortunate to have a caregiver spend the night in the adjoining bedroom two or three nights per week. They checked on Thomas's needs through the night, helped to roll him over, which he needed two to eighteen times per night, and took him to the washroom. This gave Kathy and me a chance to catch up on sleep.

It was mostly Kathy getting up at night. After getting up three times she usually woke me and said, "Your turn." One time, when Thomas was having a rough week, Kathy was so exhausted from getting up that she said to me, "Your turn tomorrow." I told her I would do it the whole week and Kathy was pleasantly surprised. You see, I was convinced it was becoming a habit for Thomas to wake up multiple times each night. So, in private, I talked to Thomas and said, "Hey, buddy, I think it might be a habit, you are waking up so many times a night, so here's the deal. Every night you sleep through, I'm going to buy you a great big fat chocolate bar of your choice that I'll pick up on my way home from work each day. But if you tell Mom, the deal is off." Talk about a happy camper. He could already taste the chocolate.

The next morning, Kathy asked how I had made out with Thomas. I said, "Excellent. Slept through the night." Kathy couldn't believe it. I just smiled, thinking, "Atta boy," and brought home Thomas's first of two chocolate bars. The next night Thomas woke and called for help once. Kathy still couldn't believe it, but it didn't earn him a chocolate bar. When he slept through the third night, Kathy was floored. I think I heard her swear under her breath, but I just smiled. The next night in the early hours of dawn, Thomas was struggling and said he couldn't do it anymore as it was too painful.

As it turned out, Thomas didn't sleep well the first few nights, but he really wanted the chocolate and just lay there suffering until morning. The game was up. Over the next few days, every time I looked at Kathy, she gave me the stink eye ...

It was a real treat when he actually slept through the night. Unfortunately, whenever that happened, I always thought something was wrong, so I ended up not sleeping well anyway. It was definitely a Catch-22.

In spite of the frequent awakenings, there was a special moment every night for Thomas and me. I think he loved having me tuck him in. He always felt that I had the special touch to get him settled in just the right way. Even during our many hospital stays, Thomas would get the nurse to wake me up so I could get him tucked and comfy in bed. The nurses could never get it right.

Even today, my sleep pattern is still not great. Subconsciously, I think I am hearing Thomas call out.

Amidst all the shenanigans, Jamie was always supportive of Thomas during the serious moments. At times when Thomas was frustrated about something at school, with me, or Glenn, he would vent to Jamie, who would calm him down. Sometimes when I knew Thomas was upset, I would ask Jamie to speak to him.

During Jamie's university years in particular, he was a huge help with Thomas. He arranged his schedule to have later classes so he could be home to help his brother up and see him out the door and onto the school bus. Jamie was also able to be home before Thomas got home from school. Often, he offered to be at home with Thomas so Glenn and I could get some down time on a weeknight or weekend. What a great kid we raised!

Thomas on Facebook, September 16, 2010:

Thomas Sorensen ... is glad he has a brother!

Gregg:

Many people will remember Thomas for being an avid video game player. Don't get me wrong, the dude *loved* his video games, but he was also an outdoorsman.

One of Thomas's favourite places to be was at Camp Horizon. There, he could experience the outdoors and all that came with being in the mountains. However, when the mountains were too far away, Thomas enjoyed spending time outside in the city doing various activities. Many summer days were filled with hockey and soccer games or driving (with his wheelchair) around the community. Throughout the winters, Thomas and I would skate and play hockey on the ice.

Like all kids, we played the typical sports, but we would also make up our own games. Many of the sports we invented involved Thomas being in his power chair while I used his manual wheelchair. As Thomas and I were both competitive, all these activities turned into rivals against each other. One activity Thomas really enjoyed that may surprise many people is flying kites. All I had to do was get the kite into the air. From there Thomas, was able to take control and maneuver the kite like anybody else. I think he enjoyed it because it was something he could do independently.

For years on end, we worried about Thomas's future. We looked into alternative housing where Thomas could live independently because he wanted to be with people he could relate to. We never could imagine him in a home where he would sit and stare at a ceiling. This simply was not what Thomas needed in his future. We knew he had to be engaged and have friends who shared the same dreams. We looked into his sharing a residence with other boys in Thomas's situation for when the time came for him to leave home, and we looked to parents with children who had similar disabilities. There really wasn't much out there for these kinds of kids.

The reality was that as Thomas grew older, he wanted to be a regular teenager. He wanted to stay up late and make his own choices, and Glenn and I were getting older and tired. We knew Thomas wanted an increasing amount of freedom to make his own decisions. Looking for appropriate accommodations for our son was inevitable but also disheartening.

One thing that annoyed him was the fact the some of his friends with disabilities chose to finish high school and then simply stay home to collect Assured Income for the Severely Handicapped (AISH). AISH is a small amount of funding available to Albertans who have disabilities. Thomas couldn't fathom anyone just doing nothing. He wanted to make a difference. He always thought that people with disabilities who stayed at home to collect AISH were giving others a bad name.

The Dream

With Thomas in grade 12, the end of high school was fast approaching. He had exams to write, which counted toward 50 per cent of his grade 12 marks. The pressure was on for Thomas to do his best. He was also planning his future, and he definitely wanted to continue his education. His goal was to study biology—viral vectors, to be specific, which, in my simple understanding, involves the injection of viruses into living cells to cure disease.

Thomas came to me one day and said, "Mom, I want to go to Carleton University in Ottawa. They have a program for kids with disabilities, and I want to go."

I remember this moment as if it were yesterday, and I laughed out loud and said, "In your dreams." I couldn't imagine our son living four provinces and a five-hour flight away from home. Living on his own at a university was beyond my belief. However, we took his request into consideration and ultimately decided it was worth a go.

So, the challenge began. Thomas applied for early acceptance in November of 2012, before any term exams.

He'd put all of his eggs in one basket and applied only to Carleton. He didn't want to even try to go to university near home. If he were to go to a Calgary university, it would require hiring a full-time caregiver who would attend classes with Thomas. Taking transit, fighting the snow, needing accessibility to the campus, and requiring full-time assistants would all come into play. The University of Calgary did not have the accessibility Carleton had, nor did it offer any help in personal care.

We filled out the application forms and applied for the Attendant Services Program at Carleton. The program provided twenty-four-hour care and assistance to students with disabilities. The attendants helped get the students up and out of bed, showered, and dressed. Attendants also packed the students' bags for classes with books, laptops, and any other necessities. They helped with laundry, meals, bedtime, and all other needs. Thomas not only needed to be accepted at Carleton, but he also needed placement in the care program in order to go to Ottawa.

Thomas's fall marks in high school were exceptional, and he was granted early acceptance to Carleton University in December. He was over the moon; his dream was coming true. He would be given a placement with the Attendant Services Program and have his own private, wheelchair-accessible room on campus.

It was around Christmas when we heard this news, and his acceptance was the best present he could have hoped to receive. He enjoyed Christmas with the family and the traditional Christmas Eve visit from Santa Kim. He spent his own money buying special gifts for each member of his family. I remember he bought me the new hard-covered Danielle Steel book that had just come out. He purchased a Batman coffee cup for Jamie and a new pair of slippers for Glenn.

Thomas was still considered a child in Grandma's eyes when the traditional Danish dessert came along, even though he was almost eighteen. He still received a prize. The adults in charge, Grandma, in this case, always made sure each of the kids had an almond. Not everyone liked the pudding but I would like to think Thomas did. We only eat it once a year, and Thomas got a prize every year of his life.

🐢 🐢 🐢 🐢 🐢

Gregg came over to the house during the Christmas holiday. The two boys talked me into letting them go skating on the lake. Of course this meant Thomas would drive his power chair on the ice as Gregg skated beside him. I was always standing close to the window to watch what was going on but trying to give Thomas his independence. My heart always skipped a beat seeing what they were up to, but I knew I had to trust them. Thomas loved every moment. He loved the fresh air, the special time with Gregg, and most importantly his independence. He brought his hockey stick with him, of course, and did complete 360s on the ice when his chair slid.

Thomas on Facebook, December 2012:

Nothing is more Canadian than hockey on ice in a wheelchair the government paid for! #Canada.

We were excited for Thomas that his dream of attending Carleton was going to be reality. He would attend a university that not only allowed him to study biology but would give him a care program to suit his needs and allow him to travel from class to class without the indignity of fighting with and getting stuck in snow.

But then another hurdle came his way. We received an email from the care program informing us that up until that year, the Ontario government had funded all students in Canada to obtain its services. But now, the Ontario government was changing their funding to include only Ontario students. The program cost $100 per day, roughly $25,000 per year, in addition to the cost of tuition, housing, books, and food. This was a major blow!

Thomas on Facebook, February 13, 2013:

Funding for Carleton's 24-7 care program has been cut entirely to those outside Ontario. As of now, I am not able to go there for school. Currently, we have an Albertan MLA Kent J. Hehr writing letters to those he can and he has started making contacts with other organizations. For me to cover the funding for the program itself, it would be $25,000 on top of tuition and other *expenses. That's almost more than government income supplements would be IF I QUALIFIED over my first year AND WORKED PART-TIME!!!! With all my public speaking experience, I hope they are ready for change.*

🐢 🐢 🐢 🐢 🐢

We decided it was time to make some calls to inquire about what personal care funding was available to Thomas. We called the Government of Alberta and Alberta Health Services (AHS). If Thomas was residing in Alberta, he would qualify for support through Self-Management care, but both the government and AHS told us that the money could not be transferred to another province. We called the Alberta Ministry of Enterprise and Advanced Education (now called the Ministry of Advanced Education). It gave grants to people with disabilities to further their education, but under no circumstances, according to their rules, could the money be used to provide personal care.

We spent hours on the phone calling any agency we could think that was remotely connected to Thomas's needs. Many answered flat out that they could not help. Some people suggested other agencies to call; many had no idea where we might seek funding.

🐢 🐢 🐢 🐢 🐢

In February 2013, I was attending the Calgary City Teachers' Convention. One of the key speakers was Rick Hansen. I knew of his journey and was hopeful that he could help Thomas with his dream of attending Carleton University. I planned on attending his session and hoped to meet him and convince him to meet Thomas. I had Thomas's caregiver, Mark, on alert and ready to bring Thomas down to the convention centre to meet Rick. The stars aligned …

I attended Rick's session, and immediately after, waited in line to speak with him. I introduced myself and told him about Thomas and his situation with Carleton. Rick already had a strong connection with Carleton and wanted to help. I asked if he was available that day to meet with Thomas to discuss his plight. He obliged, and I called Mark asking him to bring Thomas downtown. Rick and Thomas met up within the hour, and

Rick assisted Thomas by writing a letter of support to Alberta's Minister of Health. This letter was the kick-starter to Thomas's campaign to get his personal care approved to leave the province with him.

Thomas on Facebook, February 14, 2013:

Met Rick Hansen today to talk to him about going to Carleton and their program. I also gave him a draft of my letter lobbying the government to provide a program allowing the disabled to live in residence, with assistance to allow us independence and choice of education. Good day today. Really cool guy. Great experience.

When Thomas decided to apply to go to university in Ottawa, Jamie was by his side the whole way helping Thomas organize his letters, fight for funding, and figure out just how he was going to accomplish his dream. Thomas also consulted his cousin Suzy in Calgary for advice. She was an author and had the necessary writing experience to help prepare the letters.

Thomas decided to lobby the government. He drafted a letter and mailed it out to ninety-six Members of the Legislative Assembly of Alberta. He was very motivated; he was not giving up. In the end, two MLAs decided to help Thomas out. Both Kent Hehr and our own MLA, Jeff Wilson, assisted with researching who to go to for funding and asking about moving Alberta funding to Ontario.

Dear _____ ,

I am Thomas Sorensen, a seventeen-year-old, with Congenital Muscular Dystrophy (CMD). It is a progressive disorder where every day, my muscles grow weaker and die. However, this does not prevent me from living the life I want to live. In school, I strive to succeed and aspire to become a biologist and possibly a professor if the world grants it. By grade 11, I had already achieved honours in grade 12 level Advanced Placement (AP) Biology, even achieving university credit for my work. Among my other AP classes, I have also taken AP Art, where I have been able to create great sketches, carvings, prints, and paintings independently. Extracurricular, I am a top forward on my wheelchair hockey team and league. I have even participated as a member of Calgary's Selects team and gone to a continental tournament. I also enjoy volunteering with various organizations such as Children's Wish Foundation, Easter Seals, Between Friends, Muscular Dystrophy Canada, and elementary schools in Calgary. I personally believe in citizenship, leadership, independence, and awareness of special needs.

Independence is something I struggle with every day and strive to achieve. Accessibility may be growing in urban areas as awareness increases, but my personal fight against my inabilities is an uphill battle, involving constant adaptation. Independence is a universal need that has birthed and collapsed nations. It is forged in laws and policies but is expressed through freedoms and equality. This is not traditional equality, but equality of opportunity. What most people fail to see is that disability does not separate me from anyone. All people are disabled; only some are temporarily enabled. Everyone will age. Everyone will need a little help. If this is understood, then I believe all are equal.

Currently, I try to follow enough politics—being a minor—to understand where "public" money is going in Alberta so that I can do my part to ensure we have responsible government. Lately, I have been pleased to see progress toward income support to those on AISH, so fear not, this is not another letter in a long line received by the government about increasing AISH. As I stated, my aspiration is to become a professor of biology, and I was hoping to travel to Ottawa for Carleton University. Carleton was the only university to offer a 24-7 care program for students living in residence. Until the last few weeks, the program was directly funded by the Ontario government at the cost of $100 a day per student, but now I will be unable to pursue my education and independence.

I was even accepted to start this fall. Ontario cut their funding as it was not within their budget to pay on behalf of all Canada. I feel that this is a fair judgement on their part and now look to you and the Legislative

The Dream

Assembly. I realize it would be costly to fund, but seeing as you have read this far, please consider the following. I believe that this is an opportunity for the government.

*The costs will work out to be about $25,000 a year per student, which is slightly more than one year of AISH. Once funded and educated, students in my identical situation will be left more physically independent. Students will discover what boundaries are simply put into their mind by the words "disabled" and "crippled." This will help them psychologically and financially as their need for an assistant is diminished. They will also be fully capable to be independent from the government with a career. They will not need to collect AISH. This does not mean the termination of the AISH program, but a reduction of its necessity. In just five years of work, the money saved by the government will justify a four-year degree **in AISH alone**. After other programs such as PDD,[9] and the various care facilities are left unused, it would be well worth the support of students like me. As a government that provides such opportunities, you could increase the standard of living and quality of life for thousands over the next several years. The money saved would also be astronomical as time progresses. This policy would please all manner of citizens and their beliefs as it is both humanitarian and great for the budget.*

I speak of equality of opportunity in a fresh way that I hope can be applied more often in the future. I speak of efficiency and freedoms for which Canada is known. Currently, AISH is still below the poverty line, and I am looking for other life options. I know that there are others looking to live a full life and the facts are that at $25,000 a school year before the usual costs, a full life is impossible. It is time to equal [sic] the opportunities for all. It is Alberta's turn to help its disabled citizens. Ontario has funded past students across Canada for years, and as all the provinces are finding, the budget is tight. Utilize this opportunity to invest in Alberta's citizens. Past welfare policies were created with the mindset of "dealing with the disabled," but we are a resource waiting to be tapped much like the once "useless" oil-sands we are known for. It is time for change and time for growth.

I believe this program is ground-breaking and offers much hope in Canada. I believe that with the right plan, it could help not only Alberta but

---

9   Alberta's funding for Persons with Developmental Disabilities (PDD). Thomas never accessed this funding as he was not cognitively challenged.

all provinces once they join in funding for their citizens. I believe that it offers a chance for independence, travel, and honest work with a great future for those who take part. It embodies all that Canada is and embodies every bit of our constitution and history. It would make me proud, and others I'm sure, of Canada and Alberta to see this program supported.

Thank you for your time thus far, no matter your beliefs on the matter. I should inform you that I will be sending a letter to every MLA in Alberta because I believe in this. Please investigate this further, for the sake of responsible government, if not for personal interest.

Feel free to email at or call me. Feel free to mail! Please understand that I am a full-time high school student and will do my best to respond as soon as possible.

I would also like to apologize as I realize it is a formality to handwrite letters of personal interest, but given my physical condition, this would be unrealistic. I hope my signature will suffice.

Thank you,
Thomas Sorensen

Everything seemed to be running its course until the spring of 2013, the year Thomas turned seventeen. We had friends coming from Kelowna to visit for the weekend, and Thomas had a routine echocardiogram scheduled. My friend from Kelowna, who is a nurse, came along with us for the appointment. We sat and chatted as the test was being done, and then we were asked to go to one of the examination rooms where the doctor would meet us.

The doctor asked Thomas a number of questions like, "Do you feel your heart racing?" "Are you having headaches?" Thomas responded to each question with a no. The doctor then shocked us by telling us that Thomas's heart rhythms were way out of whack. She was admitting Thomas to the ICU, where they would do a procedure to get his heart beating regularly. Thomas was freaking. He wasn't feeling unwell; he didn't feel his heart beating irregularly, nor did he feel he needed any procedures.

I called Glenn, and he soon met us arrived at the ICU room. Thomas wanted his arm pillow and favourite blanket, and I figured I had time to drive home to get them before they took him in for surgery. Retrieving these items for him was a small task to give Thomas some comfort. Jamie was three hours away in Edmonton for a job, but he was ready to hop on a bus and get back to help out. I told Jamie to hold off until we had more news. While I was on the way back to the hospital, Glenn called and told me, "No rush! They called off the surgery. It looks like Thomas scared himself so much that his heart is now beating regularly!" Thomas was, of course, relieved. He was sent home with a monitor to read his heart's activity for the next forty-eight hours.

We had a follow-up appointment to talk about the results of the monitoring. The doctor felt that there was no need at this point for medication and stated that she would keep an eye on Thomas for the next few months.

It was shortly after that when Thomas woke one morning saying he had pain in his chest. He wanted to go to the hospital. Thomas rarely asked to go to the hospital, so I knew something was awry.

The same cardiologist, Dr. Clegg, came down to the emergency room to see Thomas, and another cardiologist accompanied her. Dr. Clegg explained that Thomas's condition baffled her. She didn't understand what was going on and had to consult with other cardiologists across Canada. Furthermore, she wanted to schedule surgery to do an ablation to remove scar tissue that usually occurs with muscular dystrophy. Thomas was only a couple of months away from finishing grade 12. He didn't want that year interrupted, so we decided to do the surgery at the end of June. We were told to keep an eye on him and asked the school staff to do the same. His situation was, to say the least, worrisome.

In the midst of all this excitement, I flew to Ottawa for a weekend to check out the university and, particularly, the care program. Luckily, I was able to stay with our niece Jennie and her family to save the hotel costs. A special treat for me was that my sister Sue, from Nova Scotia, was also visiting Jennie for the weekend. I was able to reconnect with Sue and spend some time talking about Thomas's health, his excitement for graduation, and his dreams of attending Carleton.

The staff in the Carleton Attendant Services Program were fabulous. They spent several hours over each of two days showing me the campus, the services, the rooms provided, and the added provisions to the facilities that accommodated students with special needs. They had proximity readers at the doors of all the school buildings where the students could use their card readers to open the doors. This meant that Thomas could drive up to a door with his key card attached to his chair and the door would automatically open. They showed me the classrooms with easy wheelchair access and seating. They toured me through the five kilometres of underground tunnels, which meant students didn't have to go outside in the winter to access the classroom buildings.

Best of all, they gave me a special viewing of the personalized room each wheelchair student had: an oversized wheelchair-friendly bedroom, an oversized washroom with a drive-in shower, and a shared kitchen, which was for two students. The services included a 24-7 call service for students requiring assistance. This meant that any time a student needed help rolling over at night, getting a drink, using the washroom, having a meal prepared, doing laundry, or simply getting materials out to study, the attendants were available.

The assistants also set up schedules to get the students up, showered, and dressed every morning in time for their classes, and to get them in bed at night. This all seemed too good to be true, and it also made it very tough for me to veto Thomas's plans and say, "No, this will not work."

I was facing the prospect of letting our son go after seventeen years of providing him 24-7 care. I was on the verge of trusting someone else to take care of him entirely. I travelled home to Calgary and shared my thoughts with Thomas and his dad. It all seemed very wonderful, and yet, we were still very unsure.

Through all of this, in April, Thomas was staying positive and continued to give back to the community. With a little help from me, he organized a fundraiser at my school, Canyon Meadows. The fundraiser was a Hop-a-Thon for Muscular Dystrophy. We had bunny ears for each child and a selection of fun dance music ready to go, including, of course, the "Bunny

Hop." Students completed their fundraising sheets at home, asking family and friends for donations.

Thomas was well-known in my school by this time and most families were eager to help out. We found great prizes for the kids, at our cost, and brought them all into the gym for the fun. The E.P. Scarlett Leadership class helped out, too. It was a great day, warm with friendship and fun.

Thomas on Facebook, April 16, 2013:

Organized the Hop-a-Thon for Muscular Dystrophy and raised the most in Canada!!! $7,000! The next up only had $2,500!

Funding the Dream

We began receiving feedback from various MLAs. Many passed the buck. One MLA had his secretary call and do the dirty work herself. She was quite negative and told Thomas that when she went to university, she had a job to pay for her courses. She was so mean and nasty that Thomas could not get a word in edgewise, and finally she hung up without saying goodbye. She had totally missed the point.

Carleton was keeping in close contact with us regarding our search for answers. They were planning on Thomas arriving in September. We were amazed to learn their plans:

Thomas on Facebook, April 16, 2013:

Carleton has set aside $100,000 just for renovating their bio department! They've never had a wheelchair person take bio!

Thomas decided to start an online petition called "Thomas Deserves Carleton." He also started a blog called "Thomasatcarleton.wordpress.com." He was trying his best to do whatever it took to make his dream come true.

Meanwhile, the three of us were researching and applying for scholarships. There were some scholarships available specifically for people with disabilities. Some were open to anyone with a disability who wanted to attend a post-secondary school. Many were specific to the type of disability and the subject areas to be studied. Others were scholarships to Albertans but not those who were studying in a different province, and still others were only for Ontario students. Some scholarships were specific to books, residence, or even tuition only. The process was overwhelming. We weren't sure where to look for scholarships that applied to Thomas's needs. Each application had different requirements and many questions to be answered. We decided to apply to any we thought might work for Thomas. Any amount he might receive would be of help.

Thomas began writing essays, answering each scholarship's criterion. Character, goals, citizenship, volunteerism, sportsmanship, and subject areas were just some of the elements of his essays. Many scholarship applications asked about daily challenges facing the applicants.

He applied for ten scholarships. Again, we waited for results.

Thomas on Facebook, April 5, 2013:

Heard back from a few scholarships lately, with one more in the mail today. All turned me down. Also, one more lead for funding turned up dry. I was feeling down until I opened my email to discover I have made it to be a finalist for a $28,000 scholarship!

One scholarship, the Terry Fox Humanitarian Award based in BC, responded asking for an interview. We were all excited.

On Saturday, April 20, Glenn and I took Thomas to the Westin Hotel in downtown Calgary for his interview. This was a huge scholarship that came with a great reputation. The scholarship would give $7,000 yearly while Thomas was in university. I am not sure who was more nervous: Glenn, me, or Thomas.

Thomas wore his dress shirt and tie, believing that proper attire was important for such an impressive occasion. Many interviewees before Thomas arrived wearing jeans and T-shirts. We waited in the reception room of the hotel for Thomas to be called in. After he was called, he was in the interview for close to an hour. When he came out, three women, who were previous recipients of the award, followed Thomas out, all smiles. They shook our hands and congratulated Glenn and me on raising such a fine young man. They told us that over 9,000 students had applied for the scholarship. One woman said that Thomas had an aura around him and one just felt good being close to him. We were very proud and hoped her comment was a good sign.

Three months into our search for support, we had followed every available lead and exhausted every possible avenue. We decided to go to the media. Every media outlet in Calgary jumped on the opportunity to tell our story. Two major television stations and our city's two major newspapers sent reporters to our home.

When the story hit, we immediately began getting responses from AHS, and we received a call from the Minister of Health's secretary. She informed us to be prepared for a call from the minister. The news reporters followed up and kept up the pressure.

Thomas on Facebook, April 28, 2013:

News teams arriving within the hour.

Thomas on Facebook, April 29, 2013:

Calgary Herald!

We received a call from the Minister of Health, Fred Horne. He wasn't terribly helpful and had no suggestions as to where to go for funding. Then we heard we were to receive another call. It was going to be a conference call between the folks at AISH, someone from Alberta Enterprise and Advanced Education, and the Minister of Health. I had to rush home over a lunch period to take the call.

After three months of inquiries, the decision had been made. Alberta Enterprise and Advanced Education would grant $20,000 toward Thomas's personal care and allow it to transfer to Ontario. Not only did we win that fight, but the Alberta government also said they would "break the rule" and allow Thomas to receive monthly AISH support. This AISH funding had been previously designated to support only people physically living in Alberta. Thomas was ecstatic.

We were still short $5,000. Thomas was not yet eighteen and was currently receiving funding through an agency called Family Supports for Children with Disabilities. This agency provided personal care and respite for our family. We called and asked if we could still collect the funding should Thomas be attending university in another province. Robert was our contact for the agency and he began making the inquiries. It wasn't long before he let us know that they, too, would break the rules and allow Thomas to continue to receive the funding even though he was not going to be living in Alberta.

We had done it! We had managed to find the $25,000 for the Attendant Services Program for Thomas's first year of university. Not only had we succeeded, but we paved the way for future students in Alberta to be able to do the same.

The other exciting news was that once Carleton found out that Alberta was on board to support its students, two other provinces also agreed to do the same. Manitoba and Nova Scotia were going to support a student from each of their provinces who wished to study at a post-secondary school outside of their own provinces. History had been made.

Thomas was psyched for his hockey playoffs in May. This year his team was called the Machines.

The playoffs were a fight to the end, but they won the championship. Thomas was grinning ear to ear as he held the enormous trophy for pictures. On top of all that, he won more awards at the hockey banquet. He received the Todd Mitchell Memorial Award for Regular Season Assist Championship, and the Danny Oulette Memorial Cup. And for the second year, he was chosen to be on the Calgary Selects team for the national tournament, the PowerHockey Canada Cup.

Sports were so important to Thomas. He not only had the excitement of the games and strategies to look forward to, but he engaged so closely with his teammates. He inspired the young rookies by offering his experience in the game, and he encouraged everyone, no matter their level of playing, to do their best. This engagement, I believe, was instrumental in building Thomas's character throughout his teenage years.

Thomas's hockey was only on Saturdays. He wasn't up early or late during the week because of his sport. He had the weekdays to reflect, plan, and discuss with his teammates the moves they were going to make the next weekend. For Thomas, it was a great balance. He needed his sleep, and yet he relished in the anticipation of the next game the following weekend.

🐢 🐢 🐢 🐢 🐢

Right after the hockey finals, Jamie finished his university education in Calgary with a degree in business. We were all so very proud of his accomplishments. Tickets to the graduation were limited, so only Glenn, Thomas, Grandma, Grandpa, and I could attend his graduation. We were thrilled to see him in his cap and gown. We took lots of pictures and clapped loudly as Jamie crossed the stage. It is always a proud moment to see your children achieve their potential. We celebrated afterwards with a family dinner.

Jamie had lined up a summer job with Lafarge. He would be designing a new catalogue for them, and he would start working for Glenn in the fall in the masonry business.

🐢 🐢 🐢 🐢 🐢

Thomas's high school year was coming to an end. Final exams were underway, and graduation was approaching. Relatives from Vancouver wanted to travel to be part of Thomas's graduation, and ten members of our family attended the ceremony. Thomas looked dapper in his cap and gown. The school had arranged for the ramp required for Thomas to be able to cross the stage for his diploma. When Thomas's name was announced, the crowd erupted; he received a standing ovation. The applause seemed to go on forever. It was a magical moment.

Gregg:

With much perseverance by all of the Sorensens, Thomas and I were able to attend the same high school, Dr. E.P. Scarlett. After eight years of attending different schools, we were inseparable throughout high school. At our graduation ceremony, Thomas crossed the stage with the rest of us. Most students crossing the stage received a small round of applause with the occasional individual getting some louder cheer. Thomas received the loudest of cheers of any of the students, which showed how much respect the student body had for Thomas. He was a well-known and well-liked guy at our school.

When Thomas finished crossing the stage and the next student was called, Thomas realized he could not get down on the "exit" side of the stage. Only one side of the stage had a ramp. He had to go back across the stage in front of everyone. This was particularly awkward because students continued crossing the stage in the opposite direction as their names were being called. Embarrassed, Thomas went back across the stage as best he could without causing too much of a distraction. The ceremony stopped and Thomas received another round of applause, which turned into a standing ovation from the students, staff, and parents. This was not just people showing sympathy for Thomas as he was forced to backtrack across the stage; this was a show of respect and an understanding of what Thomas had to go through on an ongoing basis.

A few weeks after Thomas's graduation ceremony, the phone rang, and the caller ID showed a BC number. The gentleman on the other end asked to speak to Thomas. I passed the call to Thomas and put it on speakerphone because he couldn't hold the phone on his own. Both Glenn and I were home.

It was a lawyer from Vancouver who happened to be on the board of directors of the Terry Fox Foundation. He informed Thomas that there were thousands of applications for the scholarship and that only nine applicants from Alberta had been chosen for the interview. He thanked Thomas for his application, congratulated him on his outstanding accomplishments, and then let Thomas know that he was the only Albertan chosen to receive the scholarship. Thomas was beaming, he was so excited. I was trying to hold back my tears as he finished the conversation.

When we hung up, the three of us laughed, I cried, and then we shouted from the rooftops with happiness. What a day! It was indeed a very proud moment for both Glenn and me, and for Thomas.

Thomas on Facebook, June 17, 2013:

Just got a phone call from a director of the Terry Fox Humanitarian Award, and I WON $28,000!! I am lost for words. Thanks to everyone who has written letters and nominations for any of them …!

Congratulatory letters and phone calls started pouring in. Thomas also won a $1,000 scholarship from the Maurice Izzard Memorial Foundation in Ontario, $5,000 from the Phyllis Davidson Easter Seals Scholarship, $2,000 from the Danish Canadian Club in Calgary, $5,000 from Safeway and Muscular Dystrophy Canada, $2,000 from a disability scholarship, $800 from the Alberta Teachers' Association, a $3,000 Alexander Rutherford Scholarship, and a $300 award from the Robert J. Stevenson Memorial Fund.

Thomas's tuition, room, and board would be fully covered. He was more than ready to attend his first year of university.

Thomas loved his turtle, Frank. He woke up one morning worried that Frank was ill. He did not like how Frank was looking. It was a Sunday, and Thomas convinced me to take him and Frank to the vet. We went to one vet who told us that they did not see turtles in their clinic. We had to wait until the afternoon to go to one that specialized in turtles. So we returned home only to head out again shortly after.

When we arrived, the vet admitted that they couldn't do much. They could not do an X-ray because of the shell, and they really could not take any blood to test. The vet sent us home with a cream to apply to Frank's behind. Thomas seemed relieved that Frank had been seen.

We began preparing for Thomas's move to university. Finding a new home for his pet turtle was tough. We managed to find someone who adopted reptiles in need of a safe haven and arranged for the couple to come to the house to collect Frank. Thomas sat for over an hour and a half saying goodbye to his beloved pet. I had been at work and half expected Frank to be gone before I got home, but the couple and the turtle were still there. The couple had been very kind and patient while Thomas was saying his goodbye. I walked into the family room and finally put my foot down and told Thomas it was time.

It was shortly after Frank left home when Thomas received a call from the gentleman who had adopted Frank. It turned out that Frank was actually "Frankie," and she had laid an egg! Apparently, just like a chicken or a duck, if a female turtle doesn't find a mate and get fertilized, her eggs will appear anyway. The egg was not fertile, but Thomas was thrilled to find out that Frankie was okay!

Thomas on Facebook, June 2, 2013:

Friday my turtle moved out. Today Frank laid an egg! I thought he was dying, [sic] the vet said health was poor. Basically, I'm the best grandparent ever. Feeling old.

"Frank" was really a "Frankie!" Who knew?

🐢 🐢 🐢 🐢 🐢

It was now the end of June, and Thomas was into his grade 12 final exams. Then the flood hit. Calgary and surrounding areas were overwhelmed with water. It was the last week of school, and the entire city shut down. Schools were closed, which was extreme for Calgary, and final exams were cancelled. The area where we lived was untouched, but the whole situation seemed surreal. Everyone was advised to stay home. Thomas was happy he didn't have to write any final exams. His marks would be based on his term's work. During the chaos of the flood, we were also preparing for Thomas's procedure of the ablation of his heart. Thankfully, the roads were finally open several days after the flood and we were able to get to the hospital.

Because it was unusual to perform this procedure on a patient so young, Thomas was scheduled to have the ablation done in one of the adult hospitals in Calgary. He was petrified. The doctor prescribed Ativan (a sedative) to be given to Thomas before we left home to help calm his nerves. By the time we arrived at the hospital's pre-op room, Thomas was looped. He said, "The doctors can do anything to me as long as they give me Ativan beforehand!"

🐢 🐢 🐢 🐢 🐢

Glenn, Jamie, and I remained in the waiting room during the procedure. The doctor said it would take up to four hours. She also promised Thomas a coloured picture of his heart.

After only two hours, the doctor met us in the waiting area. When they went in, she found there was nothing to ablate, but she saw a lot of scar tissue on his heart. That made sense because Thomas's kind of muscular dystrophy was a slow deterioration of the muscles, and the heart is one. All the same, the doctor was still puzzled with what she saw and did not see. The doctor was looking for a reason for Thomas's irregular heart functions.

We were able to see Thomas in the recovery room, and then he was going to be transferred by ambulance to the Children's Hospital, where we would meet him. He wanted me to ride in the ambulance with him, but the attendants said that I could not.

When we arrived at the Children's Hospital, Thomas was still pretty looped. He made us all smile with his comments. So many of them didn't make any sense! He was trying to tell us about the ride over. He told the EMS attendants that he wanted the "Wee Wee" on. They had no clue what he was talking about at first; it turned out he wanted them to put the sirens on. They explained that they weren't allowed to use the sirens since it was not an emergency ride. Thomas was disappointed.

We spent a couple of days in the hospital before he was given the okay to go home.

Thomas on Facebook, June 28, 2013:

Had surgery, came back. Heart and jugular were scoped, and no problems. Told I can't lift more than ten pounds. Hehe. Doctors.

Camp Horizon 2013

Thomas was looking forward to going to Easter Seals Camp Horizon the following week. We felt a bit relieved this year, as his cousin Mikael had been hired as one of the camp nursing staff. We knew that Mikael would keep a close eye on him.

Mikael on Facebook, July 13, 2013:

And we laughed, and we cried, and we had a really, really good time!

Elisa, a fellow camper at Camp Horizon, Easter Seals Youth Ambassador for 2011:

I swear Thomas was Socrates reincarnated :-). For those who are confused by the reference, Socrates was a Greek philosopher who taught that being afraid to die led to living mediocre life as a way to avoid the morbid aspect of the unknown. This was certainly not my late friend's point of view, not by the maximum stretch of the imagination. :-)

I remember one time in 2010 when we were playing wheelchair *Angry Birds* and though it was probably completely against the camp rules, Thomas was made the base of our tower. Basically, we taped cardboard boxes to his wheelchair and body. :-) For those of you who don't know the object of *Angry Birds*, it's to knock the other towers down with "bird poop," which we simulated with dodge balls. Now, I have a phobia of things flying at my head and body because I can't deflect. But Thomas, he went flying, right in the smack dab middle of the battlefield with his very own battle cry. :-)

Looking back, I see that my friend's participation in the game was a metaphor for how he lived his life. He went into life full tilt, knowing that at any moment, one of the balls may hit him with a headshot or bust his chair and take him out of the game for good. Yet, he still played and knocked several of the other towers down before he was out.

When Thomas arrived home from camp, we noticed that he was tired and somewhat off. One side of his chest was quite puffy. We took him to the emergency room at the Children's Hospital. A young female doctor examined him, but she didn't have any answers. We did ask for a cardiologist to examine him, but our request was ignored. The young doctor suggested that Thomas get an appointment with a general surgeon. This would take time, but she didn't have any major concerns at the time pertaining to Thomas's condition.

That same day, Thomas worked hard to convince us that he wanted to be part of one of Easter Seals' fundraisers called the Banded Peak Challenge, which was happening the next day. Banded Peak entailed a team of participants dragging Thomas up a mountain in a makeshift wagon. Glenn and I were not feeling good about this. Thomas was still recovering, but he insisted on taking part. He said the fundraiser was short of people and he needed to do this for the cause, so we gave in. We drove Thomas to the event, and Glenn and I hung out in the small town of Bragg Creek (about a thirty-minute drive west of Calgary) for a few hours before his adventure finished.

Thomas on Facebook, July 15, 2013:

This Saturday, in support of Easter Seals and my second home, Camp Horizon, I will be a part of the Banded Peak Challenge, where I will be HIKING up MOOSE MOUNTAIN. As many people have experienced, this year has been rough. Disability cuts, gas leaks, and floods have had their way at Camp Horizon. As I understand, this year's Banded Peak Challenge will be huge in ensuring they can continue to operate. Please support me, and this huge fixture in our community! Please pledge donations and SHARE!!!

When we got Thomas home, he was exhausted. He did manage to sleep for a bit, and then right after his nap, he wanted to go and lie on the couch. When Thomas got up from lying down, he almost blacked out. He panicked and wanted me to call his cardiologist. He also wanted Ativan to calm him down. Sadly, his doctor was not on call. The doctor who was didn't feel comfortable prescribing anything and said if things got worse, we were to bring him to the hospital. In the end, Thomas managed without having to go to the hospital.

Throughout that summer, Thomas's health was not great. We ended up in the emergency department at the Children's Hospital three or four times. Each time, they found nothing of concern but could not explain why he was having health problems. His chest was filling with fluid and they had no explanation. Thomas was beginning to question the aftermath of the ablation.

Not every trip to the doctor had a serious and sombre mood. A funny incident happened on one of our clinic days. Thomas was seventeen and he was being interviewed by a semi-retired doctor to help prepare him for the transition into the adult world. The doctor asked all the same old questions about his eating habits, school, extracurricular activities, and general health. All of a sudden, the doctor asked him how old I was. I thought this was a strange question, but I kept my mouth shut, allowing Thomas to answer the questions. Without a blink, Thomas smiled and said, "Oh, Mom is twenty-seven!" The doctor's mouth dropped and then he smiled, too. (I was fifty-three at the time.) My boys held my age of "twenty-seven" for many years. It was one way they tried to keep me young.

That same summer, doctors at the Children's Hospital asked Thomas to be part of a special study. Dr. Anne Rutkowski, with the Cure CMD organization in the US, and a muscular dystrophy specialist from Europe were coming to Calgary. Dr. Rutkowski felt that they would be able to better establish exactly what kind of muscular dystrophy Thomas had. Thomas filled out questionnaires and had several telephone conversations with her while she was still in California. I was pleased that he was able to speak with her. She encouraged Thomas to use his BiPAP machine on a regular basis, as this device helped give him air and remove carbon dioxide from his lungs during sleep. Thomas was actually listening to her advice. She was impressed with his knowledge and was looking forward to meeting him at the end of the summer.

Meanwhile, the swelling continued in Thomas's chest. We got an appointment with the general surgeon, who asked many questions but concluded that all was well and that there was nothing to worry about.

As if the summer was not already busy enough, Thomas was pumped to have been chosen to be on the Calgary Selects power hockey team, which meant he would travel to London, Ontario, for the national tournament (PowerHockey Cup), once again, with Jamie by his side. Thomas wasn't feeling great by the time they arrived in London. He slept whenever he could and played as often as his health allowed. Glenn and I watched some of the games online. It was definitely a highlight in Thomas's hockey career when the Calgary Selects won gold! Their trophy is now in Canada's Hockey Hall of Fame in Toronto, and Thomas's name is on it.

Thomas on Facebook, August 8, 2013:

I've been home now for two days, but I need to say, this last weekend was great. I met lots of new people and experienced great hockey. For those who don't know, WE WON NATIONALS!

I will miss playing with everyone here but look forward to playing against everyone in the future. Thanks, CPHL (Calgary PowerHockey League)!

He was now only a couple of weeks away from leaving for Ottawa to fulfill his dream of studying biology at Carleton University. However, Thomas was more lethargic than ever and the swelling was continuing. I finally had a heart-to-heart chat with him. I told him that Glenn and I were concerned, that we wanted to return to the hospital, and that we would not leave until we had answers. It was not wise for him to fly anywhere at this time. He agreed that he was getting worse.

Although I had already made the decision, I had Thomas's approval to call his neuromuscular specialist to explain what was going on and express our frustration at being constantly sent home with no results. We needed answers. The specialist contacted one of the cardiologists and told me to take Thomas straight to the cardiology department.

When we arrived at the cardiology clinic, the technicians took Thomas in for an echocardiogram. The test showed a major amount of fluid building up around his lungs, heart, and abdomen. They couldn't explain why this was happening, and they decided to admit him for further observation. Within the next twenty-four hours, all hell broke loose; Thomas swelled up like a balloon.

He was administered all sorts of drugs. Then, the doctors decided to put in a chest tube to drain the fluid. Thomas was freaked out. Glenn and I had to dress in surgical gowns so we could accompany him up to the operating room, where doctors would insert the tube. The staff wanted Glenn to help adjust Thomas on the operating table and me to be there for moral support. I was not allowed in the operating room this time. I wanted to be there for Thomas but had to wait in the hallway. Thomas was scared, and they gave him Ativan to calm him down. Once he was sedated, Glenn had to step outside of the operating room and wait with me. Our hearts were pounding as we waited to hear the results, but we were also so worried about Thomas and his emotions.

After the procedure, they put him in a different room where the staff could monitor him. As he was recovering, his mood changed drastically. He became angry and mean. He told the attending nurse that if she hurt him, he would poop all over her! This was so unlike him.

As I sat beside Thomas, he said to me, "Mom, I don't want to die!"

I was terrified. I didn't understand what was happening. I knew Thomas was not well, but we still didn't have the answers we needed. I didn't want to lose our son. I didn't even know if that was the reality we were facing. I felt so helpless. I could see the fear in Thomas's eyes, and I didn't want him to see mine. Every fibre of my body needed to be strong for Thomas, and yet, I, too, was out of control. It was the worst feeling in my life to date.

As if on cue, the muscular dystrophy specialists arrived, opened the door, and asked to meet with Glenn and me. I didn't want to leave Thomas, but I had no choice. Their time was limited, and our questions for them were so important. We hoped that they could provide answers as to why Thomas was so ill. We were also hoping they could tell us exactly what kind of muscular dystrophy Thomas had and how we could help. We were in a seriously crucial moment, literally.

They asked a lot of questions and looked at the pictures of Thomas throughout his life that we had brought at their request. They reviewed our family histories. The one question about my family that never has been resolved was that my mom had had a brother with severe disabilities. He was, in those days (the 1930s), "kept in a room" away from the public eye. My grandmother looked after his needs. He was loved but never spoken of, my mother never told me about him, and I still have never learned about his condition. My sisters and I tried to find out, without any success. I believe he passed away before the age of twenty.

One specialist believed that Thomas had a form of muscular dystrophy called Emery-Dreifuss, a rare and progressive genetic type of muscular dystrophy, and wanted another genetic test done to confirm this hunch. Up to this point, the genetic specialists at the Children's Hospital had not been able to do this test. It was rare and expensive, and it had to be done in the US.

As our meeting was taking place, Thomas was transferred to the ICU. We were unaware of his transfer during our meeting with the specialists. When we came out of the meeting and heard this, we were in shock. He was now in critical condition. Everything was happening so fast, and we still didn't understand what was going on. Not only was the fluid continuing to build, but Thomas seemed to have had an allergic reaction to the Ativan. The Ativan was working the opposite way it should, which was why he had become so angry and mean.

When we arrived in the ICU, we saw wires and monitors everywhere. A chest tube was draining fluid from his body into a sack, and his heart was hooked up to monitors. Some medications were being given to him through an IV in his wrist, others in pill form. As usual, the pill method was a challenge for Thomas, and he gagged as they entered his mouth. It took about forty-five minutes and a lot of patience from all of us to get three pills down.

Two female doctors were in charge, along with several interns and nurses, and they were all puzzled as to what was going on. We kept asking about his heart, but they believed something else was causing the swelling. One by one, teams of three or four specialists from different departments entered Thomas's room to ask questions. They were lined up in groups outside of his room: specialists from infectious disease, gastronomy, pulmonary, even bug bites. I honestly don't remember all the different areas these doctors represented.

We were grasping at straws. In desperation, I even called a cousin who is a department head at a children's hospital in Texas. My sister Sue had a conversation with a cardiologist friend, who thought there was a problem with the function of Thomas's heart. My gut kept telling me the same. I kept pressing this with the team of doctors and interns until finally, the lead doctor stressed to me in front of the entire team, "It is not his heart! You need to stop talking about this and let us do our work. We know what we are doing!"

Dumbstruck, I felt humiliated and defeated, and I was so angry. I bit my tongue and held back my tears.

Glenn later set up a meeting with the doctor and *made* me apologize. I didn't want to, but I did it. This whole episode changed the way I was around Thomas's doctors from that moment and into the future, which is something I regret. After that incident, I was hesitant to question anything, although every fibre of my being told me that I should continue to challenge them.

After the wrist slapping incident, the same doctor initiated a meeting with seven additional specialists. The purpose of the meeting was to tell Thomas he needed a tracheotomy tube put in. She had chairs set up in the room for each of them, and the meeting lasted forty-five minutes. I recorded the meeting on my phone while they each said their piece and then asked Thomas what he thought.

He had made connection with the key points they made, and he argued against each one. Thomas was very clear and concise, presenting both medical and emotional reasons for his decision. I remained quiet, observing; there were no interruptions while Thomas was speaking. Then, he let her have it. He was calm, collected, methodical, and very polite but firm and decisive.

After he had said his piece, they all left, but after a moment , one came back—a respirologist—and she said, "Thomas, I have two things to say. First, I want to say how brave you were during the meeting and secondly, I want you to know I'm in total agreement with your decision to not have the tracheotomy. I was coerced into coming to this meeting."

Thomas spent three weeks in the hospital with no conclusive results, at least not with regard to the cause of the swelling. One of his lungs had collapsed after several days, and during the entire three weeks, he had a chest tube draining fluid from his body. He was given several combinations of medications, not to mention the numerous daily tests for blood levels. The doctors wrote it up as a "mysterious illness."

The only positive throughout the entire experience was that we did receive confirmation that Thomas had a rare form of muscular dystrophy called LMNA, which is:

> a condition that primarily affects muscles used for movement (skeletal muscles). It is part of a group of genetic conditions called congenital muscular dystrophies, which

cause weak muscle tone (hypotonia) and muscle wasting (atrophy) beginning very early in life.[10]

It was under the umbrella of Emery-Dreifuss. This form of MD was a relatively new find, and it was only after Thomas's death that we learned this type of MD was totally related to the heart. One piece of information we learned after his death was that in terms of how to treat this kind of MD, patients who have this should never be given oxygen. The other: Thomas was one of three people in the world to have it.

It was during this hospital stint that we first imagined that we could lose Thomas. The fear of the unknown is always the scariest: we were terrified, not understanding what was happening, not being able to get or give answers. We saw the urgency on the faces of the doctors and nurses, but as parents, we were helpless. We saw the numerous specialists arrive and leave without any suggestions or answers to what was causing the swelling. We saw our son, lying powerless, vulnerable, and in pain, suffering. We waited patiently time and time again for results of the multiple tests that were being performed. We felt paralyzed, anxious, and afraid. There is no greater wish a mother has than to protect and help her children. I was in the position where I could do neither.

I spent every night of the three weeks in the hospital with Thomas, going home only to shower and change clothes and only when Glenn or Jamie was with Thomas to relieve me. One night in the ICU when Thomas was on heavy meds and monitors, and I was trying to sleep on the window seat, he called out, "Mom, could you crawl into bed with me, please?" The attending nurse looked at me and all the monitors around Thomas, and she helped me clear the way. I carefully crawled in and settled beside him. It was comforting for both of us.

Finally, after two weeks, Thomas began to get better. He requested to see one of the interns he preferred and asked if there was a chance of this swelling happening again. The intern thought that it was not probable but did not make any promises.

---

10 Courtesy of MedlinePlus from the National Library of Medicine: Medline Plus, "LMNA-related Congenital Muscular Dystrophy," last updated August 18, 2020, medlineplus.gov/genetics/condition/lmna-related-congenital-muscular-dystrophy/.

Word had gotten out about what Thomas had been through. Friends and family knew right away that he was in the hospital, and everyone wanted to come and visit, but most were not allowed until that third week. As soon as visitors were permitted, he was overwhelmed with visits from his friends.

Thomas on Facebook, September 4, 2013:

THROUGH THE GLORY OF MORPHINE I RISE!! After sixteen days in bed, this is my first time [getting] up independently! As of today, only physical healing of cuts and bruises. CARLETON IN TWO WEEKS!!! WHAT ELSE YOU GOT 2013!!!! HAHAHA!!!!!!!!!

Thomas on Facebook, September 9, 2013:

After twenty-one days, three weeks exactly, I'm home. I'm bruised, sore, and tired, but healthy. Carleton on Saturday.

A University Student

Thomas was so happy to get out of the hospital. Now, even though he would be late getting to Carleton, he could begin realizing his dream. The doctors set him up with a new regimen of drugs, and we got several weeks' worth of medications in blister packs for his use in Ottawa. In preparation for the move, the doctors contacted another cardiologist in Ottawa who told us Thomas was still eligible to be treated in children's hospitals because he was not yet eighteen.

Four days after his discharge, Glenn and I were on a plane to Ottawa to set up Thomas for his first year at university. He and I left for Ottawa a day before Thomas and his brother. We spent several hours getting Thomas's dorm room ready, scrubbing and polishing his living area—the floors, the walls, and above and inside the kitchen cabinets. Glenn and I went so far as to lay down wax paper on the top shelves of the kitchen cabinets to make it easier for the next clean. We scrubbed the floor tiles in the kitchen and applied new wax to them.

Glenn and I went shopping for supplies. We tried to think of and purchase absolutely everything Thomas would need for living away from home: new dishes, spices, utensils, pots, saucepans, frying pans, cleaning supplies, shampoo, and toilet paper. We picked up a new computer and monitor. The large screen would work for his schoolwork and video games and also serve as his television. Before leaving Calgary, we had ordered several items from Ikea, and our niece and her husband had picked them up for us from the Ottawa store. Chris, our nephew, was also so helpful. He was given permission to enter the dorm and worked hard putting together Thomas's desk and dresser.

We also picked up some wall art. One piece was large—an approximately eight-by-ten-foot wall hanging of a forest with the sun shining through the trees. Because of its size, we had trouble getting it to fit into the rental car but managed to hang it out the back and fasten it to the bumper. We also couldn't resist a wonderful painting of zebras.

Gregg had given Thomas a *Star Wars* lamp for graduation, and in Ottawa, Glenn and I found a second, similar one to complement the one from Gregg.

We also found a periodic table shower curtain. A new bed was delivered from Sleep Country Canada while we were setting up his room. We had actually ordered two of these beds prior to leaving for Ottawa, and the first was already at our home in Calgary. Our hope was that if Thomas had a bed with the same mattress in both cities, he would have a smooth transition from home to university and adjust easily.

After many hours of work, Glenn and I went to the airport to meet the boys.

When the elevator door on the arrivals level at the Ottawa airport opened, we were thrilled to see both Thomas and Jamie, and we could tell that Thomas was so excited he could hardly contain himself. We took a picture of the two boys getting off the elevator. Glenn and I had rented a wheelchair-friendly van to pick up the boys. Thomas was wide awake after the five-hour trip, taking in all the scenery on the way to Carleton University, his new home, his dream.

Thomas quickly learned that he had the nicest room on campus. It was a large room with two huge windows, an accessible washroom, and a large kitchen he would share with another student. Both Thomas and his kitchen mate were happy with the supplies and the decor Glenn and I had found to brighten up their kitchen.

After touring Thomas's suite, we explored the university both above and below ground. The tunnels went on and on, making the entire campus easily accessible in the winter. From his room, Thomas could get to any building on campus without going outside. The tunnels had art work from previous years' students commemorating their area of study and the year they had attended. We almost needed a map to understand just where we were on campus, it was so large. Thomas needed to learn each path that led to his upcoming classes but he quickly got it figured out. He was adjusting so well.

The Paul Menton Centre at Carleton University (PMC) was established in January 1990 to assist students with special needs and is one of a kind in North America. The science professors knew their students and their capabilities. They were apprehensive about having Thomas in their classes because a student in a wheelchair had never been in the science faculty prior to Thomas's enrollment. A few of them wanted to meet with Thomas before agreeing to include him in their classes. They wanted to see exactly who they were dealing with and what his abilities and needs were. But once they met him and listened to him speak about science, there weren't any more questions or doubts. The competent staff at the PMC saw to it that Thomas had notetakers and a lab assistant available to him. They actually worked with Thomas and the lab assistant to make sure everything was in place to set him up for success. The university even spent additional money on the proximity readers for the science buildings and installed special lab tables for Thomas to use.

While we were in Ottawa, both Glenn and I wanted to meet with the new cardiologist at the Children's Hospital of Eastern Ontario in Ottawa. Thomas seemed happy with him and promised to keep up with the scheduled appointments and regular blood work.

The second hardest moment in my life was leaving Thomas in Ottawa. He was so excited and so looking forward to his dream, but I didn't want to say goodbye. We took several pictures of Glenn and Thomas, then of Thomas and me. I can still envision Thomas sitting in his chair at the main door with the biggest smile on his face. Glenn practically had to pull me away and drag me to the airport. I cried all the way home to Calgary. I couldn't wait for the Christmas break to see Thomas's face again.

Upon arriving home, I was emotionally and physically drained. After the hospital experience and having to leave Thomas in Ottawa, I was, fortunately, able to take a leave from work to recover. On my first day back to work, a stunning flower arrangement with a card was delivered to my school. It was from Thomas. He wished me the best on my return to work. The words on the card were from the heart and made me cry: "Thank you, Mom, for being there for me. I love you so much." It was an unexpected and beautiful surprise. It made me proud to have raised such a thoughtful son.

Needless to say, that fall was different for both Glenn and me. Thomas was in university, and Jamie was living his own life with his girlfriend. We were now empty nesters, and we both felt a huge void in our home and in our lives. We weren't quite sure what to do with ourselves after being on call 24-7 for seventeen years.

Glenn and I tried to get out of the house often because we could. We didn't require a caregiver in order to go grocery shopping or see a movie. Our empty household and our sudden, new-found freedom felt odd.

When Thomas moved to Ottawa, he didn't stop volunteering and playing sports. He offered his time to the student centre, helping other people with disabilities. Thomas would hang out at the centre to do whatever he could for other students: helping with their studies, offering up coping advice and strategies, listening when they needed a shoulder, being supportive in any way he could. Later in the school year, he applied for a paid position there.

Thomas also became involved with the Ottawa chapter of Muscular Dystrophy Canada, attending meetings and offering assistance wherever they could use his help.

He joined the Ottawa Power Wheelchair Hockey League. He played for the Gators and assisted the team with filling out applications for funding they could use for acquiring equipment and improving their facilities.

Jeff Barrett, fellow CPHL player:

In Ottawa, Thomas talked about joining the hockey league. If I were to join a new league, I would be nervous, but not Thomas. He was excited about joining the Ottawa league and saw even more potential growth for himself and the players he met there. He was making a difference in the sport in a new city.

Taylor, Thomas's first-year kitchen mate at Carleton University:

His name was simply Thomas Voss Sorensen, and yet his personality showed something much more than that. When I first met Thomas in September of his freshman year at Carleton, I knew I was coming face-to-face with an unstoppable force of nature. He was an invincible mix of the studious and the silly, the courteous and carefree. He possessed a zeal for life and a purpose for living, which have been matched by few people I've had the pleasure of knowing. In spite of more than his fair share of physical challenges, he had an unmistakable grin on his face through it all, and a first-class sense of humour to match.

On one occasion, I remember Thomas, myself, and a good friend of ours, Vanessa Collins, making our way to the university cafeteria for dinner. For some unthinkable reason, three gigantic football players, showing no sign of injury whatsoever, thought it would be a good idea to ride in the elevator with us instead of taking the stairs. Well, that just wouldn't stand in the eyes of my good friend Thomas. Any other person would've objected in no uncertain terms. But Thomas, his dry wit and good humour always at the ready, found a tongue-in-cheek way to analyze the situation. As our unexpected company departed the elevator, he said, in just enough of a loud voice so that they heard him without having to turn around, "I didn't know stupid was a disability." Any other person would've read the riot act to try to explain to the football players the perceived injustice of the situation, but as anyone who knew him, including myself, will tell you, that was just Thomas through and through.

I also had the pleasure to experience firsthand the love that Thomas felt for his family. He was close to his brother, Jamie, and perhaps most of all to his mother, Kathy, and dad, Glenn. I observed his fondness for them on one particularly memorable occasion when Kathy treated Thomas and me to dinner one night at Oliver's, the undergraduate bar on campus. It was clear to me from this brief encounter with the two of them, and from the numerous phone calls and Skype calls to his parents and grandparents, that Thomas had a deep love and admiration for his family and very much enjoyed being in their company.

I also had the pleasure to come to understand Thomas's softer and more sophisticated side. Despite his numerous physical challenges and the hardships of being in Ottawa, away from his family while they supported him from afar in Alberta, he showed as much passion and dedication to his studies as he did to his friends. His lifelong goal was to become a biologist or professor of biology in order to understand and educate others about the nature of disease. He was also extremely active in support of the fight against muscular dystrophy, the very affliction which would ultimately cost him his life. In spite of his ongoing battle against this disease, coupled with a heart condition which further ravaged his body, Thomas was never broken in spirit.

Jon, a caregiver at Carleton University:

I was lucky enough to be a part of the Attendant Services Program the year that Thomas was at Carleton. So, I'd like to share a story to demonstrate what a special person he was.

One of my fondest memories with Tom came on an occasion when we were cooking dinner together. I am no master chef; I barely get by living away from home. Now, Tom wanted Kraft Dinner. However, the way Tom preferred his KD was a little unorthodox. Instead of using milk, he substituted a can of tomato soup. I call it the "Tom Sorensen Special." Using a can of soup instead of milk was fine by me, but then I came to the harsh realization that I had never used a can opener in my life. So, I went to get the can of soup and bring out the can opener, and I fiddled around with it and absolutely botched the entire process. Midway through the debacle that was me fumbling around trying to use this can opener, all I heard was that sly voice, "Oh my God, you have never used a can opener before, have you?"

Tom had a great sense of humour and loved mocking me, so he further prompted me with "Jon, how long have you lived on this earth?"

"Twenty years, Thomas."

"Twenty years, Jon, and you have never used a can opener? How on Earth have you gotten by?"

With that, Tom taught me how to properly use a can opener, we made the KD, I sat down, and I helped feed him the meal. As we sat there, Tom looked me directly in the eyes and said, "You may fail at life, Jon, but I still appreciate you."

Thomas's humour continued as he plugged away:

Thomas on Facebook, September 27, 2013:

The sign by the elevator at my new doctor's office read "Take the stairs and improve life expectancy." I'm worried I chose the wrong doctor.

Thomas called us every day to keep in touch, and he assured us he was studying and doing his best. He had already missed three weeks of classes because of being hospitalized and had to catch up.

He loved university life, but he was busy. Of the two biology courses he was taking, one required additional lab time. A chemistry course and an archeology course rounded out his first semester, giving him over thirty hours of classes per week. Thomas felt the workload was not allowing him to keep up on his schoolwork, so he dropped the chemistry course.

On top of his schooling, he needed to attend doctor's appointments on a regular basis as well as do recurring blood tests to check his potassium levels and other markers.

Thomas on Facebook, November 7, 2013:

While reviewing a mid-term ... I suppose it would only be too convenient if Nebuchadnezzar II was succeeded by Nebuchadnezzar III. My bad.

Vanessa, a caregiver at Carleton University:

When I look back on the short time that I knew Thomas, I'm amazed at how much of an impact he had on my life. There isn't a day that goes by when I don't think about him.

Thomas came to Carleton as this young, bright student looking to better his future and push the boundaries that people tried to put on his life. I met Thomas through the Attendant Services Program, which offers students with disabilities the chance to further their education, gain new experiences, and turn dreams into reality.

Thomas was a special character. I think it took me some time after his death to really embrace those happy memories and the little things that made our relationship so special. Whenever I was around his parents or friends and they were exchanging stories about how funny Thomas was, I realized there were things that he told me that he hadn't talked to anyone else about, and there were people back home that I was only privy to knowing about because he wanted to share them with me. He could keep you entertained for hours and never make it about himself one bit.

I immediately connected with him; we had a ridiculous brother-sister relationship. He would bicker at me and I would squabble at him, but we always enjoyed each other's company. I would pick on him and he'd tease me. He cracked witty jokes, was quick to make comebacks, and always had a "did you know" fact ready to tell me. When you spend so much time with someone through a program like this [the Attendant Services Program], you tend to create bonds that are so personal that the relationship doesn't even seem like a job anymore.

The program was a gateway into a friendship that wasn't about the program. When I wasn't at work, we'd be hanging out. When it was the weekend and he'd finished calling all his family to check in, we'd go on an adventure. Mind you, there were a few doctor's appointments we had to go to, but even then we got to go together, and he was always just so happy to be doing whatever. He hated his blood being drawn and when we had to go do to that, he was adamant I be there with him. He didn't want to go by himself, but he also never wanted to show people that he had vulnerability and that he was scared. He was always so adamant about being positive.

I'd come on shift and just go hang out in his room, or when he'd get Lego, he'd come to the office and I'd spend hours building it with him (he could manage some pieces but not all). Sometimes we tried cooking some of his mom's recipes like her stroganoff or her asparagus soup, and I'd always mess it up and get lectured. My cooking never measured up to his mom's. Now, I think about how much I miss those sassy comments and I just laugh.

🐢 🐢 🐢 🐢 🐢

Thomas called one day in November and pointed out to me that December was approaching. He was really asking (indirectly) if he was going to get the annual Danish Advent calendar even though he was living in Ottawa. Thomas loved waking up each day, ready to tear open the wrapping and receive a gift. He was already looking forward to receiving his calendar gift every day, planned his shopping excursions to buy gifts for the family, and wondered what the Christmas pudding dessert prize would be that year.

I played dumb on the phone, pretending that I was super busy at school. I told him I would try to do what I could. What Thomas didn't know was that I was one step ahead of him; the calendar was due to arrive the following week in Ottawa. As an added bonus, that particular year, Thomas would get all twenty-four presents! I had even arranged for our niece Jennie to pick up a small artificial tree with lights to put in his room. That was present number one. I added some decorations for his tree, a Terry's Orange chocolate ball, which was always one of his favourites, the must-have licorice, and an assortment of practical things like a new toothbrush and new kitchen gadgets.

Glenn and I were so excited for both Christmas and Thomas to arrive. I went all out decorating the house. The tree was up, and the mantle decorated with all our *Nisse*, Danish male and female elves. Thomas loved having even the washrooms decorated. I always did his with a snowman theme and the guest powder room with Santa Clauses.

I was busy, too, making some of his favourite recipes. He loved my asparagus and meatball soup, which is actually quite easy to make. I don't even use a cookbook or measuring spoons anymore. The meatballs consist of simply ground pork with a bit of onion and allspice. We had purchased a kitchen gadget in Denmark that forms the balls, which I cook in a pot of boiling water with some salt. Once the meatballs are cooked, remove them from the pot and put them aside. Into the pot, add butter and flour, then the asparagus juice, chicken broth, and cream. Finally, add the sliced white asparagus and put the meatballs back in. And you are done.

I had trouble containing my excitement, waiting for Thomas to arrive home for Christmas.

"Home for Christmas"

In early December, the fluid build-up started again, but Thomas didn't say anything to me about it. Jamie flew to Ottawa to accompany him back to Calgary. We suspected the fluid had built up again based on a picture Jamie sent us shortly after his arrival. The photo was of Thomas beside the Christmas tree that was part of Thomas's Advent calendar. However, even Jamie didn't say anything about his brother's condition until they arrived in Calgary.

It was tough for Jamie to do a turnaround flight in twenty-four hours. There was the flight time, the two-hour time change, and having to care for Thomas before and during the flight. Travelling with Thomas wasn't easy. Parts of his power chair had to be dismantled and fastened together with tape, wraps, and straps in hopes it wouldn't get damaged, as it had to be checked in as luggage. Thomas needed to be transferred into a push wheelchair to get to the plane. And once he was on the plane, it was also a struggle to get him seated and comfortable during the four- to five-hour flight. He needed adjustments in his position every fifteen minutes. Then there was … the washroom! Have you ever tried to take someone who is completely helpless to an airplane washroom? Need I say more? Jamie was invaluable. We couldn't have asked for a better big brother.

When they got off the plane in Calgary, I was shocked to see Thomas was indeed full of fluid again. He appeared heavier and puffy, as he described himself. He looked like he had gained 30 lbs. My heart ached. Thomas simply didn't look like his usual happy self. He was also tired after the long trip and wanted a home-cooked meal and sleep. We headed straight home. I had already made him his favourite Danish cream of asparagus soup, which he devoured a bowl of, and then he promptly took a nap.

"Home for Christmas"

After he awoke, we talked. He claimed the fluid build-up hadn't gotten "bad" until a couple of days earlier. He already knew what I was going to say, and so at my insistence, we promptly headed to the Alberta Children's Hospital, where I spent the night with him. Being as it was Christmas Eve, not many of the specialists were around. The doctors who were there had no answers. They decided to discharge him because it was Christmas Eve, knowing that we would see his heart specialist the following week. They were short on staff because of the holidays, and they also wanted to send him home so he could spend Christmas with his family. We brought him home, knowing we would be back in a few days.

Thomas was happy to be home, but he was worn out. The *Calgary Sun* requested to interview him. They wanted to follow up with him since he had now completed one term of university, and they ran a story on his progress in Carleton.

Although he was swollen from head to toe, we still managed to go to his grandparents for Christmas Eve celebrations: the traditional Danish dinner, and the annual visit by Santa Kim.

Thomas's only wish for a gift was business cards. They simply read: *Thomas Sorensen: Disability Advocate*. The cards also had his cell number and email address on it. He wanted to pass these out to his new friends at Carleton at the student centre, should anyone ever want his help. They were also meant for anyone who wanted him to speak at an event.

Thomas was all about helping others and raising awareness for anyone with a disability. Because doing so was extremely important to him, he gave his time and his passion for this cause. He was selfless through it all, and no matter his health he always found opportunities to educate people about disabilities. When a child asked why he was in a wheelchair or why his legs didn't work, instead of cringing or wincing, he always answered with a smile. These seemingly simple business cards spoke volumes about Thomas and represented his conviction that everyone is equal and deserves a chance at life.

Thomas on Facebook, December 31, 2013:

Well, I was hoping for a bit more time in Calgary. #surpriseheartsurgery.

The week after Christmas, we met his cardiologist. She had been in contact with Thomas's doctor in Ottawa, and they agreed it was time for Thomas to have an implant. The implantable cardioverter-defibrillator (ICD) was a device that would not only monitor Thomas's heart 24-7 but also act as both a pacemaker and a defibrillator. The surgery was scheduled for the following week.

This time, we were sent to the "adult" hospital. There was a great discussion as to whether or not Thomas would be intubated, a procedure involving a tube being inserted into a patient's throat and windpipe to make it easier for air to get in and out of the patient's lungs. Thomas did not want this, but the only other option was for him to be given a local anesthetic and be awake during the procedure. He *definitely* did not want that. So the doctors decided he would be put under with intubation. Thomas made them promise to take out the tube as soon as possible.

Glenn and I were both allowed to enter the operating room to get him adjusted so the doctors could do their work. There were so many monitors, screens, doctors, and nurses present. It was overwhelming for us, let alone for Thomas. The fear of the unknown is always on the patient's mind in an operating room, but a parent in that situation has only one wish: to take the child's place.

Jamie, Glenn, and I paced the hallways waiting for Thomas's procedure to be complete. These waiting periods always seemed so long, and we always wished for the best but worried about the worst.

After the procedure, Thomas was transferred to the ICU in the same hospital. When we arrived in his ICU room, we saw he was hooked up to numerous monitors and the tube was still in. We asked why the tube was still in place, and the doctors replied that they were not used to having such a young patient and were scared to take it out. They were hoping that he would be transferred to the Children's Hospital, where it would be removed.

We waited several hours for Thomas to wake up from the anesthesia. His little body looked so small in the big bed and room. He finally woke up and started trying to tell us something, but with the tube still in his throat, Glenn, Jamie, and I couldn't figure out what he was trying to say. It took quite some time before I thought of asking him questions, starting with his head, and going down to his toes to try and figure out what he wanted.

I asked if he wanted a scratch on his head or his nose. He shook his head, no. I asked if he wanted to be adjusted. I asked if he was in pain. With every question, he shook his head no in frustration. I couldn't think of anything else until finally I asked, "Do you need to use the washroom?" His whole body shook violently! That was it! I felt so bad, but we all had to laugh with nervousness. We were a bit embarrassed we hadn't thought of that sooner.

Thomas really wanted the tube out. We kept pressing the medical staff about this. They insisted that they wanted the Children's Hospital staff to remove the tube. At last, the doctor came in and expressed his concerns, but we convinced him to remove the tube. Poor Thomas probably had that tube in for close to nine hours. He had a few choice words to say to the doctor once it was out.

Glenn:

When they finally pulled it out, for the next five minutes, everybody got a piece of Thomas's mind. The verbal abuse from Thomas was something I'd never seen before. But the funny thing was, he never used a single swear word to tell everyone off.

Thomas on Facebook, January 4, 2014:

Most tubes and lines are out! Docs want to play with my meds before I go home and would like me playing hockey sooner rather than later (2–4 weeks). Being transferred to the Children's Hospital this afternoon!

He could not wait to get out of that adult hospital, and he was soon well enough to be transferred to the Children's Hospital. Thomas insisted that I ride with him in the ambulance, and this EMS team was okay with the idea, which made Thomas happy. It wasn't a long ride to the Children's Hospital, no more than a few kilometres, but Thomas and I talked about his disappointment of not having the sirens on during the last trip. Both the attendants smiled. "Okay, Thomas!" said one. "Get ready! We'll give you the full meal deal."

With my cell phone, I recorded the experience. I began by scanning the inside of the ambulance showing the small narrow bed, the lights, the emergency kits, and the attendant. It was a cold, grey day, and the road was bumpy. Thomas was lying on his side with an IV in his hand and bandages everywhere. He was wrapped in blankets, and his face was flushed and puffy, but he was happy his mom was there after a long, terrifying day. I could see his anticipation. His eyebrows moved up and down, and his eyes were wide. Then I could see the grin appear from ear to ear as the sirens began. Thomas exclaimed, "Oh there we go!" He was so happy. His eyes widened as did his grin. The sirens blared continuously. "Well, this is ten times better than last time!" he said.

It was a cool experience, and it helped so much to lift his spirits. Seeing his excitement brought tears to my eyes. I still have the video on my phone.

Thomas on Facebook, January 6, 2014:

Morphine feels nice.

Thomas spent another week and a half in the Children's Hospital recuperating, and I was there every night with him. Both Glenn and Jamie were fantastic in relieving me, and Thomas had plenty of visits from family and friends. He was going to turn eighteen soon, and he knew this was probably his last visit to the Children's Hospital. An end to yet another chapter.

Again, he was set up with new meds, and the doctors planned that a special heart monitor would be placed beside his dorm bed in Ottawa. This monitor would remotely send regular updates to the Foothills Medical Centre in Calgary, in the adult world, so they could keep an eye on his heart's activity.

Thomas on Facebook, January 8, 2014:

Finally, home. Ottawa on Tuesday!

As we were preparing to return to Ottawa, Thomas was back in his power chair. Something was not right. We knew that baggage handlers had dropped his chair on his way home at Christmas, which we had thankfully reported at the airport by filling out the necessary paperwork. At the time, we thought the main casing that held his batteries in place had cracked. Because Thomas was in the hospital most of the break, we hadn't thought of investigating further.

When we took his chair to have the casing replaced, we found that the damage was substantial. Long story short, the chair was a write-off. The vendor told us that the replacement cost would be $10,000. WestJet was truly amazing. Of course, they questioned why it took us more than two weeks to inform them of the discrepancy in the damage report. However, they were very understanding once we described how our previous few weeks had unfolded.

We were able to make sufficient repairs to the chair in order for Thomas to return to Ottawa, and plans were made to order a new one for Thomas, to be delivered at a later date.

Thomas on Facebook, January 10, 2014:

Getting off the plane from Ottawa, we found a crack in my chair. Damage was estimated at $200. Today we looked inside the chair at the shop and it went smashy-kablew! $10,000!

After Thomas had a few days at home to recuperate, he, Jamie, and I flew back to Ottawa on January 12 to get him ready to start his second term two weeks late. Fortunately, my school board gave me yet another leave of absence. Jamie was able to come along to help with the lifting and with the plane ride. He was a godsend, never complaining about having to provide extra help to accommodate his brother's needs. He and I stayed with our niece and her husband, saving us hotel costs. We were able to get Thomas back to his dorm room and update his caregivers as to his needs.

Thomas wanted me to stay a few extra days to make sure he was comfortable. Jamie returned home. I helped Thomas get a phone line for his heart monitor. With the campus tech people, we had to go on a hunt to find the appropriate channels to make the connection work. We finally resolved the issues and were able to connect a line to the hospital in Calgary.

I made a variety of low-sodium meals at my niece's house to put in Thomas's freezer. He now had to watch his fluid intake and output, which meant he had to stick to a salt-free diet.

Because of the surgery, he also had new, specific instructions for being lifted, which stipulated no lifting him from under the arms. The lifts had to be a side-lift or done with a sling. He was also told not to sleep on the side with the ICD for a total of eight weeks (you could actually see the shape of the ICD under his skin), but the most dismal instruction of all was that he was not allowed to play power hockey for eight weeks.

After ten days, he finally assured me that he was okay and that I could return to Calgary.

Thomas on Facebook, January 14, 2014:

You think you can keep me from Ottawa?! HAHAHAHA!!! I'm IN STITCHES!!!

About three weeks after I returned home, Thomas called. He told me that he was invited to a special reception. He had made the Dean's List for the first term.

Thomas didn't even know what this meant at first. He didn't realize that his marks from the first term were so high that he was in the upper echelon of the science faculty's student ranking. He didn't think the reception was a big deal, but we talked him into attending. We asked our niece Jennie if she could accompany him to the event. Jennie went over to Thomas's dorm to make sure he had on a pressed dress shirt and tie.

In the end, Thomas was happy that we had convinced him to attend. He sat with the Dean of Science and was introduced as a recipient of the award. He began to understand what a big deal this was.

The Faculty of Science department at Carleton had also decided that Thomas's first-year biology course was too easy for him. For the second term of his first year, he was registered in second-year biology. Shortly after the awards reception, he was invited to apply for a paid internship for the summer working with the biology professors. This invitation was offered only to a select few. We were into March by this time, and Thomas seemed to be holding his own both in school and with his health.

Dear Thomas Sorensen,

Congratulations on your excellent grades during the Fall 2013 semester. **I am writing to inform you about an exciting paid summer research opportunity.** *The Dean of Science offers paid summer internships to the top first-year Science, Computer Science, and Mathematics students. The Dean's Summer Research Internships (DSRI) allows students the opportunity to work with professors and conduct research. This year, we have a limited number of research internships available and we invite you to apply for one. Students who receive these competitive research internships will be paid ... to work with a professor in the Faculty of Science.*

The DSRI application requires you to discuss who you want to do research with, to identify the top two professors you wish to work with, and explain why you want to join their research program. While you can get substantial information from the faculty websites to learn which professors' research interests you and why, we would highly encourage you to contact faculty members directly to discuss possibilities and for you to get a good idea of the type of work conducted by the particular professor.

Regards,
Dwight Deugo,
Associate Dean of Science

Thomas was now eighteen, which meant he had to begin to establish a whole new network of doctors who would take care of his medical needs and appointments. We had been given names to contact, but with wait times involved, it was up to Thomas to get his care team established. All the doctors and specialists for children are under one roof, but as soon as you become an adult, you need to see doctors and specialists who are spread out all over a city. These practitioners don't seem to communicate with one another like they do in a children's hospital, which makes seeking care very challenging. Thomas was trying to the best of his ability to meet with the new specialists in Ottawa. Everything was taking time. He did, however, see his on-campus doctor, and he continued having his blood work checked on a regular basis.

During his second term, Thomas was still volunteering at the student centre at Carleton. He had made lots of new friends and loved university life. He wanted to become even more involved in the university, so he decided to run for Vice President Academic Candidate for the Carleton Student Science Society. He made a web page showcasing his background and his reasons for running and posted the following:

> Being your next VP Academic is how Thomas wants to transfer the skills he has learned to create a better Carleton Science Student Society. That includes Monthly Networking Events to better connect students with the faculty and prestigious alumni alike, lobbying the university for increased funding for Peer Assisted Study Sessions (PASS) within the department (which currently holds the lowest number of sessions university-wide), and increasing event accessibility through promotion and cross-departmental partnerships.

He printed off posters outlining his platform and put them up around the campus.

Through all of this activity, Glenn and I were increasingly worried about Thomas's health as we knew he wasn't sharing everything about his health with us. There were many unspoken words between Glenn and me, but we both knew we felt the same way. Our number one concern was for Thomas, yet we had to be there for each other and be strong as a family. We tried to remain positive.

I had returned to work, and my school's spring break was approaching. Glenn and I took advantage of this break because we needed some "us time," so we booked a cruise. Glenn's parents, who were approaching their late 70s, asked if they could come along. Of course we said, "Yes!" Unfortunately, during our trip, Glenn's dad, who had previously been diagnosed with lung cancer, got sick on the boat. He and Alice would not admit just how unwell he was for fear of being "thrown overboard" for medical reasons. We pretty much worried about Hans the whole trip. As soon as we dropped them off at their home when we returned to Calgary, they went to the ER only to confirm that Hans had pneumonia.

It wasn't even a week later that Thomas called. He said he was "puffy." We knew that meant his whole body was full of fluid. Thomas had only begun to receive his adult medical care. Glenn and I decided that I should fly down for the weekend to check up on him. I needed to put my eyes on him to make sure everything was okay. I packed a small carry-on bag for the plane. When I arrived in Ottawa and saw him, I also saw instant relief in his eyes. He said, "Thanks for coming, Mom. I love you so much."

I also knew immediately that we were going to be back in the hospital, but with the long wait lists, Thomas hadn't yet managed to make contact with the new doctors he needed. I called a few of them, and they all said the same thing: take Thomas to the ER.

Getting medical help for him was a bit chaotic. Because the adult world of care was so new, my phone calls to his pediatric doctors were fruitless. It felt like I was starting all over again in trying to find proper care for Thomas. In spite of the frustration, Thomas was so happy to have me by his side. He kept saying over and over, "Thank you, Mom," and "I love you so much!"

Daily Accounts of the Hospital Stay in Ottawa

Thomas had been in the hospital so many times—days and weeks—over the years. When he was admitted in Ottawa, it was the first time that both Glenn and I documented each day. This honest account of our days in April of 2014, helping Thomas meet his needs should give some insight to what life was like with him in a hospital. We sent these updates to friends and family via email each day that Thomas was hospitalized. Please note that we did miss a couple of days of documentation.

Day 1

We were in the emergency room for hours today and saw several doctors, all of whom were asking question after question. They wanted blood work, and that was an issue since we know how difficult it is to find a vein to draw blood. Each nurse was only allowed three attempts. We were trying everything—warming his hands with heating pads, massaging his hands, and holding his hands upright to try to get the blood flowing—but nothing was working. Nurses from other departments were coming to try to draw the blood. Meanwhile, the doctors were asking more questions. One wanted to send Thomas home. Another dropped his jaw when Thomas described his condition using medical terminology. He asked Thomas to slow down because he didn't understand what Thomas was saying. Finally, after several hours (perhaps twelve), one doctor said that Thomas needed to be admitted. It must have been about one in the morning by this time.

I went back to Thomas's dorm to get his BiPAP machine, his arm pillow, and his favourite blanket. It was pouring rain. I was worried, scared, and frustrated with what was happening. Furthermore, as I was not familiar enough with Ottawa to get back to the university on my own, I used Google Maps and ended up on a dead-end street. Finally, I got to his dorm room, retrieved what I needed, and made my way back to the hospital.

The nurse on the nightshift was young and sweet. She was trying her best to make Thomas comfortable and feel welcome. I was exhausted, and perhaps it showed. She helped me convince Thomas that he would be okay for one night so I could go to our niece's house to sleep. I promised him I would return early tomorrow morning. (That was one out of only three nights in five weeks that I didn't stay with Thomas.)

Day 2

I arrived bright and early to be with Thomas. I slept last night, although not soundly because I felt guilty that I wasn't there beside him. He was happy to see me arrive.

The doctors came and checked Thomas's neck veins to gauge his heart function. They wanted to do an echocardiogram and maybe a nuclear scan. This type of scan uses radioactive material inside Thomas's body to help see how his heart is functioning. Also, the doctors felt that a drug called Lasix would take care of the extra fluid that is building up throughout his body. They are hoping to drain one litre per day by giving him Lasix via IV and then switch to pill form. They predicted they would finish up all the procedures and release Thomas from the hospital in a week.

By the end of the day, we were still waiting for the echocardiogram. It turns out that it will be tomorrow instead. Meanwhile, the cardiologist wanted to confirm that Thomas's heart was the cause of the fluid build-up and check whether his heart was failing. I was able to convince the doctor to get in contact with Dr. Anne Rutkowski in California for a consultation. Dr. Rutkowski recommended that Thomas get back on prednisone to aid in reducing the fluid build-up.

Thomas was holding up okay, but he was terrified that they might want to put in another peripherally inserted central catheter (PICC line)—an IV that goes directly into a major vein and is then used for drawing blood and administering medication. These lines are one thing that Thomas especially dislikes because the procedure inserting them is painful and unpleasant.

Day 3

Thomas was sore and in a lot of pain. The swelling was continuing, but the hospital staff finally started the Lasix procedure by IV. After twenty-three attempts and having to finally use an ultrasound machine, they got an IV into his arm. Thomas was scared and didn't want to watch the IV go in, so he had his eyes closed while I squeezed both of his hands.

They performed an echocardiogram finally, but the quality was poor. All the doctors said was that his heart is not functioning properly. The doctors followed the "echo" with a CAT scan, but nothing unusual showed. Afterward, the congestive heart failure team were called.

The nurses also weighed Thomas today. In five weeks he's gone from 108 lbs to 138 lbs with the excess fluid filling up his body.

While all of this was happening, Glenn arrived in Ottawa and booked a hotel room. (I have been staying at the hospital.) Both Thomas and I are happy he is with us; we need Glenn for his love and support. He always keeps a level head when situations get tough. Glenn also injects much-needed humour into everything that is happening. He is great at lifting Thomas's spirits and finding comedy in any situation. He's committed to arriving bright and early every morning bearing a fresh cup of coffee for me. I'll then fill Glenn in on the news of the previous night and sneak away for a shower and a nap.

And in particular, Glenn can assist Thomas with his washroom needs. This particular exercise is excessive: Thomas is on diuretics to reduce the fluid levels in his body, so he has many washroom breaks during the day.

The medical team decided to get a PICC line in. They told us it would be a twenty-minute procedure, but with Thomas, it took two-and-a-half hours with three attempts and again, the use of an ultrasound machine. I was allowed to remain in the room while this procedure was being done.

Thomas received two doses of Lasix, which helped with his fluid build-up. He voided 1,300 ml of liquid, the best output yet. He was in a fair amount of pain, so he was given morphine every six hours plus Tylenol and yet another painkiller every four hours.

The congestive heart failure team finally arrived. They are still thinking that the cause of the fluid build-up is Thomas's heart, but they have no definite answers yet. We managed to get Thomas out of the bed and into his wheelchair (thankfully, with Glenn's ability to lift him). With him sitting upright, we hope that more of the fluids in his body will drain out.

In spite of all that is happening to Thomas, it is a real treat to see him doubly happy that both of us are here to help him.

Day 4

Thomas slept well last night. However, because of so many announcements over the PA, I was easily wakened throughout the night.

The doctors started treating Thomas with steroids today with the hopes that the meds would help him improve in some way. Also, his fluid output was low again today, so the IV Lasix treatment was increased. He was also given Aldactone, heart medication in tablet form, which retains potassium to aid in heart function and is intended to help protect the heart. The scheduling of the medication is tricky, trying to ensure they don't overdose the potassium. The Aldactone comes in the form of *huge* horse pills that we need to cut in half to get them down. Thomas is balking at taking them, knowing they will put his potassium levels way too high.

Generally, Glenn is with Thomas during the day and I come back as soon as I can after getting some sleep. I spend time with both of them, then remain to spend the night with Thomas. Our niece and nephew, Jennie, and Chris, relieve us every now and then. They have also made some meals for us and are allowing us to use their laundry room to wash our clothes. Thomas is enjoying playing cards or games on the computer with them. Their visits allow him to get a break from seeing Glenn and me. Even some caregivers from the university came to give us a couple of hours to go and hold hands or share a meal in a restaurant. These small reprieves are beyond words because it is during those times when we can simply just *be* a couple.

Day 5

Another good night of sleep for Thomas. His fluid output, however, was not good: he is still retaining.

I was trying to help ease Thomas's pain during the night by lying behind him in the bed, rubbing his back. His shoulder blades were painful and at this point, he is accepting any pain meds the doctors will allow.

Day 6

Thomas was scheduled for a nuclear test of the heart today. This was something new for all of us and we weren't sure of the process.

Thomas was wheeled down through the corridors and tunnels to another building, the Ottawa Heart Institute. The technician doing the test was good at explaining to us exactly what would happen. They drew blood from him, mixed it with radiation, then injected it back into Thomas's bloodstream. Then, we had to wait thirty minutes for this concoction to work its way through Thomas's body. We were then taken into the testing room where Glenn and I helped Thomas get adjusted into the position they needed him to be in. A huge machine rotated up and down and around Thomas's chest. It was taking pictures … many pictures! Once all the pictures were processed, the pictures showed 3-D images of Thomas's heart, which will give the doctors a better idea of his heart's function.

Thomas managed to make it through the test. He was brave going through all of this process without knowing what it was about to begin with.

Day 11

Overall, we haven't seen a lot of change in Thomas's condition. Today marked day three of the steroids, and the doctors decided to change the steroid cocktail—750 mg of steroids three times each day—to a 50 mg steroid tablet for Thomas to take instead. The doctors stopped two of the long-term heart meds, the ramipril and the Aldactone, in hopes the steroids would work better without them. They kept him on a beta blocker in order to help improve his heart function.

Thomas continues to have sharp pains in his right shoulder blade, although we are not sure why. We rub it and apply ice, and Thomas takes all the pain meds he is allowed.

On this day, Glenn and I noticed that Thomas's breathing was more laboured. The doctors said there was no crackling in his lungs but they ordered another X-ray.

Thomas managed about four hours sitting in his wheelchair today. The chair is a small relief from constantly lying down, and we also hope that sitting upright will help the excess fluid exit his body.

The doctors discovered Thomas's kidneys are dehydrated and therefore they reduced his Lasix dosage. A chest X-ray showed more fluid around his lungs, but a tube to drain it wouldn't be inserted as the fluid is not centralized. It is scattered throughout Thomas's chest. And Thomas's fluid output is still less than his input.

Also, with the assortment of prescription drugs, Thomas has started to learn to be consistent with his pain meds. At first, he only wanted the pain meds for pain, but that resulted in him being sick to his stomach. He is learning that if he takes the pain meds on a consistent basis, not only will his stomach better handle them, but the pain is easier to manage. Meanwhile, the doctors are continuing with regular blood work to check his potassium levels. No other major tests were discussed today.

We keep asking about a timeline for recovery, but the doctors have no answers.

Day 12

The fluid output today was fantastic—2,800 ml! The more output of fluids, the better his kidneys function, so we are hoping this output means Thomas's kidneys are okay.

Thomas was weighed again, and the results showed some weight loss. Glenn is now able to pick him up and weigh him while holding him, and therefore the measurements seemed accurate.

Last night was a tough one, though. I didn't get much sleep. Thomas was in a lot of pain and just could not get comfortable. The BiPAP was bothering him, and he was not mentally at ease. He had to constantly pee. The doctors did another round of mega steroids and increased his Lasix again to 60 mg, but Thomas is still very much filled with fluid, so we were thrilled to see the increased fluid output during the day.

Dr. Rutkowski had advised me to push for yet another test, one to check Thomas's protein in his bowel. However, the doctors here had never heard of this test. The test has to be done on a stool sample and cannot be done if the patient is on steroids, so for the last few days, I was literally carrying around a stool sample. It was wrapped in tissue in my pocket because I was waiting for the doctors to decide to do the test. The sample has to be sent to the US to be tested. Unfortunately, now that the doctors have learned enough about the test and agreed to send the sample to the US, Thomas has already been on steroids for several days. The sample I had been carrying around was too old, and a new sample would be useless because of the steroids. I was so happy when Glenn arrived this morning to take over. Last night was simply mentally exhausting.

We had a surprise visit last evening with Thomas's best friend's grandparents. They live in Ottawa and heard of our situation through Gregg and his parents. They were very sweet, both in their late eighties. They wanted to help any way they could. Glenn and I were honoured they came to visit but we didn't want to leave Thomas at all. Thus, we turned down an offer to go for coffee or supper with them.

Day 13

Positive news today: Thomas's weight is down again. He has lost 9 lbs of fluid! The doctor announced that his kidneys are fine and his heart is working better to get the fluids moving. There are also indications that less fluid surrounds his heart.

They continued the steroids and are deciding whether to keep them going by IV or switch to the pill form. The doctors are still not giving any estimates as to when Thomas can leave the hospital.

Day 14

Thomas was sleeping well until about 3 a.m. last night. Then everything started going downhill. He woke up and began asking for help every twenty minutes. No sleep for me.

Today is Easter Sunday, and Glenn and I were where we needed to be—by Thomas's side. In spite of a rough night, Thomas was grinning from ear to ear this morning, moaning with glee, as he was treated to a breakfast of runny egg, hash browns, and hollandaise sauce made by his cousin Chris. It was so welcoming to see a familiar face. Chris and Thomas had a good visit, with Chris filling Thomas in on how his sons and wife (Jennie) were doing.

Since it is the Easter weekend, Glenn and I purchased goodies for the nursing staff. We made sure there was lots of chocolate for them. We bought fruit and veggie trays, too, and new whiteboard markers for their workstation. We feel very welcomed here. They allow us access to the room to get bandages, pee bottles, wipes, or whatever we need. I believe they know that they can't take care of all of Thomas's needs and they appreciate our support of him and the goodies we brought for them.

It is strange being in an unknown city, not really knowing our way around. We know the route from the hotel to the hospital and from the university to the hospital, but that's about it. We are surprised that Ottawa shut down for the Easter weekend. Nothing is open. The hospital cafeteria was closed today, and it was tough to even find a fast-food restaurant that was open. We did find a farmers' market grocery store with great ready-made food we could heat up. We went there a lot throughout the weekend. Thomas especially loved its roasted potatoes!

Day 15

Thomas had another rough sleep last night. I was totally exhausted by last evening, so Glenn insisted on spending the night so I could try to catch up on sleep at the hotel. I felt much better this morning.

During the day, Thomas's fluid output was good. We are on the right track, and Thomas was weighed again. He has developed a sore on his side, caused by the chest tube he had in Calgary months ago, and the doctors are hoping to do an ultrasound to check it out. They also decided to switch his prednisone meds to 50 mg. The only disappointing thing today was the construction happening two floors down! The hammering, vibrating, and drilling began early and continued all day.

Thomas on Facebook April 20, 2014:

After like two to three weeks at the hospital, I wanna know why my IV pumps have "helpful tip: books and instruction manuals" on them? How often are the people treating me needing reminders like "try not to let the patient bleed out," or "dripping stuff is super cool, but try not to poison anyone?"

Day 18

Thomas slept well despite the hospital renovations below our floor continuing. It was very loud and his room shook!

What was way more encouraging was that Thomas had a record output on this day: 3,045 ml! They switched his Lasix again to 120 mg twice a day, and he is still on IV for steroids. The lump on his side is becoming more pronounced and painful.

We managed to get Thomas in his chair for quite a while and did a tour of the hospital, all six floors.

Our niece Jennie came for a couple of hours to give Glenn and me a break to get out for supper.

Day 19

Glenn:

I thought that after Thomas being here in the hospital for nineteen days and you guys getting daily emails from Kathy, maybe it was time I did one.

Being here daily with Thomas and Kathy has been interesting, being part helper and part observer and trying to do what I can. Thomas is a remarkable young man and I'm proud to be part of his journey. I can think of nowhere I'd rather be.

When the doctors talk to us, I sometimes think Thomas understands more than Kathy and me because he asks questions using language that I'm not sure Kathy or I understand. He is still in a lot of pain and quite sore, and he takes morphine and any other painkiller they will give him, but I think his situation is getting better.

The nurse is here right now trying to draw some blood from a vein. She can't use the PICC line because they want clean blood. They want to check for viruses in the blood. His white count was high today, but the nurses think that is due to the side effects from the prednisone, and they just want to make sure there is no infection.

We go for tests almost every day. Today, Thomas had an ultrasound for a large bump on his rib cage, and five other people were waiting. The staff lined all the beds six inches apart in a little alcove while patients waited their turn. Thomas and I waited quite some time with me standing ten feet away when Thomas said, "Dad, I need to pee NOW!" Boy, did I have to scramble. I managed to find a urinal (urine bottle). I had to reach up from the end of the bed, pull down his pants, get the urinal in place and say, "Okay, Thomas, go." At that moment the technician came over and said, "Who's Thomas Sorensen? We're ready for you now." Wow, nothing like peeing under pressure with four other patients watching and a nurse waiting!

Thomas has more freedom with us being here because we can do a lot of what he needs at a moment's notice: scratch his head, nose, back fifty to a hundred fifty times a day; feed him five to eight times a day; lift him from his bed to the weigh scale every morning and from his bed to his wheelchair five or more times a day; help him find something to watch on TV; go with him to all these tests that need to be done; and use the washroom—wow—fifteen to twenty times a day because of the Lasix. It's all good.

He is down about 9 lbs in the last seven days. I think we're a third of the way there. The doctor hinted that maybe after another week we can start thinking about going home, but there are still many more tests to be done. The one that has me worried is his heart. Hopefully it hasn't deteriorated anymore and they can give him heart meds to stabilize it.

I so hope Thomas will get to realize his dream and go back to school and finish the next three years.

I believe humour is some of the best medicine, and I make sure we have a good laugh several times a day. When Thomas and I are alone, we go down to the cafeteria, buy ourselves a big ice cream, and find a spot where we can sit and enjoy it with no nurses or anybody to disturb us. When we are having ice cream, all is well in the world.

Kathy and I are really tired. This experience is more demanding than a full-time job, but I'm happy to be here. If it weren't for Jennie and Chris coming over almost every day giving us a little respite, we would still be here but would be much more haggard. Thank you, Jennie, and Chris!

Thomas is really happy we're here and is always thanking us and telling us he loves us. We love and will do anything for our kids and help them any way we can. But the one thing I've learned it doesn't matter how good a father you are, you will always be second to mom. A mom's touch is magical.

Thank you for your thoughts and prayers as we continue on our journey.

Day 20

Thomas had a good night's sleep. However, as he has always slept with the BiPAP mask on, he wanted a break from it and convinced me to take it off for just one night. We both got our wrists slapped by the medical team. The purpose of the BiPAP is to provide oxygen and remove carbon dioxide, and as luck would have it, this morning they did a check on his levels. Aahh, the one night we went without!

In spite of that, all of the blood tests for infection came back negative. The ultrasound test on the lump on his side showed a swollen, inflamed tissue, which should go away. The results of the chest X-ray were positive as well. No fluid in his lungs, no pneumonia! Thomas's weight is now down to 123 lbs. This is all good news.

The doctor feels that Thomas will stay on the IV for the next few days and granted him a weekend pass to get out for a bit. If all goes well, in a few days we can take Thomas for a couple of hours this weekend to get some fresh air and a change of scenery before returning to the hospital. Thomas is wishing for a trip to the mall. He is completely ready to have a change from the walls of the hospital.

Thomas on Facebook, April 23, 2014:

Day twenty of being in the hospital for puffiness ... Things are going "swell."

Day 21

Glenn nicely reprimanded me for not having enough humour in my daily emails! I have been just so exhausted that I was simply trying to pass on the daily reports to the family.

As it would happen, after a rough night's sleep, Thomas wanted a back, head, and face rub. As I was rubbing and scratching, I was apparently missing all the spots that were itchy and sore. Thomas said, "Come on, Mom! You are only giving me half the love! Quick, Mom, put your arm around me and pretend we are still sleeping!" Thomas always tries to find the humour in everything we do!

His output was great this day: 2,061 ml. His weight is down to 120 lbs. He has lost 20 lbs and has another 10 lbs of fluid to go. The IV prednisone treatment continues. The cardiologist popped in and was pleased Thomas's weight is down.

Thomas is becoming well-known in the ward. He's the youngest patient, and the nurses are all googling him to see his accomplishments. I have been asked more than once if I am a staff member as I am so familiar with the surroundings and help myself to supplies Thomas needs when the nurses are too busy to get them for us.

We also found out that Thomas's dormmate is moving out. There is a chance we can stay in the dorm room instead of the hotel. That would definitely help cut down on the expenses.

Day 22

Thomas had yet another rough sleep. He was in pain and uncomfortable, and his mask just didn't feel right. Glenn arrived early in the morning, and I went back to the hotel for some sleep. Luckily, Glenn and I were able to move to Thomas's dorm room, so after getting some rest, I packed up our stuff, checked out of the hotel, and moved.

We have no humorous stories on this day. We are just so very tired. The doctors came in and announced it would be another ten to fourteen days before Thomas could be released. This was certainly not the news we had hoped for.

There are two camps of thought concerning the fluid build-up: the cardiologists and the general doctors. No one can figure out why the fluid is present. It could be that congestive heart failure is causing leaky blood vessels. On the other hand, it could be something entirely different. Also, because Lasix and prednisone are being used together and had been started at the same time, the doctors don't know which is working. However, a decision was made to quickly wean Thomas off the prednisone, and the Lasix is going to be switched to tablet form from 125–20 mg for three days, then 10 mg for three more days.

Thomas was feeling that "things" were slowing down today, meaning he had more concentrated urine and less output. The reduction of the swelling varies throughout his body. His right arm swelling has gone down quite a bit, but his tummy, although better than it had been, is still very large. His legs and feet are skinny. One nurse even called them chicken legs (the humour for the day—I guess there was some after all). It is hard to say if this change in Thomas's swelling is a good thing or bad.

The doctors don't want to do another nuclear test of the heart for at least two more months as it is too dangerous to do right now. On the positive side, Thomas is still allowed a day pass to get out of the hospital. He wants to check out a new watch and try some new headphones.

Last night, I was caught a bit off guard. It was 3:30 a.m. and Thomas was in pain. I came out of his room and found a nurse who said, "Who are you? And where did you come from?" I told her I was Thomas's mom. She then asked, "How do you do it? Sleeping here every night and being here almost every day?" I simply said, "We love our son."

Day 23

Thomas slept really well. He is down another pound. That puts him at 24 lbs lost. His right arm is much better and his tummy seems smaller, too.

The nurses came for another blood culture. Two different nurses tried, and they managed to get some blood but weren't sure if it would be enough. They needed a big enough sample because they wanted two negative readings for bacteria in the blood. In a previous screening, there was one positive result that may have been due to the prednisone. The nurses didn't think Thomas had a bacterial infection, but they wanted to be sure.

Thomas's prednisone was reduced to 20 mg today. He will have this dosage for two more days, followed by three days of 10 mg. His Lasix was also reduced to 100 mg through pill form.

Thomas was so excited to get out for a few hours. We called a cab to get a ride to the mall. He wanted to look for new headphones. And he wanted mall food! He was craving a big, fat, juicy burger with bacon, some French fries with gravy and ketchup, an ice-cold root beer, and definitely a huge ice cream cone. We were worried about overdoing it on our excursion, but we knew it would be good for his spirits to get out even though it was raining and cool.

Glenn spent the night in Thomas's dorm room and was quite comfortable there. I went to the dorm room to freshen up before heading to the mall. We had a great couple of hours at the mall, eating at the food court and shopping for headphones. Vanessa, one of the caregivers from Carleton, went to the hospital after our outing to relieve Glenn and me for a couple of hours.

It was a happy day.

Day 24

Well, we had yet another very rough night. I was up every hour with Thomas. The staff agreed that we will look at new masks for the BiPAP machine today. We thought that the mask was stretched and with all the weight Thomas has now lost, it wasn't fitting properly.

On a bright note, we discovered a new way to wash Thomas's hair. The nurses have a prepackaged hair washing kit! We just have to pop it into a microwave, warm it up, rub it on Thomas's head, and dry his hair.

Thomas's weight was down again. He is now down to 115 lbs, which is pretty much his normal weight. Sadly, his white blood count is up and the doctors are not sure why. We also found out that an X-ray done on his lungs showed an "empty space." They think it could be pneumonia, so they want yet another X-ray done to compare, and they are considering putting Thomas on antibiotics. Thomas has no fever, cough, or "sickly" symptoms, so we are hoping all is good.

Day 25

Another rough night. I managed to find my way to the VitalAire medical supply store to look into a new mask for Thomas. Our thoughts were correct! With all the fluid Thomas had gained, his mask was totally stretched out of shape! We were able to purchase a few new nose pillows for Thomas to use. (A nose pillow is a breathing mask only placed over the nose rather than the whole face. Much less cumbersome than a larger face mask!)

Thomas's weight stayed the same today, too. We are hoping this means we are close to the end of draining all the additional fluid. Also, there was a consensus among all the assorted doctors that we will stay for another week to a week and a half. The cardiologist wants to increase Thomas's heart medication over time and regularly monitor him, starting with his first appointment at the end of next month [May.] On top of that, another nuclear test will be done in about two to three months. We have three days left to wean Thomas off the prednisone, and the doctors are waiting to see if Thomas will gain or lose more fluid after that.

When I went back to Thomas's dorm to shower, I discovered that his key for access to his room had been deactivated! It took me a while to find the correct office on campus, and they were more than happy to help me out. I was thankful that Glenn was not the one to discover the key not working because he always returns when all the campus offices are closed, so he would've been locked out for the night.

Day 26

Thomas's weight is down again today, to 114.8 lbs. The new BiPAP mask worked much better last night, and he had a great sleep! And another new doctor was in, yet again. I have to say that it is frustrating having so many rotation changes amongst the doctors because it is difficult to feel that all the procedures and protocols pertaining to Thomas's treatments are consistent. But Thomas does really like this new doctor, who discussed establishing a regular doctor for Thomas after his discharge. They also talked about Thomas being able to somewhat control his own dosage of Lasix.

After all these weeks in the hospital, we are more than ready to get out. Glenn and I were a little excited today because one of the caregivers from Carleton is coming tomorrow to relieve us for a few hours. We desperately need a change of scenery.

Day 27

It was cold and rainy today. Overall, Thomas seems to be sleeping better with the new mask, and through the night he had a great fluid output of 1,800 ml. His weight is now down to 112 lbs. Twenty-eight lbs lost overall!

A dietician came in today and talked to us about Thomas's sodium intake. He will be allowed 2,000 mg of salt per day and 1.5 l of fluid.

Thomas and I sat in the cafeteria and played some cribbage. This seemingly simple moment was such a wonderful change of pace for us—and Thomas won the game!

We had to return to the car rental office today to renew our rental as it has already been a month since we got it. It seemed silly to have to renew the rental knowing we'll leave Ottawa soon, and it was a bit of a pain having to drive back to the airport just for the renewal.

We also received a call from a WestJet airlines representative. The representative thought we were in Ottawa in order to bring Thomas home after exams, and when I explained what was going on with the unexpected extended hospital stay, she generously put $200 on our travel account.

Day 28

Thomas is feeling better. The doctors want to see if his body will balance his fluid input and output without his losing more weight. His kidneys are showing high readings again, though (which is a bad thing!), so the doctors want to wait a couple more days before discharging Thomas.

Day 29

Thomas's kidneys are simply not co-operating, and the doctors are worried they might shut down. They don't want to increase the Lasix dosage, but at the same time, the fluids might start building up again. Thomas's sodium levels were down today, too, and he weighed only 111 lbs.

Day 31

Last night, Thomas had another rough sleep.

We are still playing the waiting game—waiting to be discharged from the hospital. Waiting to see if Thomas will be fine. Just waiting …

The doctors are fiddling with the medications to control the potassium, sodium, and kidney function. There is another new doctor on board who was doing his interpretation of care today—trying to decide what to do—but he also had no idea. He stopped the Lasix, then reintroduced it.

There has been so much rain in Ottawa during the past three weeks that people are making jokes about the animals lining up in pairs to get onto an ark.

Day 32

We are happy the weekend is finally over because one of the previous doctors has returned. It was frustrating having the weekend doctors who thought they knew what to do without even looking at Thomas's history. The intern we had last week had written in detail what needed to happen to keep Thomas on track, but the weekend doctors didn't pay much attention to the instructions. Also, Thomas had probably the roughest night yet. His whole body was sore, and he just could not get comfortable. We were also told that another new team of doctors is to start treating Thomas tomorrow.

I managed only about three hours sleep in Thomas's dorm room last night, but it helped me immensely. Thomas's new dormmate at Carleton has also moved in.

Now that we are anticipating his release, Thomas has begun expressing that he wants us to go grocery shopping with him when he gets out. He is already planning new meals and naming foods that he wants to help lower his sodium intake. And he really wants a haircut.

Thomas has also been asked by Dr. Rutkowski in California to make a video to share his experience for the doctors who are studying and researching LMNA in France. Thomas feels honoured by her request.

Day 33

We are hopeful that Thomas will be discharged tomorrow. His assorted levels are all going the right way. A new doctor arrived and she agrees that if tomorrow's blood work is good, we will all be released by noon.

Thomas was giving us a hard time today about our daily emails to the family. He sees everything through different eyes than Glenn and I do. He is more scientific about all that has been happening to him and is sometimes annoyed that we aren't use words like *myotonic*[11] or *hypertrophy* (a thickening of the muscle fibres).[12] Granted, he definitely understands the terminology better than Glenn or I do, but we felt we were relaying the information accurately.

Day 34

Finally. Our last day at the hospital!

The nurses removed the PICC line and Thomas met with the pharmacist. He was armed with questions about his medication. After that, we happily brought Thomas back to his room at Carleton.

We had an interesting last evening, though. When Thomas's fifth roommate of this past month appeared, he quickly realized why his dad and I were with him. Glenn had gone outside for some fresh air when the new patient was brought into the room. The curtain was drawn, so Thomas and I couldn't see who was being rolled in. We were watching a TV show, sharing an ear bud each. This male patient starting shouting, swearing, and yelling out threatening remarks! We weren't sure what to do. There was just a flimsy curtain between us and the new patient. The man scared the

---

11 "Myotonic dystrophy is characterized by progressive muscle wasting and weakness. People with this disorder often have prolonged muscle contractions (myotonia) and are not able to relax certain muscles after use. For example, a person may have difficulty releasing their grip on a doorknob or handle. Also, affected people may have slurred speech or temporary locking of their jaw." Courtesy of MedlinePlus from the National Library of Medicine: MedlinePlus, "Mystonic dystrophy," last updated August 18, 2020, medlineplus.gov/genetics/condition/myotonic-dystrophy/.

12 Merriam-Webster.com Dictionary, s.v. "hypertrophy," accessed November 27, 2021, www.merriam-webster.com/dictionary/hypertrophy.

living daylights out of both of us. He was a delirious seventy-nine-year-old whose language was certainly an eye-opener for Thomas. Thomas had never witnessed anything like this before.

As soon as the nurse left the room, the man started yelling out obscenities. He said he was going to kill everyone and destroy everything. Every other word out of his mouth was vulgar. Thomas and I were frozen in place.

Finally, one of the nurses heard the shouts and came in to ask the patient if there was a problem. She looked at me with questioning eyes, wondering what was wrong. Thomas and I used that as an opportunity to escape from the room.

Apparently, this patient had been transferred from the psychiatric ward. When Glenn returned and we told him what happened, he announced that he would sleep with Thomas in the room that night, much to our relief. And they actually moved the other patient into the hallway for the whole night …

A Reprieve

Thomas had a total of five roommates during his stay in the hospital. The first was an East Indian gentleman in his seventies who only had one visitor, a lady who was his neighbour. Sadly, he was left alone most of the time. The nurses rarely came in to check on him. He simply lay in bed or sat in a chair. And he never spoke. He passed away one night while sleeping. When the neighbour returned the day after he passed and asked questions about his last days, the nurses actually lied about the level of care he had received. Thomas and I heard and saw all of this. It was a real eye-opener for both of us. This was a major reason why Glenn and I, and even Thomas, realized we needed to be there for our son. We understood the nurses were overworked, but as parents, we knew that the care he required would not have been met unless we were there.

The second roommate was an elderly woman who was only there for three days. We didn't know why she was in the hospital. She never said much and had only one visitor—her son. We found it strange that a woman would be rooming with Thomas.

The third roommate was an eighty-four-year-old Italian gentleman named Michael. His English was not very good and his wife was a sweetheart. She was always getting into trouble with the nurses for bringing in her homemade meals—food that Michael was not supposed to have. He was eventually transferred to another ward. When he was discharged, his wife came to say goodbye to us. We exchanged phone numbers and I gave her a picture of Thomas. She had tears in her eyes when she left. She did call us, months later, after Thomas had passed, and I had to tell her our sad news. All I could hear on the other end of the phone was her crying.

The fourth roommate was Wilf. He was a young-looking eighty-year-old who, up to that point, had been healthy and active. His wife, Diane, and I shared many conversations during their stay. Wilf had a brain tumour and sadly, he passed a couple of weeks after being discharged. Diane and I met after his passing, and we kept in contact through email for a couple of years.

Thomas's final roommate, the fifth, was there for only one very memorable night. Thomas was happy having his dad as his "guard dog" for the night.

Thomas's least favourite staff member was a female orderly who never listened to him. She was rough and grumpy. One morning, she came in to change the sheets as Thomas was just waking up. She wanted to roll Thomas onto his other side. Thomas asked her politely to wait a few minutes if she could, as he was not feeling great. She ignored his request and began to move him. Through no fault of his own, Thomas threw up all over her.

There were many other orderlies, interns, and doctors, as well. We discovered that even with the best, most well-organized staff members, there was no way they all were able to completely care for him. They were grateful Glenn and I were there. Glenn and I learned what the many codes over the PA system meant: heart problems, security, violence, lost patients, fire. We saw some patients had security posted outside their doors for various reasons. In all, it was overwhelming to think that an eighteen-year-old would have had to cope with all of this on his own if we weren't there. We knew we had to be there for him.

Thomas went through so many invasive procedures, ones that no eighteen-year-old should ever go through, let alone one who had experienced so much already. He wanted us by his side for comfort, knowing in his heart how much we cared. In spite of all the stress of these weeks, there were many nights when Thomas and I would lie awake whispering, so as not to wake the patient on the other side of the curtain. He told me how appreciative he was that both Glenn and I were there. He knew that the regular nursing staff was not able to attend to his needs. Thomas and I would talk about his dreams, his power hockey, and what he was going to do after he was discharged. Those were such special times.

Thomas's being in a hospital for such a long time showed us that hospitals are a different world unto themselves. The daily goings-on weren't only about our son, but also others who passed through the institution and Thomas's two-bed semi-private room. Doctors came and went. Sadly, they were on four-day rotations, and there was a different doctor on weekends. The schedule was out of our control. The problem was that each new doctor would do what they thought was best, even if it had been tried before and failed. Glenn and I had to constantly advocate for Thomas's care. The doctors didn't listen to Thomas, as he was just another patient and was only eighteen. Most had never experienced his condition before and were following "textbook" information and procedures. Many times, a new doctor would come in and prescribe the same medication that another had already prescribed but then discontinued. We knew certain approaches were not working and had to be very vocal when it came to not going along with their opinions. Furthermore, everyone was puzzled as to why Thomas was full of fluid again. I was constantly and desperately trying to get any of the doctors to get in touch with the Calgary muscular dystrophy specialist as well as the specialist in California.

As a parent, my gut was telling me that the local doctors were not listening. I was feeling that Dr. Rutkowski in California had the newest information regarding treatment with muscular dystrophy patients. She had had several conversations with Thomas and had him during some of his worst days at the Alberta Children's Hospital. She was also connected with the research that was happening in Barcelona. Dr. Rutkowski, in my opinion, had revelational ideas that might save our son.

I have to admit, too, that after my experience with the Calgary ICU doctor, "slapping my wrists," I was hesitant to pursue my thoughts with the doctors. We were, after all, in the national capital city's hospital, where one would hope the "best of the best" in doctors were available. It was so emotional and conflicting at the same time.

🐢 🐢 🐢 🐢 🐢

Once we got back to the dorm room after his discharge, Thomas was exhausted. Glenn and I were also dog-tired. Neither of us had had a decent night's sleep in weeks. We were sleeping in strange beds and were unfamiliar with the surroundings. In fact, we'd lived most of our twenty-four-hour chunks of time in the hospital and after doing so for weeks, were physically and emotionally drained from the sleep disruptions and the day-to-day worries about Thomas's health. We were hoping we could all have a nap the afternoon we took him back to the dorm. Glenn and I had to book another hotel room, and it was great to have a hot shower and a little sleep.

Thomas had prepared a grocery list of items with low sodium. The school cafeteria was closed, so he had to prepare his own meals, with help of course, from me and the Carleton care program staff. Glenn and I took him on the shopping trip he had been looking forward to and helped him with getting some home-cooked meals in his freezer.

Glenn, Thomas, and I then met with Thomas's new family doctor, whom we felt comfortable with. She was friendly and set Glenn and me at ease, assuring us she would keep an eye on Thomas. Thomas was able to speak freely with her, and she listened to him. Glenn and I also picked up his new medication, made sure Thomas had everything he needed, and then returned to Calgary.

We had been in Ottawa for five weeks. It was tough to leave Thomas behind but that was his wish. He wanted to write his exams and continue with his dream. Once again, Glenn and I were forced to leave Thomas miles behind, hoping all was well.

The doctors never really discovered what caused his fluids to build up. They did know that his heart was not functioning as it should but could not say that was the cause. I made a point of getting CDs made with all of Thomas's test results in case we needed them in the future. Through Dr. Rutkowski, we had learned about research into MD taking place at the Barcelona Children's Hospital, and so I sent the disks containing Thomas's test results to the children's hospital in Barcelona, Spain, when they requested them, in hopes that researchers might find them valuable in helping other patients with muscular dystrophy.

The Neuromuscular Diseases (NMD) Unit at SJD Barcelona Children's Hospital is made up of a multidisciplinary team with **experience in diagnosing, treating, and researching** the different pathologies within the sphere of NMDs. Our unit, linked to the Neurology Department, has CSUR accreditation (Reference Centres, Services and Units) in Spain and forms part of the **EURO-NMD** European Reference Network.

We are **pioneers in the treatment of patients with Duchenne muscular dystrophy** and spinal muscular atrophy, among other diseases. We collaborate with organizations and centres all over the world and we have developed an ambitious research programme focused on patient and family care.[13]

I could not have made it through the rough five weeks in Ottawa without Glenn. We were living in an unfamiliar city managing the best way we knew how to. Glenn was stressed, too, of course, with Thomas's situation but also from being away from his work. He had left his partner high and dry for several weeks and was feeling guilty. But we had each other to lean on during one of the most challenging periods of our young son's life.

Thomas found and read an article in May 2014 titled, "First Human SMA Gene Transfer Therapy Trial Opens," which reaffirmed his reasons for attending university. He wrote a response to it:

Thomas on Facebook, May 8, 2014:

This is exactly what I am at school for! If it works, it should be able to cure cancer and every other type of genetic defect. Viruses work like tiny needles

---

13 Sant Joan de Déu Barcelona Hospital, "Neuromuscular Diseases," accessed November 27, 2021, sjdhospitalbarcelona.org/en/children/neuromuscular-diseases.

injecting their own DNA into cells. By changing the DNA from virus to human, the viruses can then go in and inject a one-time cure for any genetic disease. Since there are no transplants or surgeries, recovery time would be nonexistent. Muscle cells can also compensate for cell death meaning fifty cells can be as strong as 250. People with muscular dystrophy and associated disorders could rehabilitate.

In May 2019 the FDA published an update on this gene therapy: "FDA Approves Innovative Gene Therapy to Treat Pediatric Patients with Spinal Muscular Atrophy, a Rare Disease and Leading Genetic Cause of Infant Mortality."[14]

Shortly after his release from the hospital, Thomas prepared for his four final exams, which had been deferred due to his illness. He managed to write three but could not complete the fourth; he was back in emergency. After a three-day episode of severe swelling, the doctors adjusted his meds to drain more fluid. Fortunately, they had great success.

Determined, Thomas returned to campus to attend summer classes for calculus. He was seeing the cardiologist and also trying to establish relationships with the new adult doctors, but the wait times to get appointments were long. The cardiologist was allowing Thomas to self-direct changes to his Lasix intake as he saw fit. This, however, caused a problem with the manager of the Attendant Services Program at Carleton. He didn't trust Thomas's judgement. In all fairness, if the prescription said A and Thomas said B, how were the caregivers to know what was right? I guess there were likely liability issues in play, and it was confusing for the caregivers. But it was also frustrating for Thomas because he knew what he needed. To get everyone on the same page there were several phone calls

---

14 FDA U.S. Food & Drug Administration, "FDA Approves Innovative Gene Therapy to Treat Pediatric Patients with Spinal Muscular Dystrophy, a Rare Disease and Leading Genetic Cause of Infant Mortality," May 24, 2019, fda.gov/news-events/press-announcements/fda-approves-innovative-gene-therapy-treat-pediatric-patients-spinal-muscular-atrophy-rare-disease.

back and forth between us, Thomas, the director of the care program, and the doctor.

Thomas was planning to finish his exams, then come home to Calgary for two weeks in July. As much as he wanted to play full-time in hockey that year, his health would not allow it, but he did attend the games and help out with the team's needs. He had attended the awards banquet in Ottawa for the Ottawa Power Hockey League in May and after that, focused on his studies before coming home in the summer.

Thomas on Facebook, July 11, 2014:

Arrived! Made it to Alberta in mostly one piece! Woop!

Last Chance to Be a Kid

Thomas wanted to plan every moment of his trip home. Glenn was hesitant; he felt Thomas needed rest. I, on the other hand, wanted Thomas to enjoy some downtime after all he had been through, and we were both looking forward to him coming home. We arranged for Vanessa, an amazing care attendant from Carleton, to travel with him back to Calgary. Thomas was so excited. He wanted to see his friends, eat my asparagus soup, go to a Billy Talent concert, and have a road trip with his friend Gregg to Thomas's grandparents' cabin three hours away.

Thomas's first full day back in Calgary started with a Stampede Breakfast[15] that Kent Hehr, the MP who had first told Thomas about Carleton, was hosting. For the rest of the day, we tried to take it easy after his long trip the previous day. We spent the afternoon swimming in the lake, relaxing, and enjoying his favourite foods.

The next day featured a Billy Talent concert at the Stampede grounds. Thomas was over-the-top excited for all of it. Vanessa and I toured Thomas around the Stampede grounds, taking in all of his midway must-dos: the corn dogs; the natural root beer drinks; and Thomas's favourite game, Whack-A-Mole, which I had to play for him. Thomas talked me

---

15 The Calgary Stampede is a world-renowned celebration held every July. It encompasses the true meaning cowboy culture, including chuckwagon races, rodeo events, a live grandstand show, and midway games and rides. Stampede breakfasts are hugely celebrated every day around the city for all ten days of the celebration. Various organizations, including the Calgary Stampede themselves, politicians, and private corporations host free pancake breakfast at various venues throughout the city, many of which are open to the public. Those hosted by corporations are usually by invitation only.

into buying him an oil-free fryer at the exhibits. I knew he was concerned with his sodium and fat intake, and he thought the fryer might help with his meal preparation when he returned to Carleton. I didn't particularly enjoy Billy Talent's music, but I saw the excitement in Thomas's eyes, and that was enough for me. We even got special seating on a raised platform, as Thomas was in his wheelchair. It was a long, hot, tiring day, but one I won't forget.

What Thomas did not count on were the appointments in Calgary with the new team of doctors in the adult world of medical care. He thought they were a waste of time. He was not impressed that I took him to two different hospitals to meet with the different doctors, although all the meetings were pretty low key. We shared information with the doctors, but they didn't seem to care much about Thomas's previous hospitalizations or any concerns we had, and they told us nothing new. I found it interesting when I asked them to look at the sore on Thomas's side from the chest tube from almost a year prior. The doctor consulted with his "wound" team. Two female nurses came, looked, and simply said, "Keep it clean and put a Band-Aid on it regularly."

Glenn and I decided to end Thomas's trip home with a dinner at the revolving restaurant at the top of the Calgary Tower. We also wanted to treat Vanessa as a thank you for all she had done to make the trip possible. It was a great evening, with delicious food from appetizers to dessert. We were able to take in a 360-degree view of Calgary because of the restaurant moving slowly to end up where we began. (One full rotation of the tower takes exactly an hour.) Glenn taught us all so much about the city and its history as we viewed the different buildings and landmarks crawling by during the meal.

Thomas and Vanessa returned to Ottawa after the two weeks in Calgary. We were relieved that Thomas looked healthy and the fluid was not returning. He was slim, his colour was great, and he had no complaints. He was sleeping well and felt well-rested.

I had wanted Thomas to do all that was on his summer wish list, and he did it all! Looking back, I am so glad he did. Not only did he check everything off his list, but he was somewhat of a celebrity. He was interviewed by one of the local TV stations about his first year at Carleton. And he got to see his favourite place: Easter Seals Camp Horizon. Thomas also took the time to meet up with one of his best buddies, Brodie, who was also in a wheelchair. Brodie's method of communication was to use a keyboard to type what he wanted to say, and the technology vocalized his thoughts. Thomas and Brodie had played both soccer and hockey together when Thomas was in high school. Brodie was so pleased that Thomas took the time to visit him on his short break at home.

Vanessa:

Thomas and I took a trip to visit his parents in Alberta. We spent ten days hanging out, attending the Calgary Stampede, taking shopping trips, and eating so much delicious food.

We also did our first cottage trip without his parents, which Thomas was excited about. We went up to Invermere, BC, with two of his friends, Gregg, and Evan. We started by touring the little town and then ate more food. At the cottage that first evening, we played some board games and watched movies. The four of us had so much fun together. We all took turns picking on Thomas, and boy, did he dish it back.

Being young, we of course stopped at a liquor store. This was the first time Thomas was going to get to drink! Go wild! But in the end, I ended up buying him orange-flavoured coolers that tasted like juice.

The second day we were there, I was making breakfast and he asked me if he could have one of the coolers. He was finally of age, so who was I tell him he couldn't have one? He ended up drinking his first and last cooler for breakfast. It was nice to see him try things for the first time, especially like a tasty drink for breakfast.

The whole time we were at the cottage I couldn't get over how close he and his friends were and how relaxed and happy he was. He had been having a rough go in Ontario with us, in and out of doctors' appointments. This trip was the first time I saw him carefree and enjoying being a teenager. I know he appreciated the freedom I gave him and the opportunity to be a teenager with his friends, but I don't think he realized how much fun I was having, too, and how happy it made me to see him so relaxed and enjoying life. Something so simple like going to a cottage for a weekend with friends meant so much to him, and he kept thanking me over and over again. I'd do it all again if I could. There was never a time over the weekend when his disability played a factor. I cherished every joke, every minute, and every bug bite that weekend, and I know Thomas did, too, which was the best part.

Gregg:

It had always been our dream to go on a big road trip together. We had talked about travelling across Canada. When Thomas was eighteen, we had the opportunity to go on a summer excursion to Invermere, BC. This was a big deal for us, as we had never been on a trip like this before. Along with the two of us came a mutual friend from high school, Evan Steinke, and one of Thomas's closest friends from Carleton University in Ottawa, Vanessa Collins.

The drive to Invermere was like any drive with Thomas, complete with bickering about the music choices as Evan, Thomas, and I all enjoyed different styles of music. To avoid being a part of the "fun," Vanessa slept in the back. The plan for the weekend included playing board games, going to the weekend market, and enjoying being away from the city (and the parents). I think Thomas enjoyed playing board games even more than his video games. He absolutely relished playing Monopoly while everyone else hated it! So, we played Monopoly and Risk for hours.

We had decided that this was a good chance for Thomas to try alcohol for the first time. While Vanessa, Evan, and I brought beer to drink, Thomas had brought some beverages that were a little tastier, some coolers. This was especially funny because halfway through his first cooler, he thought he was drunk. The three of us went along, making fun of him.

One of the afternoons, we left the board games behind to go check out the local weekend market. We spent the entire afternoon exploring the shops and stands throughout the small downtown. Vanessa and I even had the chance to embarrass both Thomas and Evan by having a sword fight with balloon swords that we got from one of the stands. Thomas and Evan were less than pleased to be seen in public with the two "adults" who were fighting with balloon swords.

This trip is very special to me, as it was the last big adventure Thomas and I had together.

As much as Jamie wanted to be available during Thomas's visit, it was the summer of 2014 when he was feeling the itch to move out. Yes, he loved Thomas, but he was young and in love. He had his own mission and goals, and he wanted independence. He had a full-time job, had already paid off his car, and had amassed a great down payment for a house. Jamie made time for Thomas, but he did not realize Thomas's time was nearing the end.

Glenn and I always pushed our boys to aim high, and we encouraged him that it might be the right time to purchase a house. And so Jamie started the house hunt. In mid-July, he announced he had found a house he was excited about. He made an offer, had a house inspection, was approved, and bought the house. Shortly after he had the home inspection and all was in place, though, we discovered that the mortgage agent had made a serious mistake; she had qualified Jamie based on double his income. Jamie was shocked and scared. Glenn and I stepped up to the plate to support him. We knew that he was capable of home ownership on his own and knew that he could manage the monthly payments. In order for the purchase to go through, Glenn and I needed to co-sign for the mortgage. We did that with no qualms. To this date, Jamie has indeed managed on his own without a penny from us. His house is now almost paid for.

By the time Thomas's time at home was nearing an end, Jamie had bought the house but didn't yet have possession and so he wasn't allowed inside the house. Thomas wanted so badly to see Jamie's new house, but the best they could do was a drive-by. So they drove past the house and talked about how exciting it would be for Jamie to have his own place. Thomas was looking forward to visiting his brother in his own digs on future trips home. Jamie was proud, and Thomas was excited for Jamie.

Thomas flew back to Ontario and four days later, July 31, Jamie got possession of the house. I went over to help him clean and get ready to move in.

The house needed a lot of work. Glenn had talked Jamie into waiting to move in so we could fix the holes in the walls, clean, paint, replace missing baseboards, update light fixtures and such. Glenn bought a commercial paint sprayer and freshened up the entire interior of the house with a new wall colour. Glenn called in a few favours from his good friend Steve who installed new baseboards and window trims, and he attached new doors on all three floors at no cost; he refused to accept any payment. Jamie was one lucky new homeowner. Steve simply said that one day when he needed a favour, Jamie could help him out.

Steve has been Glenn's best friend for decades. They were a year apart in high school, but a lot of common interests brought them together at that age—fishing, playing games on Friday nights. It's the kind of friendship where two people who haven't seen each other for months can pick up where they left off. He has been generous with offering his time and carpentry skills over the years, doing favours for our family such as helping Jamie put those finishing touches on his new house.

I had gone to Jamie's house to help clean when Thomas called to say that he was back in the emergency room in Ottawa awaiting results of some tests. He wasn't feeling well, and the fluid build-up in his chest and body had reoccurred. Over the course of three or four phone calls between me, Thomas, and different nurses, I tried to get the full story of what was going on. Everyone at the hospital I talked to said that Thomas would be released right away and sent back to the university. He was lying on a gurney, waiting for blood work. Vanessa had brought him in and they had been there for hours. It was an extremely trying time, trying not to think the worst. Was Thomas getting the care he required? Was the fluid build-up greater than it had been? How bad was it? Would I be flying back to Ottawa to be by his side?

Miles away, I was feeling desperate. I was torn between being with Thomas and assisting Jamie. Maybe I wanted the distraction of helping spruce up Jamie's new home to somehow stop Thomas from being in the hospital. I spent eight hours working on the kitchen, cleaning it to my standards while trying to avoid "the call" saying that I needed to fly to Ottawa—the call that would mean that Thomas needed me, that he was not doing so well after all.

For three days, I waited to hear what was going to happen. Glenn and I were on pins and needles from one message: he would be sent home soon. But we didn't know what "soon" meant. Being so far away was excruciating. Vanessa had to work her regular hours with other students, and her boss told her not to go back to the hospital after her shift. As a result, it was getting more difficult to get any news at all. Finally, I got through to the nurses' station after four days of waiting, and the nurse I talked to told me that Thomas had been transferred to the Ottawa Heart Institute. That was the final blow. I was in a panic. The hospital hadn't even called to inform us of his transfer. I guess because Thomas was now of age, they felt they didn't need to keep us in the loop.

I looked into flight schedules. There was a flight to Ottawa leaving at four o'clock that afternoon, so I wouldn't land in Ottawa until after midnight, which wasn't ideal, but I booked it. I was an emotional wreck thinking of Thomas being on his own, not knowing where he stood health-wise. It felt like such a long flight, and my emotions were running high. The plane could not fly fast enough for me.

Bringing Our Boy Home for Good

Upon arrival, I rented a car and headed straight to the hospital. By the time I arrived, it was 1:45 a.m. I had to find an entrance and was literally running around the building looking for a way in. A security guard asked who I was and why I was there so early in the morning. He let me through the doors, and I found my way to the ward and asked where Thomas was. The nurse on duty was kind. She said, "You must be Thomas's mom. He has been waiting for you."

Not surprisingly, Thomas was waiting up for me. He told me over and over how much he loved me and thanked me for coming. He had sweet-talked the nurse into setting up a bed for me on the floor beside him.

Thomas was even more swollen than he had been in April. I was in shock to see how quickly the fluid had built up since we had seen him the previous week. We hugged, smiled, cuddled, and tried to sleep. Thomas was up every twenty to thirty minutes all night long asking for adjustments to get comfortable. He was in a lot of pain. He was already receiving two doses of 80 mg of Lasix by IV.

I was finally able to get Thomas comfortable in his bed and lie down on my makeshift bed on the floor. We talked for a while, and somehow the conversation turned around to bedtime prayers. Thomas shared with me that he said a prayer every night before he went to sleep. He was confirmed as a Lutheran and certainly raised as a Christian, but for some reason, Thomas couldn't remember the childhood prayer I had learned as a child and then taught him. Thomas had to know what it was:

Now I lay me down to sleep,
I pray the Lord my soul to keep.
If I should die before I wake,
I pray the Lord my soul to take.

Thomas wouldn't leave it alone. He wanted to memorize every word. We lay there for a long time repeating the short prayer, and every now and then, Thomas would say, "Mom, I love you so much." The memory of that night still brings tears to my eyes.

The weekend was upon us and a different doctor was on duty than the one Thomas had had the previous few days. This one wanted to give Thomas the massive pills to help his potassium. We had been through this so many times with other doctors. Thankfully, the previous doctor had written in her report to trust both Thomas and me on our thoughts for medication. Both Thomas and I explained that the potassium pills would put him over the edge with overly high potassium readings and we would be back to square one. This doctor listened and did not prescribe the pills. Thomas's potassium levels remained fine.

I was completely in my role helping Thomas, up several times every night helping myself to the supplies. The nurses were appreciative since there was no way they could attend to all of his needs. Literally, he needed to use the washroom up to twenty-three times a day. The Lasix was working again, and within three days he had dropped 11 lbs.

I was still concerned about the worsening sore on his side. I asked the nurse if we could have a consult with the wound care team. The wound care specialist was also concerned but showed me how to care for the wound. It was quite a process. I wore gloves and had to sterilize the wound by pouring saline on it. Then, I used a special bandage and gauze to cover the wound without touching it. Thomas was happy that I knew not only how to do it but that I was doing it. It was a painful process for him, though. I have to admit that we cleaned out the supply of the special bandages in the storage room. Luckily, the nurses were okay with that. We couldn't purchase this type of bandage in Canada, so after Thomas was discharged, we had Glenn's sister special-order the bandages from the US. Thomas kept asking me to take pictures of the wound with my cell phone so that he could see what was happening and how it might be improving.

We were in the hospital for a full week. The swelling went down, and he was back to normal again. He was tired but wanted out. I asked the doctors what their thoughts were about the cause of the fluid build-up. Again, they had no real explanation. They were happy the swelling had gone down and felt his heart's functions were under control. I asked if Thomas could remain at Carleton for his studies, and they felt confident that he could continue.

Meanwhile, both Thomas and I had missed Glenn's birthday. Glenn and I had planned a trip away, which we had to cancel. He had booked the time off work, and so he decided to come to Ottawa with his mom and dad to visit with Thomas instead.

Thomas was thrilled that his family was coming. There were so many sights in Ottawa that he had not yet explored, and he wanted to share them all with us. He talked and talked to me about all the museums and attractions he wanted to see. When Thomas was discharged, we made a trip to the grocery store before spending a couple of days together back in his dorm room.

As was the case with his previous release from the hospital, Thomas wanted to find low-sodium food and asked me to prepare some healthy meals to freeze for future use. We must have spent over two hours shopping. He wanted to read every label of all the products to see which the best was to purchase. He was focused on eating healthy foods that contained little or no sodium. He would ask me the amounts of ingredients, quickly do the calculations in his head, then tell me yes, it was good, or no, try another brand. Again, this was a moment where Thomas was just Thomas, not some young man with an illness. Looking back, it was an amazing few hours watching our son, who was so determined to do the right thing as if nothing was wrong in his world.

Glenn, Hans, and Alice arrived two days later to visit with Thomas and see the sights of Ottawa. I went to the airport to exchange the rental vehicle for a handicapped van and pick up the family. I brought everyone back to the dorm room where Thomas was tired but wanted to visit. We stayed for a while in his room and then agreed to let him get a good night's sleep and see him the next day for our adventure in Ottawa. The Carleton attendants were on call to care for Thomas that night.

When we arrived at the dorm the next morning, Thomas was still in bed. He'd had a terrible night's sleep. One of the caregivers was there, attempting to get Thomas up and showered. Getting him dressed took much longer than usual. I showed the caregiver how to change the bandage on his wound. During all of this, Alice and Hans waited patiently.

We finally got Thomas ready and headed out to his first wish: breakfast at a well-known egg restaurant called Eggspectation, but Thomas didn't have much of an appetite. We finished up and headed off to get the same promissory blood work. Sadly, Thomas's favourite nurse was on vacation and the other staff had no luck getting a vein to draw blood. By the end of all of this, Thomas was spent. They told us to go to the emergency room the next day.

Glenn appeared to be a little frustrated and Thomas was concerned. I don't think Glenn was upset with Thomas; he just wanted answers about Thomas's health. To add to the matter, Thomas didn't want to let on just how rough he was feeling, and he, too, was feeling bad that Grandma and Grandpa were in town with us but he wasn't up to sightseeing. He wanted to rest so he could get better, but he also wanted us there to hang out with him. I felt a bit caught in the middle as I was desperately trying to keep everyone happy.

The next morning, after breakfast at the hotel, the four of us went back to Thomas's dorm room. We brought heating pads to wrap his hands and warm them up in hopes of getting the vessels ready for the blood work, a trick that we had learned in the past that worked. We went to the emergency room and watched several nurses attempt to draw his blood. No one had any luck.

Meanwhile, it was pouring outside and Hans and Alice were sitting in the van watching the rain hit the windows. Glenn and I took turns going out to update them with any information we had. It was on one of my trips to the van when both Alice and Hans admitted that they now understood the amount of time we took in our lives to care for Thomas. I was elated that they openly acknowledged our success and dedication as parents, especially in regards to Glenn and how he was raising our boys. In my mind, that acknowledgement was a long time coming.

The ER doctor was not happy with Thomas's health. There were no hospital beds available, so he moved us into the critical care area of the emergency room. The best nurses arrived for blood work; however, Thomas was dehydrated, and drawing his blood was not happening. Thomas was frustrated. We spent several hours waiting to see what was going to happen and eventually, Alice and Hans came out of the van and were allowed to come into the critical care ward. Glenn pushed me to go back to the hotel with Alice and Hans and come back the next morning. It was Glenn's turn to stay and sleep in a chair by Thomas's side.

Alice, Hans, and I returned to the hospital the next morning, and Thomas was still in the emergency department. Finally, the doctors made the decision to move Thomas back to the Ottawa Heart Institute. Alice and Hans booked a flight back to Calgary, not having seen much of Ottawa except for the dorm room and the hospital. They understood that we needed to be with Thomas, and it was time for them to go home.

Glenn decided to stay in Ottawa with me. Once again, we went into our shift mode: I spent the nights at the hospital, and Glenn relieved me in the mornings. We wanted answers, but again, the doctors changed on their shift rotations, and the same routine was falling into place. Each doctor had his or her own ideas, yet they were the same ideas everyone else had. Thomas was filling up yet again with fluid. The same kinds of treatments were given Lasix and more potassium pills. We kept trying to dissuade them from trying the same procedures that hadn't worked in the past, but our advice fell on deaf ears. Glenn and I were exhausted. Thomas was too sick to give an opinion.

After two more weeks, the doctors decided they were going to discharge Thomas since he had improved. (Looking back, though, I now feel that they had given up since they still didn't give a reason for the reoccurrence.)

Glenn and I sat with Thomas in his hospital room and discussed his immediate future. We thought it best for him to return home to Calgary with us. Glenn and I felt that his health was not strong enough to remain on his own, and Carleton couldn't help him if he required too much attention. We suggested that if he was better in a couple of weeks, he could return back to school. If not, he could do some courses online and return for the winter term in January. Carleton said they would hold his room for him.

Thomas agreed.

Glenn:

When we were being discharged, Thomas and I were in his hospital room and Kathy was at Carelton in Thomas's room waiting for the call to come and pick us up. A nurse came in to talk to us. As she gave us care instructions, I could see that this older, well-seasoned nurse was antsy and was stalling to let us go. I looked at Thomas and could tell he was packed and raring to get out of there. When I looked back at the nurse, I realized she had something she really wanted to say, and I knew it was not good. In hindsight, I think she knew.

I've thought about this moment so many times over the years and I think now that she didn't have the courage to tell me that Thomas was basically at the end of his life. I may have realized that at the time, but she must have known I wasn't ready to hear the truth. So after a long ten minutes of this nurse and I just looking at each other, she finally signed the forms and her shoulders slumped. She gave up her internal struggle on what to do. She wished Thomas and me luck and told us we were free to go.

Thomas and I went outside and waited for Kathy to come and pick us up.

We stayed in Ottawa for two more nights as per the hospital's request. The three of us returned to Thomas's dorm room, where Glenn and I stayed with him.

Those two nights were rough. Thomas had trouble sleeping and was up several times. I was on an air mattress on the floor beside Thomas's bed. Glenn was sleeping on a bare mattress in the next room.

The day of our departure, we got up early to catch our flight. None of us had slept well. We were anxious to get home. The five-hour flight was gruelling. Glenn and I struggled to find a comfortable position for Thomas, but no position sufficed for very long. Even the flight crew tried to help but to no avail.

Once again, the flight seemed to take forever, and we were all relieved to touch down in Calgary. Thomas was so tired he couldn't even operate his power chair and asked Glenn to please put his chair into push mode. Hans, Alice, and Jamie came to the airport to meet us. Alice had brought one of Thomas's favourite foods to take home with us. She had made fresh *aebleskiver*, a delicious round pastry that you dip in white sugar and strawberry jam. Thomas smiled appreciatively, but he just wanted to get home to sleep.

We all desperately needed sleep. I managed to find our previous caregiver, Mark, whom Thomas adored, and got him to spend the night in the room next to Thomas. Mark was kind and gentle. He was Australian and his Camp Horizon nickname was "Mumbley" or "Mumbleyburzamite" in its entirety because it was sometimes difficult to understand his accent. He knew Thomas well—his special positions in his bed and chair, how he liked to be tucked in with his blankets securely arranged—and he was a great friend to Thomas. We thought that perhaps with Thomas being in his own bed and having Mark nearby, he might actually get a good night's sleep. I was comfortable knowing Mark was there and decided to take a sleeping pill to help me get some much-needed rest.

All was well until a knock on our bedroom door woke both Glenn and me at about 11:30 p.m. Mark had never knocked on our door at night. He said Thomas wanted to talk.

I went into Thomas's bedroom. Thomas said he was having trouble breathing. We tried blowing his nose, shifting him around, and readjusting his BiPAP mask. He said he would try to sleep again. Twenty minutes later he called again. He said he wanted to go to the hospital. He rarely would suggest that himself, so I knew he was not well.

Glenn and I loaded Thomas into the van and headed to the hospital. It was well after midnight by this time, and the city roads were quiet. This was the first time we tried the South Health Campus, the new hospital at our end of the city. The emergency room was busy. After seemingly endless waiting, we were taken to a room. They hooked Thomas up to an oxygen reader and based on the readings, felt he was getting enough air. It took quite some time to find a vein to do blood work, but they ultimately succeeded. We waited for various test results, again. Glenn, being so considerate, suggested I go sleep in the van. I felt bad, but having taken the sleeping pill, I could hardly keep my eyes open let alone function.

We were at the hospital for three hours, until three in the morning on a Monday. The doctors on duty said everything was fine. They saw no problems, and they sent us home.

We needed groceries, and I managed to find yet another previous caregiver, Jenn, to come in the afternoon for a couple of hours. We also invited her to stay for dinner. I was making one of Thomas's favourite meals, beef stroganoff, in hopes that he would eat a good portion of food. We sat down to dinner and had barely started to eat when Thomas said, "Mom, I think we need to go back to the hospital." He just was not getting enough air in his lungs, and he was having trouble breathing.

Glenn and I headed back to the hospital with Thomas. We didn't know that Thomas would never again return home.

The Final Hospital

When we arrived at the South Health Campus, the staff immediately hooked Thomas up to an oxygen tank, which Thomas felt was helping. Glenn and I also thought, at the time, that the oxygen was a benefit.

The emergency department was so busy that they had people on gurneys in the hallway. Thomas was one of those patients. We waited a long time before they got Thomas into a room with three walls and a curtain. There was one chair for a visitor and room enough to fit three or four people standing. Once again, we went through his history, emphasizing what had happened over the past couple of weeks when he was hospitalized in Ottawa. After much discussion, the young male doctor on duty tried a new approach: a medicated patch on Thomas's back to help the heart. We had never seen that before. I do not for the life of me, remember what it was called. We only hoped that this new medication would help Thomas.

The night was turning into the morning, and we had been up for hours. Thomas, Glenn, and I were all exhausted. Glenn and I were trying desperately to keep Thomas's spirits up.

Thomas needed his BiPAP machine, so I went home to get it along with his favourite blanket and his arm pillow, which was perfect for making him comfortable and providing pain relief for his severely bent arms and wrists. It was four in the morning when I returned to the hospital.

Glenn felt guilty because he had to work later that morning. I stayed at the hospital with Thomas while Glenn went home to try and get a couple of hours sleep. The doctor on call wanted the cardiologist to look at Thomas, but she wasn't due to come in for a few more hours. Meanwhile, Thomas tried to sleep. He kept apologizing to me for what we were going through. I continued to assure him that I was there for him and would not want to be anywhere else. I was trying to catch some sleep in an armchair but also keeping an ear and eye on Thomas for his needs. The nurses and doctors in the emergency department were busy and did not come to check on us. I believe in their minds, we were on hold until the cardiologist arrived, which would be several hours later.

When the cardiologist arrived, she decided to admit Thomas into the ICU. This was a brand-new hospital and the ICU room was huge with all the bells and whistles. There was a new hospital bed, monitors ready to go, a cleaning unit for urinals, seating for visitors, and a couple of windows allowing the sunshine in.

The staff and I got Thomas set up in his bed. He was in pretty good spirits considering the circumstances, and he was happy to know that I would be there to again spend the night with him. There was even a chair that turned into a bed for me. By this time, I had already been at the hospital for more than twelve hours with Thomas.

Glenn came after his work, around five in the afternoon. He relieved me so I could go home, have a shower, and grab some sleep. When I returned around eight o'clock that night, Glenn's parents were there. I came prepared to sleep at the hospital. I was running on maybe three hours of sleep.

Thomas was not urinating. This meant that he was again retaining fluid, which, in the end, could mean kidney failure. We were measuring any output he was giving, but it wasn't much. The nurse assigned to Thomas was young and didn't really know what to do, so I was pretty much taking care of Thomas through the night. It was a long night.

I had already arranged for another caregiver, Gregg's brother Layne, as well as Jenn and Mark, to be at home with Thomas for the following two days. I was supposed to be going back to work. Layne assured me it would be no problem for him to come and spend the day at the hospital instead. That was good news for me. I could go home again for a shower, a nap, and a change of clothes. I had already informed my principal of the situation, and I was able to miss the first couple of days working with the staff before the students arrived for the school year.

When Layne arrived at the hospital the next morning to relieve me, I went home for a shower and nap. I thought I would get a few hours to sleep. After my shower, I believe I was only sleeping for about half an hour when the phone rang. It was Thomas and he was in a great panic. The doctor wanted to transfer him by ambulance to another hospital, but he didn't want to go without me. I called the nurses' station. It took what seemed like forever to find out what was happening. All that was running through my mind was that Thomas was afraid. Finally, after probably twenty minutes, the nurse informed me that they would not do the transfer until I arrived. I immediately called Glenn, and he came home to pick me up. We headed back to the hospital in the van, knowing we needed to transfer Thomas's wheelchair as well.

Glenn and I were both scared. I think we had really believed that Thomas was on the mend when he had been released from the Ottawa Heart Institute. We did not say much to each other on the way, fearing the worst. We held hands, as Glenn drove us safely to be by Thomas's side.

It was cold and rainy when we arrived back at the South Health Campus. We parked the van and ran into the hospital. The doctor who was in charge greeted us and explained that they were not equipped to care for Thomas. She told us that the young staff did not know how to follow the signs of his needs, monitoring his urine and relaying to the doctor the colour and output of his urine. Thomas had not urinated much over a twenty-four-hour period, and the staff had not informed the doctor of that. On top of that, his urine was black. She felt that his care would be better administered at another Calgary hospital, the Foothills Medical Centre. Thomas seemed okay with the transfer, but he wanted the doctor to give him some positive news.

Thomas always needed a positive focus. The doctors were planning to put him on another new type of medication and finally said, "Well, we are hoping this new medication will turn things around." That was what Thomas needed to hear—he could focus on hoping the new meds would turn his situation around. After he had that bit of encouragement, and knowing his parents were beside him, he was ready to be transferred.

Thomas wanted Glenn, not the paramedics, to be the one to lift him onto the gurney. The paramedics were extremely caring and listened to Thomas, their patient. They watched as Glenn tried to make him comfortable on the small bed. He then begged the EMS attendants to allow me to travel in the ambulance with him, and they agreed. Thomas and I went in the ambulance and Glenn drove the van, with Thomas's chair, to the Foothills hospital.

The traffic was heavy, but the ambulance driver felt the transfer didn't warrant the sirens and lights. Thomas needed a lot of adjusting on the way. The ambulance gurneys are so tiny and narrow, and his poor body was so bent that it was difficult to get him comfortable. Along the way, the EMTs and I we were trying to lighten up the mood. I could see that Thomas was scared of the unknown—of what may happen at this next hospital. The EMT in the back of the ambulance with me and Thomas was telling us about his appearance on the Oprah Winfrey show. I guess he had lost a pile of weight and somehow got featured on the show. That was when Thomas told him that I was famous and what an awesome teacher I was. I laughed and said that I was not famous, but I guess I was in Thomas's eyes. (Just as a mom looks at her child with adoring eyes, I guess Mom is always the one a child looks up to. Even up to his last moments, Thomas knew how committed I was to caring for him and giving him the best life he could have. While I still grieve him all these years later, it warms my heart to know that to him, I was his personal celebrity.) The attendant and I did everything we could to try and keep Thomas's mind off what was happening.

When we finally arrived at the Foothills hospital, Thomas and I were taken up special elevators and along several hallways through the back way to the cardiology division of the ICU. Glenn was already there to meet us. When Thomas and I arrived in the ICU, suddenly, several staff members were upon us and assisting Thomas. They wheeled him into a private room and told Glenn and me to leave. Thomas freaked. Even the EMTs suggested that we stay, knowing from their experience how difficult it was to lift and adjust Thomas.

When Glenn lifted Thomas onto the bed, Thomas burst into tears. It was a style of hospital bed he had had before and it just did not work for him (there are a surprising number of varying bed styles—some are air-filled, some have springs, others are different in size, and so on). I was trying to explain this to the staff, and they quickly found a different style for Thomas.

There must have been six doctors and nurses in the room, each doing something different. They were hooking Thomas up to more monitors, assessing him, and trying to draw blood. Both Glenn and I were trying our best to let the staff know about the difficulty of getting blood. We informed them of his weak veins, suggested they warm up his hands to increase the blood flow with heating pads, and let them know the best areas to try for success. We insisted that we knew the best route to find a vein after having gone through this so many times. Thomas didn't want us to leave his sight. None of us really knew what was happening.

Glenn was glued to my and Thomas's side trying to calm both of us. He held our hands, tried to make some jokes to put smiles on our faces, and attempted to put everything in a positive light. Glenn and I needed each other to be strong for Thomas. Both of us were on the phone, when we could, to let family members know what was happening.

After what seemed like an eternity but was only a couple of hours, the doctor finally had some news for us. Thomas had not been urinating and the fluid was continually building up, so they were concerned that his kidneys were shutting down. They wanted to try a particular drug, one that was extremely expensive. They said that Thomas was probably the only one in Canada getting it. They hoped that this drug would turn things around, but it would take at least twenty-four hours for the medication to produce results.

They wanted to do regular blood work, but Thomas's veins would not allow access. The doctor suggested putting in a port, a tube inserted directly into a main artery in his chest, to allow straight access to the bloodstream. The port could also be used to administer medication. Inserting the port was tricky—more difficult and complex, being placed in his chest—and since it was an invasive procedure, it had to be done in a sterile room.

Thomas was terrified. He insisted that both Glenn and I be allowed to accompany him to the surgical room. The staff, by this time, realized that we were better experienced to get Thomas situated enough on the table and calm him for the procedure. Fortunately, Glenn was strong enough to lift Thomas, and he tried to make light of things for Thomas in hopes of relieving his fear. Seeing the monitors showing Thomas's heart and lungs, Glenn was hoping to interest Thomas in the visual. He desperately tried to engage Thomas in the science of what was happening.

I remember some of the conversations we had while waiting for Thomas to be taken to the operating room (OR). Thomas had previously been joking a bit about his nurse and Jamie. The nurse was beautiful and efficient, and Thomas was trying to hook her up with his brother. He told her about Jamie's newly purchased house and how he was looking forward to seeing it after he got out of the hospital. Glenn picked up on this and used it as an opportunity to keep Thomas's mind off of the upcoming procedure; he tried to keep the conversation about the nurse going. Thomas continued talking about how well-suited his brother and the nurse were. He tried to convince her that Jamie was a good catch. Thomas, again, was thinking of others when he was in a critical condition.

Glenn and I waited patiently outside the OR for Thomas to be taken inside. There was no one around; it was quiet. When they took Thomas inside and Glenn and I got into the room, we adjusted Thomas on the table and placed all kinds of different-shaped foam pieces to prop him into the position that would allow the doctor to do his work. I remember the X-ray screen showing the already mind-boggling number of wires connected to Thomas both inside and out. Thomas wanted me to stay, but the staff gently ordered us to leave. The port was then successfully planted in his chest.

After the procedure, of course Thomas asked if I would spend the night, so the nurses set up a bed for me in his room. Glenn went home for some sleep. The night was fairly quiet, with the exception of Thomas needing a roll or a sip of water. He was limited in his intake, but they would allow him a Popsicle. He awoke at one point and asked for one. I sat beside him and fed him the Popsicle. He was laughing and smiling, so I asked why. He said he had just had a dream that I was pregnant! We both laughed. He told me that in the dream, I was going to have a daughter, and I was happy about this idea because I only had boys. I assured him that I was completely happy with my two boys and I certainly was not going to have any more babies at this point in my life. We talked for a long while as he worked away on the Popsicle.

It was our last real conversation, one-on-one.

The News

Throughout all of Thomas's trips in and out of hospitals, Glenn always kept to his routine of arriving early in the morning, usually between 5:30–6:30, with a coffee in hand for me. He knew that the nights were long and, come morning, I needed a good hot shower and a change of clothes. Glenn would take over the care while I slipped away for a couple of hours.

True to form, Glenn arrived early that next morning with the customary coffee in hand. However, this time I remained at the hospital.

As we began our day, everything was all too familiar. Nurses arrived to put in a PICC line. Thomas pleaded with the nurses to allow me to stay to hold his hand; they finally gave in. Everyone else in the room had to leave. I had watched this procedure twice before, and although I don't have a medical degree, I sort of knew what I was seeing. My heart sank. There were no veins available. The nurses tried their best, but after an hour they shut down the ultrasound machine they were using to look at his veins. They said they would come back on Monday to try again. (It was Friday.)

There was only more bad news to come.

Neither Glenn nor I wanted to leave Thomas's side. Doctors and nurses were coming and going. Somebody decided to get the respiratory team in to see if they could improve the function of Thomas's BiPAP machine. At this point, Thomas was using his BiPAP and oxygen 24-7. He was sleeping more and more, and his appetite had dropped right off. He didn't even want his favourite foods: a Wendy's stuffed potato, or hash browns from McDonald's. All we could do was pray that the new medication to drain his fluids was going to start working.

Again, I spent the next night with Thomas. Glenn went home, begrudgingly, for a bit of sleep. Thomas was sleeping so much that it was strangely quiet. I lay half awake all night with my mind spinning. I knew that if I drifted off to sleep and Thomas woke, the nurses would wake me to help him.

With Glenn, Jamie, Hans, Alice, and one sister from each of our families hanging out at the hospital the next day, all we could do was wait. The hospital staff was constantly monitoring Thomas. Now, the fluid was backing up into his lungs. Thomas was sleeping so much, but he knew we were there. When he woke, he would suck on a Popsicle and then fall back asleep. There was very little fluid output.

I spent the night again, and again it was quiet—just me, Thomas, and the nursing staff. It was hard to sleep. I was listening to every breath Thomas took. Every once and a while, he would call out, "Mom," and I would instantly be at his side. He knew I was there, but he didn't respond. He kept slipping in and out of consciousness. I kept telling him how much I loved him.

Glenn:

The cardiologist came in early and hooked Thomas up to a bunch of extra wires to get a better picture of his heart function. After a while, the doctor walked over to Kathy and me. He stopped, looked at us, and said in a low voice, "I'm so sorry, but Thomas's heart is barely functioning, and there's nothing more I can do."

Our hearts broke as we stood there and looked toward our son, who had no idea what was going on. Everything was happening too fast. The doctor said the situation was out of his hands now and we would need to meet with the palliative care team, who would make decisions regarding Thomas's care and tell the doctors what to do. He would set up a meeting for us to sit down with the team and discuss our options.

I asked the doctor, "What does this mean? How much time does Thomas have?" The doctor said he was not sure—a few hours to a couple of days. Sometimes people last a week. Kathy and I were in a daze. We told

The News

Jamie what was going on, but we decided not to tell Thomas yet as he still had hope that everything was going to be fine.

We had to wait until mid- to late afternoon before the palliative care team came, a man and a woman. Kathy, Jamie, and I followed them to a private room. The man did most of the talking. They looked at their charts. Thomas was eighteen, they noted. He was an adult and he needed to be told what's going on.

We asked, "Can't we just let him sleep 'til he passes away and not tell him?"

We wanted him to still have hopes and dreams. If we told him there was nothing the doctors could do and that he was going to die, we were going to scare the crap out of him. We didn't want this for our son. We fought with the team on this issue.

They said we had the option to talk to him or they would, but this conversation with Thomas was going to happen because he was eighteen. As parents, we could ask him if he wanted to know what was going on, and if he said he didn't want to know then we wouldn't have to tell him.

After hearing all of this, I told the team, "There's nothing wrong with Thomas's brain and of course he is going to want to know the truth. And when Thomas freaks out upon learning the doctors can't help him, I'm going to be really pissed at them for stressing him out for no reason." I was really irritated at this man because I thought he was cold and unprofessional and never tried to put us at ease; he was almost whispering. As we got up to go back to Thomas's room, they were on our heels. I told the guy what I thought of them and their lack of professionalism. It's hard enough to have to deal being told your child only has hours to live, but when you have a man who's cold and compassionless telling you how you are going to do things, boy, that is one hard pill to swallow.

The room was filled with tension and heartache. Kathy sat down beside Thomas's bed to be face-to-face with him. I was standing beside Kathy. Kathy asked him if he wanted to know what was going on with his health. Of course, Thomas said yes, so we had to tell him the doctors had done everything they could, there was nothing more they could do for him, and he was going to die.

Thomas said, "I'm going to die. I'm going to die. I'm going to die."

Naturally, Thomas was in shock. After his brief outburst about dying, he was speechless. And he was extremely upset, not wanting to accept his reality.

I asked Thomas if he wanted to talk to the doctor, and he said he did.

I went out into the hallway, where the doctor was waiting, and told him Thomas wanted to speak to him.

The doctor came in and sat down on a stool so that he could look at Thomas not from above but at eye level.

"Is there nothing you can do?" Thomas asked him.

"I'm so sorry, but no," the doctor levelled with him.

"You can cut my arm off if that helps."

"No, that's not going to work."

"You can even take my head off," Thomas continued, almost pleading. "I don't want to die. Is there nothing you can do?"

The doctor apologized again. "I'm so sorry, Thomas."

He paused and then rose from his stool.

As the doctor got up and was about to leave, Thomas said, "Thank you."

The doctor stopped and looked at Thomas; the doctor looked sick, as if he were about to cry. He said he was about to go off shift, and he was going to go home to hug his children.

This all happened with the palliative care team looking over our shoulder. I was seething … furious, but on the inside as I didn't want Thomas to see how I felt. I told them, "See! I said this would happen."

The first words out of the mouth of the woman from palliative care were to Kathy. "Your husband doesn't look happy."

Kathy glared at her and replied, "You think?"

At that point, the two of them rushed out the door and we never saw them again.

The doctor also left the room.

And then Thomas said to me and Kathy, "I didn't win."

Thomas wasn't upset about dying. He was angry about the fact that he felt he didn't get to finish what he had set out to do. He had such big ambitions. The work he had started as a child, advocating for himself and other disabled children, the progress he had made in bringing awareness to others about children with special needs, the success he had had in securing funding for himself and others to continue their education out of province. And of course his university studies. He had only completed one year of his degree. His dream of being a professor and being part of finding a cure for MD. It was all being ripped away from him at that moment. He was devastated. And of course, so were we, his parents, who had worked so hard for so many years to support his endeavours and help him realize his dreams.

For months, I lost a lot of sleep thinking about this: within a ten-minute span, Thomas was told he was going to die and the doctor couldn't do anything more … and my boy said, "Thank you." Still now, I don't know what to think about this. It just does not sit well.

By this time, everything had been shut off. There was no heart monitor. No oxygen. They'd removed Thomas's BiPAP machine. There was nothing at all. It would have been nice if they could have given us just a little more time to collect our thoughts first, before shutting everything down. Suddenly, without the monitors, the room was so quiet; we weren't prepared for the quiet. It all just felt so fast.

And final.

I should point out here that Glenn and I remember some of the events of this day slightly differently. You have to remember that this was the lowest point in our lives to date, and we were both feeling overwhelmed, confused, frustrated, and helpless. We were mentally and physically drained, not to mention emotionally. It has been interesting throughout the writing of this book how we disagree on certain events. We were able to verify some details, as we had someone else to ask. For other details, we just simply agreed to disagree. The last day of Thomas's life reveals some of those differences.

This is how the day went for me …

That morning, the whole family was at the hospital. The doctor came in to do a test on Thomas's heart function. The news was not good. His heart was barely beating. The decision was made to stop all meds. They simply were not working. Thomas's care team also decided to turn off his pacemaker and defibrillator. The doctor said they had done everything they could. He was going to call the palliative care team in to meet with Glenn, Jamie, and me. The three of us were in shock.

The meeting with the palliative care team was horrible. There was one male and one female doctor. The male looked like the son of Frankenstein and had a personality that matched. They asked us questions and asked our thoughts, and, in turn, we gave our answers. They had the mindset that since Thomas was eighteen and therefore an adult, they could tell him that he was dying since it was Thomas's right to know. We totally disagreed, especially Jamie. Jamie spoke out strongly saying that was the worst thing to do. We wanted Thomas to pass quietly in his sleep; there was no point in upsetting him at this stage. The two palliative doctors insisted that we tell Thomas he was dying, or they would. I could not imagine Thomas hearing such news from a perfect stranger. We had to agree to their demands.

Not only was my son dying, but I had to tell him. This was definitely the hardest thing I have ever had to do in my life. I was angry in so many ways, in the worst emotional state of mind I had ever been and absolutely heart broken. I wanted to scream to the whole world. Glenn was furious with the team. And he was very verbal telling them that this was not the right decision.

All five of us went back to Thomas's room. I was leading the way to make sure I got there first. I was shaking and trying to hold back my tears—trying to be strong for Thomas. The two doctors followed us in, making sure we were going to tell Thomas the truth.

I held Thomas's hand and woke him up. Glenn and Jamie were right by my side. I told Thomas that the doctors had tried everything they could but nothing was working. And that he was going to die.

Thomas freaked. He shouted, "No! It can't be true. No! I haven't won! I don't want to die. I'm not finished yet."

Glenn, Jamie, and I tried to reassure Thomas that yes, he had won. He had made a difference in our world. But Thomas wanted to see his doctor (the heart specialist).

When the doctor came in, he was very gentle. Thomas asked him if they could do a heart transplant, if they could cut off his arm in order to find a vein, anything to help him live.

The doctor explained calmly that they had tried everything they could. There was nothing more to do. Then the doctor got up and shook our hands and said, "I am going home to hug my own kids."

Glenn turned to the two palliative care doctors, who quickly began to leave the room, and said, "I hope you are happy. We told you this would happen."

We never saw those two doctors again.

Final Moments

The way Thomas was told was not how the scenario should have played out.

We sat with Thomas in disbelief, trying to wrap our heads around what seemed like a lifetime of events that had taken place over just the past hour.

Minutes later, the different teams came in and began their work. They turned off the oxygen and BiPAP machine, they turned off Thomas's ICD, and they shut down the medication they had hoped would turn things around. They began administering painkillers.

Everything was happening so fast. Our world was spinning.

Glenn:

We didn't let any of the family in for the first few hours. We wanted to be alone with our son, hold his hands, and try to come to grips with watching our son die.

Eventually, we realized it wouldn't be fair to the rest of the family not to have a chance to say goodbye. Grandpa, Grandma, Jamie, Kathy's sister Marj, my sister Susanne and her husband Bill, and Thomas's cousin Mikael were all waiting, relying on me and Kathy to guide them through what was happening. So we went out to the waiting room to update everyone and welcomed them to come and sit with Thomas and say their own goodbyes.

Final Moments

I had texted Thomas's friend Gregg the day before. He had misread one of my postings on Facebook and thought Thomas was doing okay. I texted that he was not and it didn't look like Thomas had much time left. Little did we know, Gregg and his two brothers immediately got in the car and drove non-stop from Vancouver to Calgary, a twelve-hour drive! Jamie saw them through the window of Thomas's room when they arrived at the hospital Sunday afternoon. When they came into Thomas's room, all three boys were shaking and crying. We stepped out and gave them each their own time to say goodbye to Thomas.

Thomas was in and out of consciousness. I don't know how much he heard or said to each person. We gave them their privacy.

For the rest of the day and evening, everyone camped out in his room. Waiting. There must have been fifteen of us if I remember correctly—grandparents, aunts, uncles, cousins, Gregg and his brothers—sitting in Thomas's room sharing stories and memories of Thomas. We were desperate to support one another. I mostly sat beside Thomas. Every now and then he would call out, "Mom!" and I would tell him that I was there and that I loved him. At one point, Thomas called out, "Jamie!" Jamie came to his side and Thomas said, "I'll miss you!" Right to the end, he was always thinking of others.

It was a long afternoon and an even longer, sleepless night. We had no idea how much longer Thomas would be with us. We wanted to make sure he was feeling no pain. The nurses assured us that he was on enough medication that he wasn't in pain. I crawled into Thomas's bed beside him and rubbed his back for a long time. It was the last time I felt his warm skin and smelled his smell.

I kept whispering in his ear how much I loved him and how so very proud I was of him. I wanted to reassure him that he did make a difference in this world. I told Thomas that it was okay to let go. I had been through this with both of my parents. I was there when they both died. This was so different. So hard. This was our son. But I had to let him know it was okay to let go, and that we were all there with him.

Glenn's parents stayed a long time, but it was late and they were feeling their years. Bill, Susanne's husband, drove them home. Glenn and I each had one sister who stayed with us the entire night in Thomas's room. The younger group—Gregg, his brothers, our cousin and his girlfriend, and Jamie—were camping out in the waiting room around the corner and at times were coming and going from Thomas's room. At one point, Glenn went out to check on them and brought blankets, courtesy of the hospital staff to cover them while they were sleeping.

Glenn had spoken with the nurse about Thomas's painkillers. She had explained that they were mixing up the meds to make him more comfortable, and she suggested that we roll Thomas to his left side. Glenn said he would do it, but he had to wait before he did. He needed to collect his thoughts, as he knew that this could be the last time he would ever roll Thomas over. It was tough.

It was not long after the rollover when Glenn and I were sitting beside each other with Thomas that Glenn broke down and started crying. This was only the second time I have ever seen Glenn cry. I motioned to everyone except Jamie to leave. They did, and Glenn, Jamie, and I cried together.

Morning was coming, and the nurses were changing shifts. Thomas had had three nurses during this hospital stay. They were all overwhelmed with him being such a wonderful, young patient, as most of their patients were typically older. They rarely saw young patients. They were moved by Thomas and all the family support he had. They, too, had become emotionally invested. They had a connection with him. Almost an hour after the shift change, the nurse who had already been on duty for twelve hours was still there. Glenn and I were saying thank you and goodbye to her. Meanwhile, Jamie was sitting beside Thomas when all of a sudden, Jamie said, "Mom, Dad, I think it's time." We rushed over to Thomas's side. The three of us told him how much we loved him.

Glenn:

It was a peaceful night with me, Kathy, Jamie, extended family, and friends sitting through the whole night watching Thomas sleep. As the hours ticked by, Thomas's breathing was getting more and more erratic and slowing down with many seconds between breaths. We knew Thomas's time on Earth was coming to an end very soon.

I went outside several times that night to get some fresh air and collect my thoughts. I decided that when Thomas passed away, I wanted a few minutes alone with Kathy, Jamie, and Thomas. I wanted to hold our hands over Thomas's body and say a prayer of thanks for having Thomas in our lives. All night I composed the most beautiful prayer in my head, and I thought I was ready.

I looked over to the family and could see their heartbreak. Thomas's nurse and the other nurse whose shift had ended two hours earlier were standing beside the bed. It was so very moving to see the compassion in these young nurses.

When it was time, I asked everyone to leave. That was the lowest point in my life: watching one of my children take his last breaths. Kathy, Jamie, and I stood around Thomas. We held hands over him and said the prayer I had worked on. As I looked at my family, however, my mind became overloaded with emotions and I went completely blank. So I just winged it, but I think they were happy with it.

The rest of the family came back to say one last farewell before leaving.

7:55 a.m.

Thomas took about three very shallows breaths, and then he was gone. We all cried. The two nurses were hugging each other and cried.

We were in shock. This was not supposed to happen.

Glenn asked everyone to leave, and he grabbed Jamie's and my hands and said an amazing prayer for Thomas. We sent our son on his way with all of our love.

When I stepped out of the room, my sister, who was a nurse for cancer patients, suggested that I ask if I could help get Thomas ready with his washing. I wanted to do that for Thomas. I also wanted that for myself, too. For me, it was a way to deal with losing him. A way of healing. A way to care and to love. A way to say goodbye to Thomas, from just me.

The nurse agreed.

It was the last sponge bath I gave him. I spent extra time washing, making sure I got all the areas that I always did. It hurt me to see the lines quickly forming in his skin as his death passed. Death was causing him to get cold and even stiffer than, in life, muscular dystrophy ever did to him.

Glenn:

Kathy asked the nurse if she could give Thomas a sponge bath and clean him up before we had to leave him. The nurse got the soap and water, and Kathy gave Thomas one last wash. I stood at the door to Thomas's room with my sister Susanne, and we watched Kathy so tenderly and lovingly give our son his last touch of personal care.

Afterward, we met with the attending doctor. Years earlier, when he was probably thirteen or fourteen, Thomas had expressed his wishes to donate any part of his body that would be helpful for others, and so we tried our best to honour his wishes, but all to no avail. We requested that a sample of his heart be sent to California to Dr. Rutkowski's muscular dystrophy clinic so she and her colleagues could use it for their continued research. However, because of the international border regulations, the heart tissue could not be sent to California. The only part of his body we were told that could be donated were his eyes, and so we made that request. Sadly, several months after his death, we received a letter informing us a special type of blood work was required in order for his eyes to be donated, and it did not work out.

Thomas's personal medical file consisted of several files, —probably a foot thick. We were told that his files would not be used for further research. They would simply be filed. We did send many reports on CD from Ottawa to Barcelona for their reference. We can only hope that his history will be used to help others. We were, and still are, adamant that Thomas's advocacy and legacy continue in any way possible.

Glenn:

There were so many thoughts going through my head as to what had transpired over the last few weeks of my son's life. My brain was scrambled. I was replaying so many moments from the past week in particular.

After Thomas's death, I had nightmares for months wondering if we could or should have done anything differently. I guess it's only natural to look in desperation for answers or solutions in a situation like this, wanting to go back in time and change anything you can so as to keep your loved one alive longer. In the end, though, I believe we did everything we could have done for Thomas. We were his parents, and for almost nineteen years, we consistently did what we felt was best for him. That was enough and, perhaps, more than most people ever could.

Glenn and I left the hospital to drive home, and we were in a daze. We were numb. Our Thomas was gone. No words could ever express what we felt. Everything had happened so quickly; it was surreal. We still didn't believe that Thomas had just passed. It felt like the car was driving itself. We seemed not to notice the all-familiar landmarks.

On the drive home, my cell phone rang. It was one of the local television news stations asking if they could do a story on Thomas's passing. The word was out and we were amazed that already, someone wanted to let the world know about Thomas's life. Glenn and I had tears in our eyes as I spoke with the news station personnel. Of course, we said yes, that it would be okay to do a story, but we were still in shock and surprised that they already knew and called.

We have no idea who told the press of Thomas's passing. Thomas made national news with both television and print announcing his death. We received calls from family and friends across Canada telling us they heard about Thomas's passing on their local news. Although it's sad to make headlines because of death, we were honoured and grateful that Thomas's story was getting out. His work, his ability to make a difference, indeed, is not yet finished.

Thomas Speaks

Children often ask me, somewhat bluntly, "What happened to you?" The parents quickly scold their child and apologize for their behaviour. The question is taboo to most, but not to me. My life goal has always been to raise awareness for those with disabilities because I have muscular dystrophy. No able-bodied person can demonstrate what being disabled truly is, which is why I believe in the importance of my goal. I take the initiative to ensure that there is deep societal empathy as well as an understanding for the disabled.

It is said it takes a village to raise a child, and this could not be truer. There are multitudes of governmental and charitable programs that do great work for those with disabilities. Many have given me an escape from my disability, and I now try to give back. I understand that I may not be able to help with the manual labour of regular volunteer work, which is why at age seven, I initiated my role of advocate.

In my youth, I drew inspiration from my older amputee cousin who won silver at the 2000 Summer Paralympics in Sydney. Today, I know a small boy and his younger sister, both in wheelchairs, and I want them to have a positive example as to what they can do despite some limitations. I want them, and others, to grow up understanding that they are normal.

I was a three-time honorary parade marshal for the Children's Wish Foundation. At age twelve, I began speaking to businesses on behalf of different organizations. At the Danish Canadian Club of Calgary, I was a lead organizer for the annual Great Dames Dinner Gala, where members step forward to organize a fundraising party for a charity of the organizer's choice. The year I was involved, we raised three times the average funds for previous and subsequent years. For the Between Friends club in 2006, I gave my first speech at a fundraising gala for two hundred people. The following year, I *spoke at the annual Giddy Up Gala and sang a solo for Easter Seals in front of an audience of seven hundred. That year, the gala raised a record $270,000 in just five hours. Easter Seals named me as their official Youth Ambassador a few months later. For the next year, I met with dignitaries and partner groups who donated generously. I made further speeches, accepted cheques, visited the Alberta Children's Hospital, and appeared in a music video with Gord Bamford, raising awareness for disabled youth.*

Children are impressionable. I speak to them in the community to help them understand my disability. I arrange fundraisers in local elementary schools, volunteer to teach art on my days off school, and contribute as a guest speaker. Over one of my high school exam breaks, I organized two sessions with thirteen elementary classes giving them art lessons. I think it is important to help society understand that disability is something we can accomplish, rather than what limits us.

Besides art, my passions include playing power hockey competitively and power soccer recreationally. Last hockey season, I finished with the second most star points based on importance and was chosen for continentals. I am also working to create a power wheelchair soccer league in Calgary.

For me, raising awareness is not about teaching. Teaching shows facts, dates, and statistics that become overused and miss the point of everything I live for. I work to help people understand. I strive to create an example of all that I can be so that others in my situation can see disability for what it is. Disability does not separate me from anyone. All people are disabled, and only some are temporarily enabled. Everyone will age. Everyone will need a little help. If people understand this, then all are equal.[16]

---

16 This is an essay Thomas wrote for one of his scholarship applications.

Planning for a Funeral

Kim Thomas on Facebook, September 1, 2014:

It is with heavy heart today that I update my profile and cover photos to honour an inspirational young man who lost his battle with muscular dystrophy this morning. Thomas Sorensen, you have been an inspiration and a leader to many as you faced head-on your battle with MD, but as your body failed, your mind grew stronger and you continued to strive to be able to help those who will follow in your path.

I will cherish the memories of my annual Santa visit to the Sorensen house on Christmas Eve. I know you knew many years ago who Santa was, but you humoured me anyhow.

RIP Thomas Sorensen.

Melanie Rose Barringer on Facebook, September 1, 2014:

Today, heaven gained the most beautiful angel ever. I first met Thomas in Legal Studies class in high school, and from there our friendship only grew stronger. Thomas was always full of life. It didn't matter what the situation was; he went at it with all his heart and determination. Thomas always made me laugh. From legal studies jokes to chasing around camp staff together during LEAD [Leadership, Education, Adventure, and Diversity—a specific program at Camp Horizon developed to help camp attendees develop leadership skills], Thomas never failed to make me smile and have a good time.

Aside from Thomas being a massive goofball and always making me laugh (even if it was diabetes jokes), he was also the strongest person I know. He could have a million things going wrong in his life, but he made sure to focus on the positive. I don't know anyone out there who could make a joke about a nurse missing his vein and having his hand fill up with fluid like Thomas could. Thomas inspired so many, and he was always looking out for others.

Thomas, you changed my life forever and I miss you so much. The world will not be the same without you. Rest easy, my friend. I love and miss you so much. Sending heaven my love xoxoxo.

To Thomas's parents: You raised an excellent man, and I am so grateful I had the pleasure of spending so much time with your son. I am so sorry for your loss.

Ben Thorne on Facebook, September 1, 2014:

Thomas, you always inspired me. I always say it's my goal to break the barrier for the non-disabled or "uprights" as you called them, but you brought it to a level I can only hope to get to one day.

My favourite memory of Thomas comes from hockey. We were playing against each other and I accidently caught him in the face with my stick. I was obviously concerned until he said, "Ow," and we started laughing. Then, he got me back later that season.

Rest in peace. You will be missed so much!

Martha Franlin on Facebook, September 1, 2014:

Shocked and saddened by the passing of our friend Thomas Sorensen. My favourite memory of Thomas is him showing up at the camp office and saying, "I'm going to Carleton next year. I need some help getting there. Let's write a letter!" This was much better than when he made me scrub between his toes with ten people watching or trying to make me uncomfortable with

Preparation H! (Thomas used that on mosquito bites! It reduced the swelling and took away the itch!)

Thomas, you were an amazing kid who I met years ago as a camper, and you grew into one of the most amazing, inspiring, and passionate friends I've ever had.

May you rest in peace and know that we will all continue your mission in your memory.

There were so many posts on Facebook, along with emails, calls, and letters. Glenn and I were in awe. We were beginning to learn that Thomas has left a legacy.

Our families had already started planning to make their way to Calgary from across Canada and the US. My sister Sue called from Nova Scotia and asked what she could do for us. I knew Sue was the "calm" sister and having her stay at our home would be hugely helpful, as she could make sure meals were done, and keep both Glenn and me on track without having to be asked. I insisted that Sue and her husband, Bruce, stay with us.

I also asked if Bruce would do Thomas's eulogy. Although Sue and Bruce lived on the opposite side of Canada for all of Thomas's life, Bruce definitely had made a bond with Thomas. When he was young, Thomas called Bruce "Captain Bruce" after a couple of special visits to Nova Scotia and several memorable rides in Bruce's boat, along with a personalized train ride, where Thomas got to ride up front, blow the horn, and have a penny stamped by the train he rode in. On one visit, Bruce and Sue also treated us to a day on the Halifax harbour viewing all of the tall ships from around the world. Bruce was number one in Thomas's eyes.

We had so much to do. We needed to find a funeral home. We needed an obituary. We needed to make arrangements with a pastor and a church. We needed an organist. We weren't sure where to even start.

We called our former pastor from the Sharon Danish Lutheran Church. Liselotte was now retired, but she was the pastor who had confirmed Thomas.

We wanted her to do the service as she could speak personally about him, and she agreed. The service would be held at the Lutheran church.

Our beloved family in Denmark sent word that they wanted to pay for all of the flower arrangements in the church for the funeral. Glenn's aunts, uncles, and cousins had been able to meet Thomas on our two trips to Denmark, and this was their way of supporting us since they couldn't attend the funeral. Both Glenn and I were extremely touched. Words cannot express our appreciation for this gift. The beautiful flowers ensured that we felt their presence at Thomas's funeral. Glenn's two sisters, Susanne, and Grace made arrangements for the flowers on their behalf.

Next, we contacted a funeral home. There were plenty to choose from. We chose McInnis & Holloway Funeral Homes, as it was close to our home and therefore convenient. We met with them at their office to begin the planning. They arranged for Thomas's body to be transported from the hospital. Jamie was already working on an obituary, so they didn't have to worry about that. Then they asked for pictures of Thomas and a program of the service. We also had to bring them a change of clothes or a suit for Thomas. They brought to our attention that even though we had decided to cremate Thomas, we still had to pick out and purchase a casket, which they would use to transport Thomas to the crematorium. Then, we needed an urn.

They took us into a room to pick out an urn. There were so many choices. We chose a green granite box, as Thomas's favourite colour was green. This urn had gold threads running throughout as well, and so we decided to emboss "Thomas Voss Sorensen" on the box in gold print.

Next, we entered the casket room. They had everything from literally a pine box to the exceedingly ornate caskets with silk lining. Glenn and I looked at each other. We were a bit surprised that a basic pine box was about $800! I thought there was just something wrong about choosing a pine box. It just did not feel right. I looked around saw a simple casket called "Horizon." I knew immediately that that was the one. I was, of course, thinking of Camp Horizon, Thomas's favourite place on Earth. The Horizon casket was $1,100. Glenn looked at me and with no hesitation we said, "That's the one."

Since we had already decided on the church, the funeral director told us they would provide staff to usher the guests in. They would also deliver to the church Thomas's urn containing his ashes. We still needed to send them the program of service, which they would print including pictures of Thomas. We filled out the paperwork, promised to return with pictures and an outfit for Thomas, and left the funeral home.

Meanwhile, the family was arriving in Calgary. It was all so emotional. We were happy to have so many family members around for support. Flower arrangements and baskets of various items were being delivered from friends and organizations. Friends were bringing us food, cards were arriving in the mail, and emails and Facebook comments continued flooding in.

And the phone was ringing off the hook. The major newspapers and television stations wanted interviews from me and Glenn so they could print Thomas's story. Thomas's passing was on both our major television stations in Calgary, along with stations in Vancouver, Toronto, Montreal, and Ottawa. The newspaper articles went national. We also received a call from the Carleton University newspaper. They, too, published an article.

A Legacy of Hope Left Behind by Calgary Teen[17]

Author of the article:

Jamie Komarnicki/*Calgary Herald*, a division of Postmedia Network Inc.

Publishing date:

September 3, 2014

Thomas Sorensen spent a year at Carleton University, and even made it on the dean's list his first semester.

This summer, he took in a concert at the Calgary Stampede and had the chance to go on a road trip with his best friend.

Each day, he worked hard towards achieving his many dreams, big and small.

---

17 Used with permission. Jamie Komarnicki. "A Legacy of Hope Left Behind by Calgary Teen." Calgary Herald. September 3, 2014. calgaryherald.com/news/local-news/a-legacy-of-hope-left-behind-by-calgary-teen.

When complications from his rare form of muscular dystrophy sent him to hospital in Calgary, Thomas remained steadfast that there was so much more he wanted to learn and see and do.

"He said he wasn't finished," said his mother, Kathy Sorensen.

Thomas, 18, died on Monday.

His bold and resolute spirit remains an inspiration for all who knew him, his mother said. "People just loved him, his spirit. He taught us so much. Probably more than we ever taught him. He just had such a love for life.

"He just shone."

Last spring, intent on one day becoming a scientist and working on cures for debilitating diseases, Thomas pushed governments to take up his cause and provide funding for a unique care program at Carleton that would allow him to attend university.

The Carleton program provides long-term care on campus for students with disabilities, but because Thomas was out-of-province, the Ontario government wouldn't fund him.

His rally proved successful, and Thomas was admitted to university with much of the funding in place for the care program.

Although a turn for the worse that sent him to hospital meant his introduction to Carleton was delayed by several weeks, he was able to start classes in the fall, Kathy Sorensen said.

"He loved it. He absolutely loved it. He loved the independence," she said.

Through the year, he spent several weeks in hospital, particularly to drain excess fluid from his body.

But he also excelled academically, making it onto the dean's list, and winning several scholarships.

He came home for two weeks in July to spend some time as a leader at Easter Seals Camp. He also took in the Billy Talent concert at the Stampede, said his mother, adding he was "so pumped."

Another special occasion was a road trip with his best friend Gregg to Invermere, B.C., something he'd talked about doing for months.

After the latest stint in Ottawa hospital in August, Thomas returned home to Calgary a week ago Sunday.

He was admitted to Foothills on Tuesday after he had trouble breathing. Sorensen praised the care her son received from nurses and doctors, but said his condition deteriorated rapidly.

"It was kind of a shock to us. We at that point thought there was something they could do to turn things around. They tried their best. There was just nothing. His heart was barely pumping Sunday morning."

Kathy Sorensen said she's been overwhelmed by the outpouring of love and condolences since Thomas died on Monday morning.

"People are writing incredible stories about Thomas and how he influenced them," she said. "I think a lot of Canada now has an understanding of what Carleton has to offer for kids with disabilities."

She said the family wants to look into ways of keeping his dreams alive, perhaps through a scholarship to inspire other young students. "Thomas, he was an amazing kid. He overcame his obstacles. He didn't let anything stand in his way," she said.

A funeral is planned on Saturday at 2 p.m. at Sharon Lutheran Church.

Music has, of course, always been one of my passions, and since Thomas embraced that love, too, I particularly wanted the music at his service to be special. Catherine Glaser-Climie is the founder of many children's choirs in Calgary and is the organist and choir director for our local Lutheran church. Our paths had crossed many times over the years, and I only hoped that she would accept our request for her to play the service. She did.

Next, I wanted someone to sing. A couple of years prior, my sister Marj had introduced me to a gentleman who was not only a pastor but a musician, composer, and singer. I had heard him perform many songs at different functions over the years, including a muscular dystrophy social event for clients and families involved with Muscular Dystrophy Canada, and I had one of his CDs. His name was Paul Rumbolt. I got his contact information from Marj. Paul agreed to perform.

I choose the congregational hymns: "Praise My Soul, the King of Heaven," "I Feel the Winds of God Today," and "Go, My Children." The last two were songs that had been sung at Thomas's confirmation. Paul sang three solos by request: "Wing and a Prayer," "Be Still," and "Blessing." With these decisions made, I felt confident that the music portion of the service was covered.

As family continued to arrive in Calgary, we helped find places for all of them to stay. Sue was managing our house and us. She answered the phone, planned meals, and asked about anything else she could look after for us. Glenn and I were walking around in a daze. We would go to do something and forget why we were in that room.

Jamie, in the meantime, had written the obituary:

Thomas Sorensen: January 23, 1996–September 1, 2014

It is with the greatest sadness we announce the passing of our youngest son, Thomas Voss Sorensen. Thomas was born on January 23, 1996. He is survived by his mother and father, Kathy and Glenn Sorensen, and his brother, Jamie. Thomas will be missed by his loving grandparents, Hans, and Alice Sorensen; his aunts and uncles, Susanne and Bill Berry, Grace and Boyse Harris, Jane and Mike Alcorn, Marj McNeil, Sue and Bruce MacIntosh, Elizabeth and Larry Ramscar; and his many close cousins across North America and Denmark.

Thomas was an incredibly intelligent and witty person, inspiring many throughout his life. Born with a rare form of muscular dystrophy, he was bound to a wheelchair from an early age. His handicap, however, only helped to fuel Thomas's determination; he never let anything stand in his way. His life was selflessly devoted to helping others and spreading awareness for disabilities. Much of his time was dedicated to fundraising for various charities and organizations. He was selected as the Youth Ambassador for Easter Seals in 2008 and volunteered extensively with Muscular Dystrophy Canada, Between Friends of Calgary, and Children's Wish Foundation, never declining an invitation to help a cause.

Even in his personal endeavours, Thomas's focus was always on the greater good. After graduating from Dr. E.P. Scarlett, Thomas achieved his dream of attending Carleton University in Ottawa with hopes of one day studying viral vectors to cure various diseases. In 2013, Thomas was the only Albertan to receive the Terry Fox Humanitarian Award, and in his first year of university made the Dean's List.

Thomas had a passion for playing power wheelchair hockey, winning nationals on the Calgary Selects Team in 2013. Thomas played a key role in establishing a power soccer league here in Calgary.

Funeral services will be held at 2 p.m. on Saturday, September 6, 2014, at the Sharon Danish Lutheran Church, 210-10th Ave. N.E. In lieu of flowers, donations may be made to Easter Seals Camp Horizon, one of Thomas's favourite places.

🐢 🐢 🐢 🐢 🐢

Everything was surreal. Glenn and I were barely functioning.

We met with the pastor and made our wishes for the service known. She was in total agreement with everything we requested.

We had to go to the funeral home and drop off Thomas's clothes. I brought his tuxedo, the one he wore at the galas he attended and spoke at. It seemed fitting to send him off in such style. We also brought his favourite blanket: a striped, fuzzy blanket in several shades of green. The one he had for years and loved. We wanted him to be cremated covered with his blanket.

Everyone was concerned that the church wouldn't be large enough to hold everyone who wanted to attend. Glenn and I had thought it would be sufficient, but after all the emails and Facebook messages, we, too, began to wonder. Fortunately, Jamie was working for a security company at the time. He approached his boss, and they were willing to set up monitors, screens, sound, and video to broadcast Thomas's funeral in the basement of the church, which would hold at least two hundred more people. We were also advised that because Thomas's death was so widely publicized, we should have a security guard at our house while the funeral was happening. Back Stage Support generously provided us all of these services at no charge.

The Beginning of a Legacy

Glenn:

We had never realized how much of an impact Thomas made on people's lives. We started to figure it out when Safeway's head office, the grocery store where Thomas had spent a lot of time advocating for muscular dystrophy, contacted us and gave us their condolences. They said they would like to supply food and drink for the reception after the church service. Thomas had many occasions to be a spokesperson for both muscular dystrophy and Easter Seals through Safeway. He was featured several times as a guest speaker on a national conference video with Safeway.

We started talking about how many might come to the service and realized the church might be too small. It was too late to change churches, as the time and place were already named in Thomas's obituary. We realized the church would be full but had no clue as to how many people would show up.

With all the family here in town, Kathy and I decided to have the whole family and some close friends for a sit-down dinner the night before the funeral. This was our way to say thank you and provide everyone a chance to mingle and talk.

Safeway generously came through with platters of fruit and sweets. We arranged for the Danish Canadian Club in Calgary to make up traditional Danish sandwich trays. The church women's group had offered to cater the reception in the basement of the church. They would set up the tables, make coffee, set out the trays of food, and do the cleanup afterward.

Glenn and I had to return to the funeral home to identify Thomas's body before the cremation. This was tough. Very, very tough.

Glenn had thought that he didn't want to go in. He initially said he wanted to remember Thomas alive, not dead in a casket.

The staff brought us to the room and said there was a rose on a podium should I feel like placing it on Thomas. I entered the room, picked up the beautiful white rose, and walked over to the open casket. Suddenly, Glenn was next to me. He'd changed his mind. Together we placed the rose on Thomas's chest. He looked so peaceful dressed in his tuxedo and covered with his favourite blanket folded nicely at his feet. I kissed him on his cheek. His skin was so cold. We told him how much we loved him, how proud we were of him, and how much we were going to miss him. That moment will be forever in my memory.

Together we left, both in tears.

During all of this, the Easter Seals Drop Zone fundraiser was happening in downtown Calgary. Perhaps I needed a reason to get away, or maybe I just wanted to be with one of Thomas's favourite support groups, but I felt the need to go downtown and witness the event. My sister Jane came with me.

There were so many at the event who knew Thomas well. Everyone was coming up to hug me and give me their condolences. It was very emotional, but also what I needed. I felt that Thomas was actually there.

One of the participants was Jeff Wilson, the MLA at the time that Thomas was fighting for the Alberta personal care funding through Alberta Enterprise and Advanced Education to be allowed to go with him to Ontario. Jeff had been extremely personable and supportive through Thomas's fight. We were touched that he was rappelling off the top of a high rise to raise money for Easter Seals in the Drop Zone event.

Jeff wrote the following speech for the event:

> *One of the primary reasons I got into politics was to ensure the quality of life for my sister, Amanda, who is a client of the PDD[18] system and faces numerous challenges daily that I could not*

---
18   PDD: Persons with Developmental Disabilities

even begin to understand. I wanted to do this drop to honour her spirit, which is why I'll be wearing the Wildrose green and pink with a proud W on my chest and A on my heart.

This week, further perspective was added to this entire event and experience, and that was when I learned of Thomas Sorensen passing away.

Thomas was a constituent of mine. I first had the pleasure of meeting him when he came to my office to ask for help with his funding to attend Carleton University. He told me all about how Carleton had created a campus that was accessible to him in his wheelchair, that they had a unique program in Canada that provided 24-7 care to students like him who required the additional support, how his dream was to pursue a career in biology, and that Carleton had accepted him into their one-of-a kind program.

I was pleased to assist any way I could and pressed the minister responsible to find a way to make his dream come true. Eventually, through Thomas's and his family's sheer determination and perseverance, the goal of securing the funding was ultimately reached.

Thomas made the Dean's List in his first year at Carleton and no doubt would have continued to excel for as long as his muscular dystrophy would have allowed.

I am so grateful that I had the opportunity to meet Thomas, to be inspired by his tenacity, his passion, his lust for life and living life to its fullest. It is for this reason, and the fact that Easter Seals Camp Horizon was one of his favourite places, that I am dedicating my "Drop" to Thomas.

It's rather fitting, considering my definition of a superhero is someone who makes the world a better place, and there is no question that Thomas Sorensen left a legacy with everyone he touched.

All out-of-town family members who planned to come to the funeral had arrived in Calgary, and family and friends who lived in Calgary opened their doors to house them. Glenn and I decided that we would host a family dinner at our home the night before the funeral. He and I planned the meal and wanted to do most of the cooking. That's just what we do.

We did have lots of family to help out. All the men rearranged our living room furniture to make room for one long table and forty-two chairs. One of my sisters came grocery shopping with me. Others tidied the house and vacuumed for me.

This was the fourth reason for a Dane to attend church: a funeral. In a Dane's life, family and friends gather to celebrate the person's baptism, confirmation, marriage, and death. Sadly, Thomas missed the third. When Thomas passed, almost the entire family showed up. The only reasons that some family didn't attend were distance and financial restrictions prohibiting them from getting to Calgary. It was, indeed, wonderful to have everyone around, and the gathering answered one question we had been struggling with for years. We did see, in the end, that family cared. We always knew that they did. From Glenn's and my perspective, though, their love was not necessarily represented in the ways we needed it to be in previous years—in the form of tangible help, supporting Thomas's day-to-day needs. Is this harsh? Maybe, but it is the truth.

I still had to go to the church to set everything up for the service. Three of my nieces came with me. We brought Thomas's wheelchair, his hockey shirt and stick, his favourite wallet (green with Yoshi[19] on it), and a framed picture of Thomas. When we arrived at the church, my niece Jennie said she would wheel Thomas's chair in. She had lots of practice moving it around in Ottawa and knew how to put it into push mode. She managed to get it out of the van but could not make it any further. It was really strange. I said, "No worries, let me try." As soon as I put my hands on the

---

19 Yoshi: the fictional dinosaur in Nintendo video games. He acts as an ally of Mario and Luigi.

handlebars, the chair moved without any effort. It was as if Thomas wanted me to take it in. Unexplained, but true.

The girls and I set up the front of the church. Thomas's urn was already there. The beautiful flower arrangements our family in Denmark had insisted on paying for had been placed as well. I felt pleased about how everything looked. Thomas would have been happy.

We also set up a display in the basement of the church for people to see during the reception including pictures, newspaper articles, trophies, certificates, and some of the awards Thomas had received.

Everything was in place. We went home to get ready for the family dinner.

When we arrived home, Glenn wanted me to go with him to see our family doctor. He was worried about our emotions taking over at the funeral and thought our doctor could prescribe something to calm us a bit without making us too numb. We went. Our doctor was great and gave us a prescription for a sedative. He also signed paperwork approving me for a leave from school.

The family dinner was wonderful. Glenn and I had prepared the appetizer—a cooked then cooled head of cauliflower smothered with shrimp and mayonnaise. We cooked two full pieces of beef tenderloin, two filets of salmon, lots of fresh green beans, roasted potatoes, and a Caesar salad. We had three platters of everything to make the servings go around the table quickly. Everyone came together to enjoy a comforting meal. We cried and laughed as we shared stories about Thomas.

My niece Suzy and her father, "Uncle Al," had been busy behind the scenes. They asked us if it would be okay to set up a scholarship in Thomas's memory at Carleton. They had already contacted Carleton University and begun to arrange to set up a memorial scholarship in his name. They had a large poster designed to display at the funeral with forms for people to take should they want to donate.

Dawnell and Jolene, two of Glenn's nieces, had also prepared a beautiful hardcover book in Thomas's memory, with his graduation picture on the front. They had printed coloured pages with photos, newspaper stories about Thomas, and special tributes from friends that had been sent through daily emails and Facebook messages. They also included several blank pages for people to write their own comments at the funeral. They had made several copies of the book for both sides of our families and for Thomas's best friend, Gregg. It is a wonderful keepsake.

After dinner, everyone sat to visit, and later, so many helped with the cleanup. Various family members helped with the dishes and putting the furniture back in its place. We all hoped that we would get a decent night's sleep.

The Funeral

The next morning Glenn and I had a quiet breakfast with Bruce, Sue, and my sister, Liz, who was also staying at our house. So many thoughts were floating in Glenn's head and mine.

Bruce drove me, Glenn, and Sue to the funeral. As we pulled up to the church, I was stunned to see all the different people already there: school staff, Thomas's friends, family, and family friends who had travelled quite a distance to pay their respects, and others who, I had absolutely no idea who they were. I wanted to go in to make sure everything was still in place.

The funeral home staff were there in their black suits, ushering people in, inviting people to sign the guest book, and assisting the many friends who were in wheelchairs. Muscular Dystrophy Canada had sent black wristbands with their logo on it to pass out to guests. Many people were stopping on their way in to give us hugs and pass on their condolences.

The pastor had arranged a room for the family to gather, so Glenn and I went in with the rest of our family. We sat all together, trying our best to keep it together. After twenty to thirty minutes, the pastor arrived and announced it was time to go into the sanctuary. Glenn, Jamie, and I were to follow Liselotte, with the rest of the family behind us. When we exited the family room, we were shocked to see that people were standing outside the building. The entire upstairs of the church was packed, as was the basement. The guests arriving later had no choice but to stand outside the doors of the church in hopes that they could at least hear the service. There were well over five hundred people in attendance.

Catherine had been playing the organ as people entered the sanctuary. We followed Liselotte inside. Everyone stood up out of respect as we found our seats. I don't think I remember seeing anyone in particular as we went in; I was just trying to hold myself together. The service began with a solo by Paul Rambolt, "Wing and a Prayer." Liselotte gave a greeting and a prayer. There were words of scripture followed by another song by Paul called "Be Still."

Layne was next with the scripture he had chosen to read. He was breaking down, and I felt the urge to go and stand beside him as he read, to help him through. Looking back, I wish I had. I did get up to give him a hug after he finished.

This was the scripture Layne had chosen:

> He gives power to the weak,
> And to those who have no might, He increases strength.
> Even the youths shall faint and be weary.
> And the young men shall utterly fall,
> But those who wait on the Lord.
> Shall renew their strength:
> They shall mount up with wings like eagles,
> They shall run and not be weary,
> They shall walk and not faint.[20]

We sang "Praise My Soul, the King of Heaven." Then Bruce delivered the eulogy:

> *Good afternoon friends, family, and admirers of Thomas Voss Sorensen.*
>
> *Thomas's life was too big and too full to condense into a six-minute eulogy. Please forgive me if I run a bit over my allotted time.*
>
> *I start this eulogy with a disclaimer: Kathy and Glenn probably asked me to do this for the family because they thought I was the only crusty old curmudgeon who might make it all the way through this service without losing it. Well, fair warning, I might not meet their expectations. And frankly, given the sadness and shortness of the life we are celebrating*

---

20 Isaiah 40:29-31, NKJV.

and honouring today, I think we are all entitled to be cut a little bit of extra slack and be allowed to wear our emotions on our sleeves.

From an early grade school project called "Thomas Time: This is Me," quote, "My full name is Thomas Voss Sorensen, but I go by almost anything. I've been called Tom, T, T-dog, T-bone, T-Moe, Mr. T, Tommy Douglas, and everything else in between. Don't ask me why because I don't know. My parents have affectionate nicknames for me like Pumpkin, Goombah, and more commonly, Magoo. To most people, I'm just Thomas."

From an early age, Thomas knew who he was. He was comfortable in his own skin. And that never wavered until the day he died.

I confess I am not a big Facebook fan. However, as I have read the flood of Facebook comments from friends of Thomas, it has shown me the sunnier side of social media. Every hour there have been new tributes, stories, and comments being shared about him online. There is one person who never met Thomas who now has a photo of him at her workplace desk. She has it there as a source of inspiration and admiration for someone she did not even know. Because of Facebook, there is a young two-year-old boy in my hometown of New Glasgow, Nova Scotia, who has a new role model in his life. He, too, has a rare form of muscular dystrophy and, as was so often the case with Thomas, his doctors don't know what to make of his MD. His parents are now familiar with Thomas's story and they are no longer adrift with fear and uncertainty. Because of Thomas, they are beginning to understand that their two-year-old son need not be defined or confined by his diagnosis.

Let me provide you a flavour of what some of Thomas's Facebook friends saw in him, and how he influenced their

The Funeral

lives. Since I'm paraphrasing and excerpting, I'll not identify the persons involved, but you will get the gist of things.

"Thomas, you were so amazing. Such an inspiration. You were able to accomplish so much. It always amazed me how positive, witty, and intelligent you were, cracking jokes at four in the morning when I knew you were exhausted and probably preferred to be elsewhere."

"My kids love Thomas. Thomas taught my kids never to be afraid of people in wheelchairs."

"His smile could fill countless rooms. He was many different things to many different people."

"My favourite memory of Thomas is him showing up at the camp office and saying, 'I'm going to Carleton next year. That's a given. I just need some help to find a way to get there. Let's write some letters.' That was so much better than when he made me scrub between his toes with ten people watching, or when he used to tease me and try to make me uncomfortable when I had to apply his Preparation H. He was one of the most amazing, inspiring, and passionate friends I've ever had."

"Thomas, you have been an inspiration and a leader. As your body failed you, your mind grew stronger."

"Aside from Thomas being a massive goofball and always making me laugh, he was also the strongest person I have ever known. He could have a million things going wrong in his life, but he made sure to focus on the positive. He was always looking out for others. He changed my life forever."

"Thomas provided me the best backpacking trip I've ever been on. He had the most positive outlook of any person I have ever encountered. I thank Thomas for teaching me what honest gratefulness looks like."

"Thomas, thank you for teaching me to laugh during hard times. To fight for what you believe in. And that being different is the best thing you can be."

And there's much more than Facebook. There's the handful of university students who worked as part-time caregivers to Thomas at Carleton, who became so much more than care providers. One of those friends, upon learning of Thomas's death, dropped everything and bought an airline ticket to Calgary in order to be here this afternoon to pay her last respects. There's the veteran intensive care unit nurse in Ottawa who was brought to tears by Thomas's concern for others as he was facing his Maker. There's Thomas's local MLA, who sent the following note to Glenn and Kathy yesterday:

"I am so grateful that I had the opportunity to meet Thomas, to be inspired by his tenacity, his passion, his lust for life and living life to its fullest. My definition of a superhero is someone who makes the world a better place. There is no question that Thomas Sorensen was a superhero. It is for this reason that I am dedicating my Drop to Thomas." He then proceeded to rappel down the side of a skyscraper as part of a fundraiser for Easter Seals.

After all of that painfully insightful and heartfelt sincerity, allow me to finish those quotes with a bit of homegrown humour from the man himself. Last fall, when Thomas first arrived in Ottawa, he had to start all over again with educating an entirely new medical team. He wrote on his Facebook page, "The sign by the elevator at my new doctor's office read, 'Take the stairs and improve life expectancy.' I'm worried I chose the wrong doctor."

Another Thomas-ism, from only a couple of months ago, while he was hospitalized in Ottawa, "Day twenty of being in the hospital for puffiness ... things are going swell."

As some of you know, even the national media picked up aspects of Thomas's fully-lived life. The Toronto Sun described him as a young man who refused to let his dreams be eclipsed by his disabilities.

The word "disability" is defined as "a physical or mental condition that limits a person's movements, senses or activities."[21] *True, Thomas's movements, senses, and activities were different from those of us not born with his particular condition. But neither "limits" nor "disadvantage" are words that spring to mind when we think of Thomas.*

Thomas took in stride what many of us would view as insurmountable obstacles. He got about his life and searched out ways to overcome whatever impediments confronted him. The thing that is perhaps most inspiring about Thomas is that he refused to see himself as handicapped.

He, of course, did have battles and obstacles and challenges. But in his day-to-day life, those were his fights for government funding, his battles against the opposing power hockey teams, working his academic tail off to make the Dean's List, or his larger and most passionate fight to push for better understanding of and cure for diseases like muscular dystrophy. He was a tireless advocate for raising awareness and funding for people with disabilities. Those were his battles. Not the fact that he was born with muscular dystrophy.

You should know that Thomas and some of his buddies call the rest of us "uprights." Thomas's father, Glenn, described a special conversation that Thomas recently had with his best friend, Gregg. They apparently were having a young-man-to-young-man discussion about dying and going to heaven. Gregg commented that maybe Thomas would be able to

---

21 Oxford Reference.com Dictionary, s.v. "disability," accessed November 27, 2021, oxfordreference.com/view/10.1093/acref/9780198832096.001.0001/acref-9780198832096-e-0819.

run when he got to heaven. Thomas apparently reflected on that for a moment and then said it really did not matter to him that much. He felt he would still be able to do what he wanted to do in heaven, as he did on Earth. He really believed himself to be just as capable as us uprights. Even in heaven, he was determined to be himself.

That's how he lived.

Let me tell you a bit about how he died. To paraphrase Shakespeare's Macbeth, *nothing in Thomas's life became him more than his manner of leaving it.*[22] *He was brave and courageous, and he refused to flinch or take the easy way out in the face of his ultimate adversary. Or, as his aunt Marj described it in a family email shortly after we lost him, "Thomas died the way he lived: on his terms."*

His mother, Kathy, described to me the ultimate definition of selflessness. She said that she did not think Thomas was afraid to die, but he was so angry because he didn't get to finish the many things he wanted to do in life, including helping to find a cure to muscular dystrophy. That anger at being unable to continue to make a difference in the world, rather than the more predictable self-pity and fear of death, is yet another distinguishing attribute of our Thomas.

So how do we put this all in context? We all need some time to allow grief to move toward healing, none more so than his parents, Kathy, and Glenn; brother, Jamie; and his paternal grandparents, Hans and Alice, who were such a large part of Thomas's life. For those of us who wish to truly honour and celebrate the impact Thomas has had on our lives, what can we do beyond the well-intended words that are so easily spoken on such a sad day as this?

---

22   William Shakespeare, *Macbeth*, Act 1 Scene 4:1-8, http://shakespeare.mit.edu/macbeth/full.html.

The Funeral

I have a few suggestions.

First and foremost, for those of us who are able, we keep a supportive watch over those who Thomas loved most. Each of us will find our different ways to be supportive of those two extraordinary parents who raised such an extraordinary young man. What they sacrificed to make Thomas the young man he became is a story in itself, one to be told another day. Kathy and Glenn, when you need more than faith, solitude, reflection, and quiet healing to get you through your difficult days ahead, know that your family will be there to support and embrace you, as you did for Thomas.

There is another strong young man who will be kept close in our thoughts over these coming months. Thomas's brother, Jamie, at an early age, had the maturity and insight to recognize that the eighteen years of medical whirlwinds that were a normative part of Thomas's life sometimes left him on the perimeter, with less than equal time. Jamie never let that medical reality affect his relationship with either his brother or his parents. Jamie and Thomas were best friends. Always, to the very end.

Thomas carried a torch of joy of happiness to his grandparents whenever they spent time together, which was often. With his passing, Thomas will expect the rest of his family members to pick up that torch and keep a caring eye on his grieving grandparents, Hans, and Alice.

So, what about those who are not so close to family. What can you do to honour and celebrate Thomas's impact on our lives?

My daughter, Jennie, and son-in-law, Chris, live in Ottawa, where Thomas went to university. They were Thomas's only family in town. The three of them became good buddies in the short time Thomas lived in Ottawa. As Thomas was in the last stages of palliative care and his passing was imminent, Jennie and Chris decided to go for a hike in the Gatineau Hills to clear their heads and sort out their emotions while they readied themselves for the loss of this special cousin and friend. As they were driving down a remote back road, they came to an intersection in a small rural village. Blocking the roadway was a fireman's boot, surrounded by local volunteer firemen who were raising funds for muscular dystrophy, as firemen have been doing annually for many years.

Call it fate. Call it serendipity. Call it divine intervention. Whatever it was, Jennie and Chris were moved to fill that fireman's boot. The rest of us can do likewise. Fundraising and research for muscular dystrophy was a passion and life-long commitment of Thomas. We honour him in pledging our donations to such worthy causes. I am also pleased to report that Thomas's family have established The Thomas Sorensen Memorial Scholarship at Carleton University, to support students with disabilities who have big dreams. You will be able to find out more on the Sorensen Facebook site.

One final observation about Thomas. Thomas loved life. He embraced it fully, perhaps more fully sitting down than most of us can do standing upright. We can all learn from that.

If Thomas loved life, he loved the people in his life even more. Not just his family and his friends, not just those who were easy or convenient to embrace. As so many of his friends have commented, he embraced everyone who came within his reach. He was different things to different people. He was totally undiscriminating with his smile and with his empathy for others, especially those with bruised or broken wings or souls. As one who had more than his fair share of

The Funeral

pain and suffering, he refused to acknowledge his own but felt and embraced the pain and suffering of others.

That is the type of living that Christ calls upon all of us to find. Most of us purport to do so but tend to dally in the shallow end of the pool. In everything Thomas did, he jumped into the deep end of life's pool. He made us all better for it.

Christ calls on all of us to love our neighbours as ourselves. On that commandment, Thomas made the Dean's List.

We had invited Susan Boivin-Law (CEO) and Anna Garcia (Camp Director) from Easter Seals to share a few words about Thomas. Both women graciously accepted the invitation to speak. So many memories were brought to mind. It was fitting that they announced at the funeral that just days prior, a huge anonymous donation was made to build a new dorm for Camp Horizon.

Our nieces Dawnell and Jolene, along with Jolene's husband, Peter, put together a PowerPoint presentation commemorating Thomas's life.[23] They asked me if I had a choice for the background music. I suggested "Tears in Heaven" by Eric Clapton, a song that Jamie had learned on the guitar. With the beautiful melody and lyrics, I felt it was fitting. The second song they included was a song by Green Day, "Good Riddance (Time of Your Life)." Both songs worked well. Every time I hear them now, I think of Thomas.

Paul sang another solo called "Blessing," and we all sang "I Feel the Winds of God Today."

Liselotte delivered her sermon in memory of Thomas:

> *"Do not let your hearts be troubled. You believe in God; believe also in me.*

---

23 This PowerPoint is still available to view on YouTube: youtu.be/v_M6kb58X00.

My Father's house has many rooms; if that were not so, would I have told you that I am going there to prepare a place for you?

And if I go and prepare a place for you, I will come back and take you to be with me that you also may be where I am.

You know the way to the place where I am going."

Thomas said to him, "Lord, we don't know where you are going, so how can we know the way?"

Jesus answered, "I am the way and the truth and the life. No one comes to the Father except through me.

If you really know me, you will know my Father as well. From now on, you do know him and have seen him."[24]

This had been the gospel reading at Thomas's confirmation a little more than four years ago. And today Thomas is at home, with "The Big Guy," as his grandfather put it when he told me Thomas had passed on Monday morning. "From now on, you do know him—and have seen him."[25]

As much as we all are going to miss Thomas—and there many, many people who will miss him—we place him with confidence in the care of his Heavenly Father and are comforted knowing that peace is now his.

Our hearts go out to his loving parents, Kathy and Glenn, and his wonderful brother, Jamie. On the last day of his life, they were close around his bed all the time, and the love between them filled the room. We share their grief today and our thoughts are also with his grandparents, aunts, uncles, and cousins, all of whom meant so much to him. The

---

24 John 14:1–7, NIV.

25 John 14:7 NIV.

The Funeral

support and encouragement he received from them all was just overwhelming.

Thomas was special in so many ways, but I think the most special thing about him was "Thomas." The person he was and what he did with his life.

The name is important. The name is something more than just a label. And without a name, a person is—nothing. But the name gets its contents only from the life and the acts of the person carrying this name.

When Thomas was baptized, he received the name "Thomas" and was baptized in the name of Jesus—the Father, the Son, and the Holy Spirit. And this name became important to him. During his time in confirmation class, again and again, he expressed how much his faith, his church, and God meant to him. Not just in a "religious" way, but in a "real-life" way.

These are Thomas's words:

"Jesus talks about this, the parable about the Good Samaritan, to show how important human lives are to God and Christians. People become so entrenched in the little details of their religion, they forget the big picture. This is why being Christian is important to me, to have a moral in daily life."

Some of the posts about Thomas on the Internet have been shared with me, and it is just amazing, what he meant to so many. Two of the posts I saw were about hockey and how he inspired others on the team. "His smile could fill countless rooms" is my favourite.

When the confirmands get toward the end of their course, I have them write an essay about what their Christian faith means to them. And guess what Thomas put into his essay? Hockey!

His faith, his Christianity, was something he lived out in everyday life. The way he treated others and the way he could support and help where it was needed. As we have heard a couple of times, he never said no if he was asked to help, and he never gave up.

My wish for Thomas and his friends in confirmation class was that they might give the name of Jesus, the name of the Christian Church, and their own name a content that will love, heal, and forgive so that their name may be a good name among their friends and family, a name that is spoken with love and respect.

That wish came true for Thomas in a way none of us would have imagined. All throughout the past week, the name Thomas Sorensen was mentioned, honoured, respected, and loved.

When Thomas was baptized, we were assured that he is a child of God and that his name never will be erased from the heart of God. And so, we know that Thomas is loved very much, not only by his friends and family but most of all by God. We cannot understand why Thomas had to leave us so early. There was still so much to do. But the legacy he has left behind gives the life he lived a deep meaning, and that is where we should follow. His life has given hope to so many, and I think it is not by chance that Thomas's word of promise four years ago was, "Those who hope in the Lord will renew their strength. They will soar on wings like eagles."[26]

Yes, Thomas was soaring. Let us honour him by hoping in the Lord and soaring with him.

---

26   Isaiah 40:31, NIV.

We give them back to you, dear Lord, who gave them to us. Yet as you do not lose them in giving, so we have not lost them by their return.

Not as the world gives do you give, oh lover of souls. What you gave you do not take away, for what is ours is ours always if we are yours. And life is eternal and love is immortal, and death is only a horizon, and a horizon is nothing save the limit of our sight.

Lift us, strong God, that we may see farther. Cleanse our eyes that we may see more clearly. Draw us closer to yourself that we may know ourselves nearer to them. And while you are preparing a place for us, prepare us for that happy place, that where they are and you are, we too may be. Amen.[27]

This church is almost too small today, and there might have been other venues to choose. But right from the beginning, Thomas's family was not in doubt: his funeral has to be from the Danish church. And Thomas would have agreed. Here is what he wrote in an essay about four years ago:

"Armed with everything in our church, I believe that I have a great moral foundation. Our church has forgiveness. If I lose my way, the church has moral lessons to be taught and teachings to tell me how to show my morals. I feel good about how our church is run, also. I know our church is special in these ways and will find a way of teaching the gospel without putting other religions down. I think our church is perfect for our faith, and I want to remain a Danish Lutheran Christian all my life."

Let us pray.

---

27 Frank Colquhoun (ed.), *New Parish Prayers*, London: Hodder & Stoughton, 1988.

And so she led everyone in a prayer followed by the Lord's Prayer, and finally, Liselotte gave the benediction. We ended the service with a congregational hymn, "Go, My Children."

Liselotte led Glenn, Jamie, me, and the rest of the family out of the church. Everyone was invited to attend the reception in the church basement. However, the church ladies needed time to clear out everyone who had been observing the service from there and set up the food and beverages, so everyone exited the church.

Glenn, Jamie, and I had made it through the service in part by continuing to squeeze each other's hands. When it was over, we tried to breathe deeply, compose ourselves, and get ready for the next phase: the receiving line. So many people were coming up to us and hugging us. They all said it was a beautiful service. Many told us later that they had not known about all of Thomas's achievements prior to the service. Even Glenn's friend Steve had no idea. Another couple told us that they felt they knew Thomas just from the many who shared their stories of him. People loved the music—both the solos and the hymns—the readings that were chosen, and the speakers' words.

There were people from all walks of life. Doctors and other staff from the hospitals, Thomas's former teachers, colleagues from both Glenn's and my work, friends of the family, Thomas's friends of course, and total strangers! One gentleman who came up to me and shook my hand told me that I didn't know him and he hadn't known Thomas, but he had been following Thomas's story through the newspapers and television. He felt the need to attend the funeral as he was so touched by Thomas's life.

Glenn brought two beautifully dressed girls to me at one point. I didn't recognize them but Glenn introduced them to me. They were the two nurses who were present when Thomas passed. They had come to pay their respects after only having known Thomas for a few days.

So many people came to the reception. Every now and then I would lose it, thinking of how touching it was that a particular individual came and remembering a special time in Thomas's life. Sadly, we don't really know just who all attended the funeral. There were well over five hundred people at the service, and many didn't stay for the reception. It was only after the funeral when we read some of the cards that we learned of some

The Funeral

of the people who had been in attendance. We also received emails from others later telling us that they had attended.

We learned something new about Thomas's funeral in September 2022, so many years after the fact: the lift in the church was broken that day, and so those attending in wheelchairs had no way to get up the eight stairs into the church. The only solution was an unbelievable sacrifice and showing of generosity. Several men were lifting these people up the stairs and into the church so that they could attend the service.

There was so much we didn't know that day—so much that was a blur or was happening without our knowledge. In hindsight, we thought it would have been great if the funeral home staff had taken pictures in front of the church so we could later view them and see who had attended.

After we managed to make it through the reception, our family helped us gather up the display of Thomas's achievements. The church ladies cleaned up the food, and Bruce drove us home to welcome our family and close friends to reflect together. We were very appreciative of all of the help.

Many friends had dropped off platters of food to the house for our family. We offered these up along with an open bar. It was a beautiful, warm fall evening, with the sun shining, so we were able to gather and sit on our deck. Emotions were running high with everyone having to officially say goodbye to Thomas. Many of the family were still in disbelief.

That evening, I wanted to lighten things up and share some love with those who were gathered at our home. Thomas had more than one hundred various kinds of turtles: stuffed, ones that lit up, glass, and statues. I thought that it would be nice to give each family member one of his turtles as a memory. Glenn thought I was bananas. I went through Thomas's collection and carefully selected a turtle for each family member. The family was thrilled, especially the young cousins!

Many of them still treasure their gift. I just could not imagine keeping Thomas's many treasures or donating them to anyone else but family.

Carleton Honours

Over the next couple of days, our out-of-town family members left. Jamie had moved out two months prior, so Glenn and I were now alone and feeling empty. We were lost.

Sympathy cards were pouring in, along with many emails. Everyone was trying to support us. Several people wrote stories about Thomas. Others offered to help out however we saw fit. Many had no words to express our loss or their sympathies; no one could truly know how we were feeling. In spite of the well-wishes of those people who surrounded us, the sombre stillness of the house and the grief of losing our youngest son led to feelings that were heavy and simply indescribable. The house felt so empty, so quiet. Glenn and I were not sure what to do, where to go, or where to sit.

The week following the funeral, we received news that Carleton University wanted to do a memorial service. Again, we were shocked. Thomas had only been at Carleton for only one year. The president of the university asked if we would like to attend. Glenn was feeling bad about not being at work and wanted to return, so we decided that I would fly back to Ottawa for the service. As much as I wanted Glenn to come, I knew he wanted to be busy. At the time, I wondered if it would have been too difficult for Glenn to return to Ottawa. The city had a special place in his heart what with everything we had gone through with Thomas there.

The president of Carleton University, Roseann O'Reilly Runte, had previously called us personally to pass along her condolences. Now, in this second call, she said that she would be presiding over the memorial service for Thomas at the university, as he had touched so many lives during his short stay there. I felt I had to do this for Thomas. We booked a flight for me to go.

When I arrived in Ottawa on Thursday, September 11, I rented a car and drove to my niece's house. Jennie had arranged for Vanessa and Jamie, two of Thomas's caregivers from Carleton, to join us for a visit. The three of them had already gone to Thomas's room to clean out his belongings. Glenn and I had requested that they take anything that meant something to them and donate other items that could be of use to other students. We so appreciated their help.

Jennie, Vanessa, Jamie, and I sat in Jennie's living room sharing stories and memories about Thomas. The girls told me about Thomas's mischievous side and how he sometimes got into trouble with the manager of the care program because of playing tricks on various people. They reminisced about hanging out in Thomas's room, and how his room was set up for his friends to come and play video games. There had apparently been many late nights with them and other friends hanging out in Thomas's room and many battles played on the Xbox.

We then went down to Jennie's basement and sorted through many of Thomas's belongings. The girls weren't sure what to do with the remaining items. As we went through everything, we continued sharing stories. Certain items would trigger someone's memory and I would hear a new story. I took a couple of Thomas's favourite T-shirts, his hockey trophies, his turtles, and certain decorations that meant a lot to him. The girls had already donated some of his belongings, and after we did this sorting together, we put the remaining items in a pile to donate to students at the university or give to charity.

Vanessa:

There was one time we went to the market (Ottawa has a massive market) and he was determined to find white asparagus. In true Thomas fashion, he explained to me that white asparagus is so incredible and that it makes the best soup. He told me that he hadn't been able to find it anywhere. I told him it sounded awful, knowing that if we found it, he'd force me to eat it anyway. We spent the entire afternoon walking around, eating lots of snacks, and cracking up.

We never ended up finding any, but I know his mom sent him some to make soup. He eventually got to make the soup and made me try it. It was not my cup of tea, but he was determined to make me like it.

When Thomas passed, I helped clean out his room and his cupboards. With everything I took out, I cried a little more. Then, when I got to his food cupboard, I opened it to find two jars of white asparagus. I sat there for about two hours after that just laughing and crying about how important these jars were to him and how no one else would have known that. They wouldn't have known that we searched Ottawa's stores for weeks to find it or that we spent afternoons at the market hoping someone would sell it. These two little jars of asparagus had to be sent to him by his mom and cooked by someone who openly told him he had the oddest taste in food.

Those two jars are still sitting in my cupboard, even after they've expired ... I mean it's not like I was ever going to eat them anyway.

🐢 🐢 🐢 🐢 🐢

The next morning, I managed to pull myself together for Thomas's memorial service. I had brought a framed picture of Thomas, his cousins' memorial book, and a variety of memorabilia. I had no idea what was ahead for the memorial service.

It was a cool, grey day with the skies threatening rain when I arrived at Carleton. My emotions overtook me when I saw the room the organizers had reserved. They had several chairs placed, a variety of trays of sandwiches, sweets, and beverages, and there were a half-dozen flower arrangements. Some of the flowers were sent from Carleton University and others were from Thomas's friends he had met during his stay.

People began to arrive. All the power hockey players from the Ottawa Hockey League came. Dormmates. People from the Paul Menton Centre at Carleton. Care attendants, classmates, and professors. Gregg's grandparents came. And, of course, the president of Carleton University, Roseann, with her assistants. I was busy trying to meet and introduce myself to everyone, asking what their relationship to Thomas was, and focusing on keeping my composure.

I had placed a framed photo of Thomas at the front and managed to figure out the PowerPoint wand to get Thomas's pictures on the screen. Vanessa sat beside me for the service. Our niece Jennie and her husband were there, too, but sat several seats behind me. I was overwhelmed at how many people were there; there had to be about two hundred.

The president oversaw the service. She welcomed everyone and spoke about Thomas's impact in such a short time at Carleton. Then she asked for a few speakers to come forward.

One was Matthew Cole, the director of the Attendant Services Program. Matthew spoke highly of Thomas. He remembered meeting me and convincing me to allow Thomas to attend Carleton, knowing Thomas's needs would be met. I was surprised to hear that he compared Thomas to Terry Fox. Matthew did admit that Thomas was not an "angel," that he was very outspoken, loved to prank, and sometimes loved to play the innocent one. He also spoke about Thomas's determination and his love for science, which led the university to add new additions for handicapped students in different areas of the university.

This is what Matthew had to say about Thomas:

> *Thomas was a lot of fun to have around, and no one accused him of fading into the background. That might be what we will miss most about Thomas. He spoke out, he stood up for himself, and he was a great advocate on campus. He was a little mischievous at times, and we all liked that about him. We still smile when we think about him and this is one of the main reasons.*
>
> *Regardless of who should be up here speaking, here I am, and maybe I still don't have the words to explain why an eighteen-year-old passes away far too soon or to offer comfort to those who also do not understand it.*
>
> *But I will share some additional thoughts.*

One of the most emotional aspects of Thomas's passing was something that Kathy shared with me. She said that Thomas was angry. He was angry that he passed away before he was able to accomplish some things he had planned in his life.

Thomas had been determined to beat the odds. He rejected any limitations put on him by his medical diagnosis. He travelled across the country to attend Carleton, but that was supposed to be just the beginning for him. Thomas wanted to leave a legacy, and he was angry when he thought that this was not to be.

But when I think of Thomas and all of the fond memories we have of him, he reminds me of a great Canadian icon, Terry Fox. Both were stubborn and fierce.

Terry Fox also thought he had failed when he could not finish his Marathon of Hope. Not one of us here today believes that Terry Fox failed, and I feel the same way about Thomas.

Coincidentally, Thomas passed away on September 1st. That was the same day that Terry Fox was forced to abandon the Marathon of Hope.

Like Terry Fox, Thomas is still with us in a sense.

And like Terry Fox, Thomas's legacy will live on. We have our memories, and I am also mindful of the support being given to the Thomas Sorensen Memorial Scholarship. This scholarship guarantees that Thomas will always have a place at Carleton and will have a positive effect in the future on students with disabilities.

Thomas left us far too soon, but he did not fail. We are sad because he only lived for eighteen years, but in those years, he did make an impact on many lives. He established a legacy, and he will not be forgotten.

I am sad that I can't remember the name of the professor who spoke next. He brought me to tears. He was a biology professor, one of the first who questioned Thomas's ability to be in his class. This professor was completely shocked when he met Thomas, and he admitted as much. He was amazed at the young boy's knowledge. And he said that in the months since Thomas started at Carleton, he loved engaging in conversation with Thomas because his understanding of science was beyond his years. During his speech, this professor actually broke down and cried. He went on to say that he wished all of his students had the understanding and passion for science and learning that Thomas had.

The student union president spoke next. He told his story of how he had met Thomas at the Paul Menton Centre and how passionate Thomas had been in wanting to help others.

It was special, too, that we heard from a few of Thomas's friends from the dorm rooms and from hockey. It was the first time I had met some of these Carleton friends. Some care attendants also shared their memories of Thomas.

Somehow, when asked, I was able to summon the strength to share Thomas's eulogy. Bruce was kind enough to provide a copy for me. I did add a couple of thoughts after Thomas's funeral, and I have included those additional thoughts below. I was grateful to Jennie for coming up to the podium to help me through. I still don't know how I read the words. Remember, this was only six days after the funeral:

September 12, 2014:

Good afternoon special guests, friends, family, and admirers of Thomas Voss Sorensen.

I am Thomas's mom, Kathy Sorensen. It is an honour to be here today to share some stories about our son. My husband, Glenn, and I always knew we had a great kid, but we have only begun to understand the impact Thomas had on so many lives in his short eighteen years. My brother-in-law, Bruce Macintosh, Jennie's dad was very kind to do Thomas's eulogy at the funeral on Saturday in Calgary. We had over five hundred people in attendance. Bruce did Thomas proud, and he has allowed me to use much of his eulogy today. Thank you, Bruce.

Thomas's older brother, Jamie, had a special relationship with Thomas. Jamie always needed to be close to Thomas to be available to help in any way he could. The night before Thomas passed, Thomas would open his eyes and simply say, "Mom." I was right beside him. At one point, his eyes opened and he said, "Jamie." Jamie came to sit beside him and held his hand. Thomas said "Jamie" again, and Jamie said, "I'm here, bro." Thomas then said, "I'll miss you." Thomas, right to the end, made sure his brother knew he loved him. He always called Jamie the "problem child" because Jamie was still living at home at age twenty-four.

Glenn and I would like to thank Carleton University for giving Thomas the opportunity to live his dream. The accessible rooms, the tunnels, and the proximity readers all contributed to Thomas's independence and success. We would like to thank Matthew Cole, director of the Attendant Services Program, for convincing us to let Thomas come. I remember a year ago April when Matthew was touring me around campus, he said, "Kathy, do you know what our biggest problem is here?" I said no. He simply said, "Mothers."

We would like to thank all of the attendants for their love and care they gave Thomas. You are all special. It is not a job most people could do. Please know that Thomas truly appreciated everything you did. He always spoke of you highly.

I would like to share a couple of stories that are difficult to explain …

First, Thomas's best friend, Gregg, was coming over to our house last Tuesday after Thomas passed to bring some of Thomas's belongings from Carleton that his father had picked up in Ottawa. Gregg's parents had just purchased a new car for their three boys. It was the first time Gregg was to drive the car. He loaded Thomas's belongings, then started the car. The car's systems all came on and were set at factory default. Gregg looked at the date that flashed up on the car. It was January 23. Thomas's birthday.

Secondly, two of my nieces came with me to the church to set up for the funeral. Jennie was one of them. She certainly was used to Thomas's chair and was pushing it out of the van. She asked me, "Kathy, is this on push mode? I can barely move it?" I said, "Yes, but here, let me do it." I put my *hands on the chair and it took no effort at all to move it into the church. I think Thomas wanted me to take him in …*

After my eulogy, the president of the university presented me with a certificate of acknowledgement for Thomas's studies in science. It is something we hold dearly to this day. Glenn and I had no idea how much influence Thomas had or how deeply he had impacted so many lives in such a short time.

Everyone at the memorial was so kind and spoke so highly of Thomas. I returned the next day to Calgary, leaving behind a mountain of memories that had built up in less than a year. Ottawa and Carleton will always be special places in our hearts.

Still Reeling

Glenn and I decided that we would get away for a week to reflect on Thomas's death, just the two of us, with lots of hand holding. We booked a flight to Cabo San Lucas for the following Sunday, a week after I returned from Ottawa. Jamie's twenty-fifth birthday was a few days before we were leaving, and we knew we had to celebrate his day. We invited the whole family in Calgary to attend a party for him on the Saturday before we were to leave.

After Thomas had returned to Ottawa in July, he had found some towels as a birthday gift for Jamie to use in his new home. After he was hospitalized in Ottawa, he showed me the towels. He wanted to find more towels with a contrasting colour to add to Jamie's birthday present. He and I went shopping, found some great ones in different sizes, and I put together a package for Jamie. We brought this gift home when Thomas, Glenn, and I returned to Calgary after Thomas's stay at the Ottawa Heart Institute. At that time, little did we know that Thomas would pass two weeks before his big brother's special day, and this gift would end up meaning so much more to Jamie.

I was busy packing for our trip to Cabo at the same time Glenn and I were preparing Jamie's traditional Danish birthday dinner for ten people. While dinner was cooking, I changed the sheets on our bed. I had our comforters outside to air out. As I was bringing in one of the comforters to make the bed, I forgot there was a suitcase inside the door and I tripped over it. As I fell backward, I realized that the glass coffee table was behind me, and I hit my head on the corner of the table. I put my hand on my head only to find that my head was gushing with blood. I realized I needed stitches for the first time in my life. I was so angry. I was thinking, *Really!*

Are you kidding? Glenn heard me fall and came running into our bedroom. He was concerned but remained calm. He immediately went to the kitchen and turned off the roast, explaining to our guests that I needed to go to the emergency room. He was extremely loving and understanding. I think he knew I was kind of on edge.

At the ER, Glenn leaned on the counter and calmly explained our situation to the nurse. He told them about Thomas's death, that we had a house full of company waiting for dinner, and that we were supposed to be leaving the next day for Mexico. They took me in right away. The doctor came, stitched me up, and sent us on our way. We were in and out within an hour. We arrived home without supper being ruined and were able to celebrate Jamie's birthday. The food was great, and I think Jamie was feeling special on his day. After an eventful but enjoyable evening, we said a good night to our family, cleaned up the dishes, and went to bed.

The next morning, we were packed and ready to leave for a week in Mexico. Jamie arrived at our house to take us to the airport. The moment we put our hands on the suitcases to leave, my cell phone rang. It was the airline informing us that there was a Category 5 hurricane on the way to Cabo and that the plane would not be leaving. WestJet informed us that it would take at least forty-eight hours before we could try to rebook another location. I don't know why, but I blurted out everything: I told the agent about Thomas, the suitcases in our hands, and that we had a limited time to get away due to work commitments and needing to be back for a special dedication in Thomas's honour at Camp Horizon. The agent said she would look into it and call me back.

It took a few hours, but she managed to break a few of their rules and arranged to fly us out the following day to Cancun. We lost a pile of money from our advanced-seating bookings and the price difference in the two resorts, but at this point we didn't care. We just wanted to run away from reality for a week.

The week away did not feel like a vacation, though. We weren't in party mood, and even the margaritas seemed frivolous. Reality was sinking in that Thomas was gone. It was good, however, to hold hands and reflect on the last couple of months. There were many times when Glenn and I didn't even have to talk; we knew what the other was thinking. When we did talk, we kept replaying the trips to hospitals, conversations with doctors, and Thomas's last hours. We shared stories about Thomas and talked about the whole experience leading up to his death. It was an important time for both of us to have a change of scenery, to be alone with no phones, no anything, just to hold hands and try to put everything in perspective. And Glenn played doctor and removed my stitches.

When we got home, we were launched into being busy. There were more cards in the mail, the new dorm at Easter Seals Camp Horizon was being dedicated, and our niece was getting married in Vancouver. We put on a brave face and attended the camp dedication.

Easter Seals was naming one of their rooms after Thomas. The camp director talked about Thomas's impact on everyone at camp and how he would always be remembered. It was a special tribute. Once again, people gave us hugs and shared their stories of Thomas. One of the guests at the reception was the CEO of the Calgary Safeway stores. He approached us to give his condolences and to let us know how special Thomas was and how he made a difference in our world. He talked about how the Safeway administration admired Thomas for his courage and for facing his daily challenges with dignity. They recognized his intelligence and his drive for learning and they appreciated his commitment to advocating for anyone with disabilities.

Immediately after the celebration, we headed to the airport to fly out for our niece's wedding in Vancouver. Although it was a wedding and a time to celebrate, it was a tough weekend for us. Thomas was gone, and we were seeing so many family members so soon after the funeral. It was difficult to conjure a festive mood. In spite of our emotional struggles, we were touched when our niece Dawnell, and her new husband, Ruben, included Thomas in their reception. The bride and groom announced that if guests wanted them to kiss, instead of the traditional clinking of the glasses for a kiss, guests had to donate to Easter Seals Camp Horizon in Thomas's memory. They raised over $800.

When we returned to Calgary, Glenn decided to go back to work. I was worried about him, of course. I felt he really had not let go and was going back too soon. As for me, I was not ready to return to work. My school board was compassionate with my situation, and fortunately, I was on a paid leave.

Over the next month, we tried to adjust. Our house was so quiet. We wanted to reorganize Thomas's room and go through his belongings. We decided that we needed to donate some of Thomas's equipment. We donated his new wheelchair to Easter Seals, along with the lift in the garage and the tracking system on the ceiling in his bedroom. We returned the shower commode chair and his original wheelchair to Alberta Aids to Daily Living (AADL). We had Thomas's van professionally cleaned. We replaced the windshield and then put it up for sale. Each time something left, our hearts ached. It deepened the reality that Thomas was gone. These were steps we did not want to take, but we knew we had to at some point.

After the funeral, Jamie started calling me on almost on a daily basis. Glenn saw him every day at work, but Jamie was looking out for me, too. He tried to drop by every now and then to give me a hug and come for supper.

Since Thomas's passing, time moved like a waterfall. From September onward, Glenn and I both took one day at a time. We were still receiving cards, emails, and gifts. Each one would bring a tear to my eye.

The Starlight Children's Foundation, an organization supporting children and families with disabilities, named a star after Thomas. They sent a beautiful certificate with maps of where in the sky his star is located. People continued donating in memory of Thomas to Easter Seals Camp Horizon, Muscular Dystrophy Canada, The Children's Wish Foundation, and the memorial scholarship in Thomas's name at Carleton University. We both felt proud of Thomas and humbled at the same time.

Kathy on Facebook, December 12, 2014:

Thomas officially has a star named after him. Star number Ursa Major RA 10h 9m 37s D 41' 51'. This star is now named "Thomas Voss Sorensen." This star is permanently filed with the "registry's vault" in Switzerland and recorded in a book which will be registered in the copyright office of the United States of America. Thank you to the Starlight Foundation!

🐢 🐢 🐢 🐢 🐢

I was invited to speak at the Prairie Firefighters and Muscular Dystrophy Conference in Edmonton on the first weekend in November. I was still on leave from work, and I felt I needed to do that speech to keep Thomas's legacy going and to share our story. Preparing the PowerPoint and the speech was somewhat therapeutic but difficult at the same. It reminded me of what a force Thomas had been and how determined he was to make a difference in our world. It also brought back so many memories, both good and bad. Glenn read over every word and helped me rewrite the script as I went along.

Only two months after Thomas's death, Glenn and I attended the conference. We both sat, shook our heads, and wiped away the tears as we heard a specialist say that muscular dystrophy patients should never receive oxygen because it builds up the carbon dioxide in the bloodstream and causes damage to the heart. If we had only known. There were so many times when Thomas was in an emergency room and the first response was to give him oxygen.

I guess the positive side, if there is one, is that Thomas was a trailblazer. When he was first diagnosed with LMNA muscular dystrophy, we were told he was one of three in the world who had this form of MD. Since then, more and more children continue to be diagnosed with the same kind of muscular dystrophy at a much younger age. Our hope is that parents, nurses, and doctors around the world will become more knowledgeable with this form of the disease and learn from Thomas's experience.

There were over one hundred firefighters at the conference, along with family members of people with muscular dystrophy. Everyone there was connected by muscular dystrophy. They were all excited to share their stories and concerns and network with one another, but more importantly, they wanted to learn more about the disease and obtain any new information that would assist their families. Somehow, I managed to get through the presentation with Glenn by my side. We received a standing ovation.

The presentation at the conference gave me a push to begin writing Thomas's story. So many people were suggesting we do a book to continue Thomas's legacy and to tell his life adventure. Glenn had also encouraged me to write. I felt that I needed not only to honour Thomas but to try to continue his legacy.

I have never considered myself a writer. My high school education in Nova Scotia never taught me how to write an essay, let alone a novel or story. But I wanted share with the world Thomas's story and hopefully give hope and inspiration to families with children with special needs. I wanted to reach out to teenagers needing that extra push to do their best, to show them what a kid in a wheelchair who may appear or feel seemingly completely helpless can do to make a difference. I also wanted to give insight to caregivers, nurses, and doctors.

As I wrote this story, Glenn continually gave me hugs and kisses every time my tears started to flow while remembering parts of Thomas's life.

Shortly after the conference, we felt we needed to take another step forward in the healing process. Thomas's favourite place was Easter Seals Camp Horizon, so I felt we needed to spread some of his ashes there. We received permission from Easter Seals to do this. Glenn's sister Susanne and brother-in-law Bill were in town from Vancouver; they wanted to be a part of this, too. Along with Glenn's parents, they accompanied Glenn, Jamie, and me.

Once we were at the camp, we decided on the best place to spread some of his ashes. Thomas loved his time around the campfire. The campfire site has a beautiful view of the Rocky Mountains. On this day, the sun was shining and it was unusually warm for that time of year. It felt like Thomas was there with us and opened up the skies to let the light shine on his favourite spot at camp. Glenn, Jamie, and I spread some of his ashes from his remains. Alice had brought some flowers she had saved, which Gregg had given to Thomas during his final days in the hospital. Everyone there was remembering Thomas and how much he loved Camp Horizon. We took turns sharing stories, remembering his incredible life and how much we all missed him.

Afterward, we wandered around the camp for a bit and then went into the main hall to look at the many pictures of Thomas in the collages on the walls showing the campers over the years.

Our family members were pleased that we had included them. We all shed tears that day.

It all felt so right.

Life Without Thomas

Glenn was worried about me and wondering when I was going to go back to work. He was thinking that I was taking too long to go back. Christmas was coming, which is a busy time for musicians. I thought that if I went back to prepare all the concerts, it would give me a new focus and a means to move through my grief. I decided to go back in the middle of November, after Remembrance Day.

My school invited me to an assembly before my return. My principal told me that the children had prepared something for me in remembrance of Thomas. The whole student body sang two songs. The one song that brought tears to my eyes was "Tomorrow" from the musical *Annie* It was moving, and the children could see my appreciation. The assembly was a good icebreaker to ease me back to work. So many children and parents gave me hugs at the assembly and I felt their support.

In hindsight, Remembrance Day was probably too soon to go back. There were many days I struggled just to get out of bed and get to school. But I kept telling myself that I had to move on, that I had a job, and that my kids at school needed me.

Christmas was approaching. And even though I was working to prepare the Christmas concerts, I had no desire to be at home over the holidays, nor did I have any holiday spirit. There were just too many memories, and this would be our first Christmas without Thomas. Glenn and I decided that we would take Jamie on a tropical vacation. We were worried that Glenn's parents would be upset, but they were in support and understood our intentions. Furthermore, Glenn's sister and her family were all coming to Calgary for Christmas, so we knew his parents wouldn't be alone.

🐢 🐢 🐢 🐢 🐢

It was the beginning of December when someone wanted to buy Thomas's van. The potential buyer was a young girl in her twenties who we had met at the firefighters' conference. She had muscular dystrophy and was in a wheelchair.

She bought the van after looking at the pictures we had taken. We arranged to meet her family in Airdrie (a small city ten minutes north of Calgary) because they were travelling south from Edmonton. She was thrilled. We knew it was going to a well-deserved home. Glenn drove the van and I followed behind in the car as we delivered it to its new owner. Tears were running down my cheeks. It was yet another piece of Thomas leaving us. We were both pretty quiet on the drive home.

Every time we see a grey van, we look to see if it is Thomas's. We had applied a cool wheelchair sticker to the left side of the back window. We would recognize that sticker anywhere. We only drove that van when Thomas was in it, and we never took advantage of the wheelchair parking when he wasn't with us.

🐢 🐢 🐢 🐢 🐢

We arranged for Thomas's interment to take place on December 13. It took until then to have the plaque made (his urn is in a columbarium).

It was a cold, grey, windy day. Jamie, Glenn's parents, my sister Marj, my niece Suzy, Gregg, and Jenn came along. I clutched Thomas's urn tightly as Glenn drove us to the cemetery. I didn't want to let it go. Up to that point, Thomas's urn had sat on our mantel.

At the vault, we had a vase attached to the plaque so we could place fresh flowers whenever we came to visit. We also had a picture of Thomas to place inside the vault with his urn. Glenn's parents brought a picture of the two of them to place inside, as well.

We were all quiet. I think we were each remembering Thomas in our own way. Glenn led us in a prayer for Thomas. It didn't take long for the staff to close the vault. Glenn, Jamie, and I held hands and said our good-byes again. And again it became quiet. Both Glenn and I felt a little strange seeing our names under Thomas's on the plaque, but we knew that one day our ashes would be placed with his. We don't want him to be alone.

We invited everyone back to the house afterward for snacks and beverages and to reflect upon the day. Another chapter in our lives was closed.

We miss seeing Thomas's urn on the mantel. Even though we now live in a different house, we again have a fireplace, and Thomas has his spot above it. His photo is there in place of the urn.

We continue to go to his gravesite at least every two weeks, if not more, to place fresh flowers in Thomas's vase. One of his favourite turtles hangs on the vase along with a red heart.

🐢 🐢 🐢 🐢 🐢

I managed to make it through the numerous concerts at my school and finish off the first part of the term. I was glad that it was over.

Toward the end of December, the three of us jumped on a plane for the Christmas holiday. We had decided to go to Playa del Carmen in Mexico. Jamie was looking forward to his first all-inclusive stay at a resort. The resort we chose was steps away from town, where there were lots of shops and restaurants. We didn't want anything too secluded. We feared Jamie might not have enough to do at the resort, and we thought the town might give him other options to keep him busy.

The weather was hot. We had a swim-out pool from our room and bottles of beverages in our room. Our hotel was right on the beach. The three of us played lots of cribbage and enjoyed delicious meals. We strolled the streets, checking out the many shops, and enjoyed a cold beverage or two along the way. On occasion, Jamie would take off to explore the resort, but he always returned for a swim or a game of cribbage.

It was interesting to be in Mexico for Christmas. The palm trees were decorated with Christmas ornaments, and the hotel played holiday music everywhere. Some of the staff dressed up and acted out the nativity story on Christmas Eve. We had to chuckle at the Mexican staff dressed as Mary, Joseph, and the Wise Men. We even saw Santa Claus ride into the pool area on a Harley-Davidson motorcycle, handing out Mexican candy to the guests.

The week flew by. The three of us agreed that it was a good decision to go away for Christmas. We certainly thought of Thomas every day, but it was easier to do that in Mexico than at home where we would have been faced with the struggle of carrying on all of our usual traditions without him.

After returning home to Calgary, Glenn and I spent a quiet New Year's Eve. We were in bed by ten. We both remembered how much Thomas enjoyed staying up until midnight. Many years, Glenn and I would fall asleep on the couch while Thomas watched the countdowns on TV. It was pretty strange not having him there with us.

Overall, we made it through the Christmas break. We didn't go out much and, I have to admit, we were very selective in answering the phone. So many people were thinking of us but they didn't know what to say or do. Most people seemed to be a loss for words. No one ever wants to go through the loss of a child. Nor can anyone ever imagine what it feels like unless they have gone through it.

🐢 🐢 🐢 🐢 🐢

Friends. Well, as I said, they came and went. I was devastated after Thomas's passing when a "friend" of mine said, "You know, Thomas has been gone for a couple of months. It is time you let it go. People gave their support at the time, and now it is done. People forget. It is time to move on."

Wow! Words cannot express what I still feel when I think about that comment. To this day, I cannot forgive her. I used to think of myself as a forgiving person. I tend to "pick my battles," but this comment hit so hard, I'm not sure I can ever let it go. It hit my core, or what was left of it.

We lost our son. There is no "letting go" of the void his death created, and grief isn't an emotion that can just be switched off and on.

🐢 🐢 🐢 🐢 🐢

Somehow, 2015 arrived. A new year with many familiar occasions that would feel different … new … like we were experiencing them for the first time. From this point forward, holidays, birthdays, other significant events would all take place without Thomas.

Both Glenn and I were back to work. It seemed more difficult for me this time. Just getting out of bed was a feat. I had lost the joy of teaching. I guess my job felt like a mundane routine. I was going through the motions rather than celebrating a new beginning with my students. It felt like there was nothing to look forward to.

Thomas's birthday was approaching, another of the "firsts." And this was a big one. There was no way I could face a full day of excited kids on the day of his birthday, so I called in sick. I knew I wouldn't be able to hold my composure, so I didn't even try.

Glenn and I went out to place fresh flowers for Thomas on the morning of his birthday. I had also booked an appointment for an angel reading for later in the day because I felt that I would be closer to Thomas on his birthday. An angel reader is similar to a psychic in the sense that she (in my case) is able to intuit what those who have passed away are trying to convey to the living. I was hesitant to tell Glenn about my appointment, as I feared that he would think I was silly in believing in such a thing, but he was totally understanding. He drove me to the appointment and sat in the truck while I was there.

The angel reading was fascinating. My reader was able to connect me to Thomas through holding my hands. I wanted to believe what she told me, so I was careful not to give any specific information. I wanted her to reveal to me things she could not possibly know. And she did.

According to her reading, Thomas knew that I had bathed him after his passing. She was able to describe my mom and dad and grandparents, who were there to meet Thomas when he passed. In celebration of his birthday Thomas was holding red balloons. (I hadn't told her that day was his birthday.)

She assured me that Thomas was by my bedside and with us every night as we went to sleep. She talked about a dried rose in a vase in our room and said that Thomas was seeing that rose. I hadn't told her the rose was there! This was the rose that Glenn had on my pillow when I returned from Mexico and he had been in Denmark.

According to her, Thomas knew I was writing a book about him and he was happy. He was busy running around and keeping an eye on everyone he cared for, including riding around with Jamie in his truck during his workdays. She also told me that Thomas was standing, and he was very tall and handsome and happy to be out of his wheelchair.

And yes, there were some things she said that did not make sense. The number twenty-two. That meant nothing to me. She told me to look out for that. (I still have no idea what significance "twenty-two" could have.)

All in all, I was calmed. I felt my son's presence. I tried to remember everything she had said so I could share my experience with Glenn.

In February, we received a phone call from the Children's Wish Foundation. They wanted Jamie, Glenn, and me to attend their annual gala. They also wanted to interview one or all of us about Thomas's wish. Wanting to continue Thomas's story, we agreed.

I also received an email about an upcoming conference for people working with students at risk. The conference focused on evidence-based programs and strategies educators can use to prevent dropouts and help students succeed. I have no idea how the conference organizer got my name, but here was yet another opportunity to share Thomas's story. The conference was in March in Calgary. Glenn helped me rewrite the script we had prepared for the muscular dystrophy conference. It would be perfect for this event.

Glenn and I were pretty much homebodies at this point. Outside of work, we didn't want to talk to anyone. We rarely went out, but we did spend all of our time outside of work together. We didn't feel like entertaining, which had been a regular occurrence only a year before. Instead, we discovered Internet access to TV shows that we had missed over the years and watched many TV series together in the comfort of our living room: *Suits*, *The Good Wife*, and the Marvel series. These programs took our minds off Thomas for a brief time. We didn't feel much like doing anything else.

My fifty-fifth birthday was another first without Thomas. Glenn spoiled me, buying me lots of presents and spreading them out throughout the day. This was something I had always done for the boys while they were growing up. I had always planned the gift-giving so they would get their last present just as they were going to bed. Glenn knew it would be a tough day for me. I would have preferred simply skipping the day in every way, but he pushed me to be positive and tried to make me celebrate. Both Jamie and Thomas always did the countdown on birthdays, mine included. They would sing "Happy Birthday" every chance they had throughout the day. This year, there wasn't much singing, but Jamie called and texted several times to wish me a happy birthday. I did end up making it through the day, but I was happy when it was over.

The Students at Risk Conference came soon after. Glenn made time to come and listen to my presentation. He stood in the back, smiling, and watching the audience's reaction. Many came up to Glenn after the presentation and spoke to him after recognizing him from the pictures I showed in the presentation. I was so pleased that he was there for support and to experience the feedback. There were approximately seventy-five people in attendance at my session. I could see from their expressions that Thomas's story and our experience raising Thomas made an impression on them. Some needed tissues, and lots of people chuckled at the humorous stories about Thomas. It made me realize that I needed to continue writing Thomas's story …

Honouring Our Son

Even though Thomas was physically no longer with us, we didn't want to end any of our relationships with the charities Thomas and our family were involved in. Both Glenn and I wanted to continue our support for various organizations that had become important to us over the years. I had remained on the executive council for the Calgary chapter of Muscular Dystrophy Canada after Thomas went to Carleton. I wanted to give back to our community and, at that time, I had the time to volunteer. I wanted to help.

Along with a Christmas party for the MD kids and their parents at the end of that year and a June barbeque at Camp Horizon, my helping our local Muscular Dystrophy Canada chapter included organizing and hosting an event in April with a specialist from Edmonton. Glenn and I had met Dr. Janice the previous November at the firefighter conference. While Glenn and I listened to her presentation, we were both shaking our heads in disbelief. She was a wealth of information on people with neuromuscular diseases. We remembered learning in November that giving a patient with muscular dystrophy oxygen not only increases the carbon dioxide in their systems (increased carbon dioxide can lead to damage to the respiratory system and the central nervous system), but it causes major damage to the heart and could possibly lead to death. She reiterated this point at the April event, and there were multiple other points she made that could have been helpful in prolonging Thomas's life. We only wished we had heard her speak months earlier. We knew she had important information for other families living with muscular dystrophy. The session was very well-received. So many individuals learned how to care for their muscular dystrophy.

Glenn and I had volunteered to act as her host for the day. We picked her up from the airport, took her to lunch, accompanied her to the speaking session, then returned her to the airport. During our time with her, we had the opportunity to speak with her about Thomas and his passing. We appreciated her knowledge although for Thomas, it was too late. But we were both happy that Dr. Janice could at least share her expertise with the participants at the event. Maybe her advice would help others in the future.

🐢 🐢 🐢 🐢 🐢

Carleton University had also contacted us at the beginning of the new year wanting to speak to us about our wishes for the memorial scholarship. Glenn thought we should go to Ottawa to meet with them. I agreed, believing it would be another healing part of our journey, especially for Glenn, who had not been back to the campus since we brought Thomas home. We flew out for a weekend in April 2015 to meet with Diane Chea, Director of Philanthropy, and also saw many of Thomas's friends and caregivers.

Before we were to meet with this department, Glenn warned me that if I was going to break down, he would ask me to leave, as he, too, was emotional. We were both thinking of Thomas and how excited he had been to attend Carleton and pursue his educational dreams. There were so many reminders all around us at the campus, from Thomas's first days to the hospital visits. We were saddened that our son was not able to fulfill his scholarly dreams, yet excited and proud to be able to start this scholarship so that other students could benefit from his legacy.

Our meeting with the scholarship department was productive. Mainly, we wanted to know that Thomas's scholarship would be handled properly, so Glenn was focused on this aspect of the process. I only lost it once, just briefly, but I made it through the meeting. The staff looking after the scholarship explained how the process with donations and recipients worked. They asked us if we had specific qualifications for the recipients and invited us to give them suggestions. We specified it was to be open to all Canadian students with a disability who had big dreams. The money could be used at their discretion. They also requested we submit a short write-up about Thomas and what he stood for. Afterward, four staff members took us to lunch, and they gave us a tour through the Paul Menton Centre, where

Thomas had received so much support setting up his classes. It was good to be back in Ottawa.

After the trip to Carleton, we came home in time to attend the Muscular Dystrophy Gala to show our support, and a couple of weeks later, we attended the Children's Wish Foundation Gala. It was a sunny, warm evening for the Wish gala, and we were dressed in our Sunday best. At this function, I was to be interviewed, which I was nervous about. Glenn and Jamie opted out of the interview but showed their support by coming to the event. We had given the organizers some pictures of Thomas on his trip to Denmark and Legoland and were happy to share these memories. Many in attendance had read about Thomas. The evening was a huge success; the organizers felt that my interview encouraged their attendees to dig deep into their pockets. Two of the Children's Wish Foundation's staff later came to visit us at our home and thank us for our support. The Children's Wish Foundation is one charity we will always embrace and support.

One of the directors from Easter Seals contacted me that month, as well. They were celebrating the fiftieth anniversary of Camp Horizon and wanted me to be a speaker for their event. They wanted something from a mother of a camper who had passed away. In their fifty years, they had never made such a request.

They also wanted to know our thoughts on where the money donated in Thomas's memory should go at the camp. Over $12,000 had been donated in his memory. We wanted something at the camp that would remain for many years to honour Thomas. Up until this point, we had not really come up with an idea, but once we met up with the camp's staff, it occurred to me that perhaps with some of the money, we could have a bench made. It would be something that could be seen and used at the camp.

Thomas had always loved the television shows *The Timber Kings* and *The Carver Kings*, featuring world-renowned log home builders from Williams Lake, BC. He enjoyed seeing the many different carvings the men created. We agreed that I would look into the possibility of having one of these men create a bench for the camp. I had no idea what the cost would be but only imagined that it would be a lot.

I was excited about the possibility of having something at camp to memorialize Thomas. I started making phone calls.

When Glenn got home from work later the same day I got the call from the camp, I was elated. I couldn't wait to share my news. I had already called Pioneer Homes in Williams Lake and connected with one of the main workers at the company. We immediately made a connection over the phone. He, too, had lost a child and understood what we were going through. He was very gracious and open to having a bench carved in Thomas's memory at an incredibly low price. Glenn was a bit upset with me, not because of the purchase of the bench, but because I didn't include him in the process. I felt bad about that but excluding him hadn't been my intention. Once we talked about it, Glenn was happy about the idea of a beautifully carved bench for Thomas and thought, too, that it would be perfect for the camp. We were hoping that it would be ready and delivered to the camp for the fiftieth anniversary event.

The anniversary event was scheduled for June 20, the fiftieth anniversary of the date the camp was established. Campers, volunteers, sponsors, and staff from throughout the fifty years were on hand to celebrate and reminisce. Both Glenn and Jamie came with me to the event in support, and Jamie helped me write a script:

> *Good afternoon, special guests, Easter Seals volunteers, staff, family, and friends. I feel honoured to have been asked to share a few words today.*
>
> *Today we celebrate fifty years of Easter Seals Camp Horizon. For countless children and adults with disabilities, it has been a home away from home, a beacon of anticipation for a summer of fun, and escape from the harsh realities of everyday life.*
>
> *It is an unfortunate reality that many who attend camp here are taken too soon from friends and loved ones, and we would like to take this time to remember all those who left a lasting impression on our lives. They could come to Camp Horizon, feel comfortable in their own skin, and help*

others in their own special way. Many are inspired by the camp to pursue their dreams in life. This was so for our son Thomas who attended Camp Horizon for ten years, gaining independence and freedom he used to pursue an education at Carleton University in Ottawa.

Easter Seals Camp Horizon has provided fifty years of inspiration and wonder for its campers. It has created generations of leaders and continues to be a pillar of happiness for those who hope to forge a legacy.

Patti had asked me to find a poem that represents our loved ones who have passed. I had trouble finding one that was fitting, so instead, I wrote the following:

Tenacity, vision, success. These are some attributes that put others ahead of the rest.

We gain insight, inspiration, and love from those that lived each day to their best.

They never complained, let nothing stand in their way.

They wanted to make a difference each and every day.

We can only hope that we can live up to their expectations in our way.

To continue their dreams, making them as proud as we are of those who have already passed away.

Here's to the next fifty years of Easter Seals Camp Horizon.

Thank you!

Honouring Our Son

Unfortunately, Thomas's bench had not arrived. The staff was also disappointed, but we knew it would come soon and be placed at the camp for Thomas. The day was about Camp Horizon.

One tough moment was when the master of ceremonies, Darrel Janz,[28] said hello to me and Glenn. Even though we had met him several times with Thomas at other functions over the years, we reintroduced ourselves. He knew who Thomas was and remembered him. He then asked if Thomas was present for the celebration. He quickly realized what he had said and covered his mouth. Glenn grabbed my hand in support. I was taken off guard. I composed myself and reminded him that Thomas had passed away, but I told Darrel that I knew he was there with us in spirit.

Thomas's bench arrived in July 2015 and now sits proudly at the entrance of Camp Horizon in front of the new dorm. We go out often to visit and always place flowers on the bench.

It was June 2015—slightly more than half a year since Thomas's passing. Another winter and another school year were coming to an end. I was so ready for some downtime, and Glenn was looking forward to summer, as well. We sat on the deck with our coffee in the mornings and played cribbage together in the evenings. We were thinking that we would have a fairly quiet summer and had only planned one trip near the end of summer to a niece's wedding in Nova Scotia.

Glenn's dad was turning eighty. This was a big milestone, not only because he was celebrating eighty years, but because he had been diagnosed with lung cancer six years prior and had been given six months to live. It seemed only fitting that Hans was throwing a big party at the local Danish Canadian Club.

---

28   Darrel Janz, now retired, was a long-time, well-known CTV news anchor in Calgary. Although he has been officially retired from the media for several years, he often MCs and attends fundraisers and other community events in and around Calgary.

All the extended Sorensen family was travelling to Calgary in July for his birthday on the ninth. We received a couple of calls and emails asking if family members could stay with us at our house and we agreed before we realized what we were committing to. The party celebration was only for one day; however, the family stayed for a week. In the end, we had seven family members staying at our house for a full week. We really didn't mind, but it was not how we had planned our summer. There were meals to cook, bedding and towels to clean, and the push and pull of family dynamics to endure. Putting smiles on our faces for a week straight and trying to be gracious hosts took a lot out of us. As much as we enjoyed seeing the family, we were happy when they left so we could each catch our breath.

The birthday celebration was festive. We wrote songs and sang them, keeping up with the Danish tradition, ate great food, and mingled with Hans's and Alice's friends. In spite of the merry atmosphere, though, I was having a tough time. Other than our niece's wedding the previous fall, this was the first major family celebration without Thomas. I was a bit saddened that Hans didn't mention anything about Thomas in his speech or even in conversation throughout the night. Maybe he thought it was not the place.

Over the years, we had had so many family celebrations at the Danish Club, and Thomas loved going there. His absence weighed heavily on us. By early evening, Glenn and I were ready to leave. My emotions were on edge, and Glenn had to work the next day. We actually asked Glenn's parents for permission to leave, but his mother was not happy. She said it was too early for us to leave. We hummed and hawed about whether to stay or go, but we finally turned to each other and said, "Let's go." I had tears in my eyes as we left. It was just too much. We were "in the doghouse" with Glenn's parents for a while, but they eventually got over it.

We had three more sets of company in July. It seemed like we were running a hotel, but we did enjoy parts of each visit. I had several opportunities to visit Thomas's gravesite and go to Camp Horizon to show off Thomas's bench to our visitors.

My first opportunity to see the bench was when my niece and her two boys were here visiting from Seattle. The four of us drove out to camp after visiting Thomas's gravesite. It was a beautiful, sunny summer day. The bench had only just arrived and was in the maintenance building to be varnished for the outside weather. Seeing it brought tears to my eyes. Thomas's name was engraved on the front of the backrest, and there were wonderful turtles carved next to his name. Many family members have since requested to go out to the camp to see the bench in person, and everyone agrees that it is a beautiful tribute to Thomas's memory, one which campers can enjoy using for years to come.

After our last group of visitors had left, Glenn and I finally had some "us time." We booked a trip to New York City for a couple of days, then a cruise to Bermuda for a week in August. In both places, we walked the sights, held hands, played crib, and answered to no one.

After the cruise, we flew to Nova Scotia for my niece's wedding. We were going to stay with my sister Sue and her husband, Bruce. It was their youngest daughter getting married, and we knew they needed help in preparations. We were happy to help out, knowing how much Sue and Bruce helped us during the funeral. We wanted to return the favour. We arrived in Halifax, where we spent two days and nights pretending to be tourists. We went to a seaside restaurant we had visited many years before with both Jamie and Thomas. It brought back many memories, and the food tasted just as good. Nova Scotia scallops, clam chowder, and fresh lobster. What a treat!

From Halifax we drove to New Glasgow. It had been several years since I had been home. Both my parents had passed away years prior, and Glenn suggested we stop and pick up flowers and go and visit my parents and grandparents at the cemetery. Our first stop after buying bouquets was the Lorne Street Cemetery. First, we found my grandparents' gravestone. Sadly, it had been knocked over. We tried to set it upright but it was too heavy. We placed the flowers on top of the gravestone.

Then we started looking for my parents' stone. The graveyard was in bad shape. The grass was long, and there was dried grass covering all the stones. We finally found my parents' gravestone and placed flowers for them. Glenn spoke to my mom, telling her that he has always regretted never meeting her. My mom passed away when I was only twenty-one years old. Glenn did meet my dad, though. His fondest memory of my dad, perhaps, is their first meeting when Dad asked Glenn how old he was. When Glenn replied, Dad's comment was, "You are just a boy! You probably don't even know who the Beatles are!" After we left Nova Scotia, my sister arranged to have my grandparents' gravestone repaired.

Throughout our journey, Glenn wouldn't let me drive. He was worried that I was too excited to be home and that I might have an accident. He drove us past my mom and dad's first house, my old high school, and the house where I grew up. Memories were flooding back from my past, and I was enjoying every minute.

We made our way to Sue and Bruce's place in the country, a few minutes outside of New Glasgow. The long, winding roads, the greenery in the trees, and the hot summer air reached out to our senses. Bruce was at work and Sue was in town shopping when we pulled up. They had the front door unlocked for our arrival. My eldest sister, Jane, and her husband, Mike, showed up at the house, and then Sue got back from town. My sister Marj was close behind. We all exchanged hugs and kisses and enjoyed a wonderful family dinner together that evening. The food was delicious, but more important were the meaningful company and conversations, catching up with all of our news. The nieces and their children came and went. Sue filled us in on the wedding plans.

Glenn and I were busy. We cleaned, we cooked, we served. We did anything Sue and Bruce wanted us to do. The wedding rehearsal party was the next day with thirty-five in attendance. We spent that day preparing food for the wedding and decorating the hall for the reception. Glenn hung out with Bruce delivering tree branches to the hall and shelling 90 lbs of lobster. He never complained about anything. That's my husband. We didn't really see a lot of each other throughout the day, but we managed to crawl into bed at night knowing that we had been helpful.

The wedding was hugely successful. It was held outside, which led to a bit of tension for most of the day; it poured rain all day until one hour before the wedding. Hay bales covered with beautiful handmade quilts were used for seating. The guests arrived to witness the country wedding of two wonderful souls. The reception was held in town at a community centre and included lots of food, drink, and dancing. The live band was fantastic. They played everyone's favourites—songs that guests loved to dance to—and they even took requests. People partied into the wee hours

Honouring Our Son

of the night. The bride and groom were happy, as were the parents, Sue, and Bruce.

After this grand event, Glenn and I headed back to Calgary knowing that not only had we returned the favour of helping but we also got to experience Sue and Bruce's world.

As much as we enjoyed our time away, it was good to be home. The only downside was that we would have to return to work. And the one-year anniversary of Thomas's death was just a few days away—September 1, which was also the first day of classes for the students at my school.

Part of me wanted to run away, but the other part was telling me to be strong and be there for the first day. Glenn asked me what I wanted to do. My principal also realized the importance of that day. He said that if I felt okay to come into work, he would let everyone know that there would be no music classes on the first day. He told me I could come and go as needed. There was always a lot going on the first day and help was needed in so many areas. I felt that I was okay to go in, and being a senior staff member, I knew I could help out in many ways without having to teach an actual class. Meanwhile, Glenn and Jamie had their own discussions about me. They were worried about me and how I was feeling. They wanted me to decide what we should do about visiting Thomas's gravesite and about our dinner plans for the evening.

After work that day, Jamie came along with us to visit Thomas at his gravesite. We did pop into Glenn's parents' house after we saw Thomas, and then the three of us went for dinner at our neighbourhood pub. Dinner itself was okay. We had all remained pretty calm all day, but we had our quiet times remembering Thomas. I was hoping that the one-year anniversary would be a major crossing point, that I would not be so emotional, that I could move ahead. I had been trying to tell myself that all summer. We were finished with the "firsts:" Thanksgiving, Christmas, birthdays, Easter, Mother's, and Father's Day.

So here we were, at the beginning the second year without Thomas. We continued to go on a day-by-day basis.

We still miss Thomas so very much.

Glenn:

So, every year on Thomas's birthday and the anniversary of his death, Kathy and I put flowers on his grave and stop somewhere for supper and reminisce.

Afterword

Thomas's legacy

Little did we know, as parents, just how much of an impact Thomas had on others. We had certainly worked with him to give back to the organizations that had supported him. We tried to fuel his passion in his areas of volunteering. Thomas glowed when it came to sharing his beliefs in making the world a better place. We are still so very proud of him for standing up for what he believed in.

When people saw how open and giving he was, they opened their own hearts. The passion and enthusiasm that poured from him was infectious, and people wanted to return it in kind. It might have been through a gift they gave to Thomas, or a donation they made to an MD-related organization, or a smile, or sharing a lasting impression that impacted their lives. We continue to receive stories about how Thomas influenced people. The donations made in Thomas's memory to his favourite charities have continued to increase over the years.

Carleton University now has two memorial scholarships named The Thomas Sorensen Memorial Scholarship. They are available to students with disabilities who have "big dreams." There are two scholarships, granting recipients $3,000 each. We are hoping that donations continue so the scholarships will continue in perpetuity, giving two $5,000 scholarships each year. We are now going to start a third scholarship for graduate studies. There are no restrictions on where the money goes. We recognize the extra costs to students such as taxi cabs, bandages, etc. Even paying for groceries may be a struggle for some of these students at times. We want these scholarships to go wherever the student needs the money.

In January 2016, during my last year at Canyon Meadows School, the parent council purchased "buddy benches" for the school playground. These are benches designated for children to sit on if they feel lonely or don't have any friends. The idea is that when a child is sitting on a buddy bench, other children can see that this child needs a friend and can go and sit with them. I was overwhelmed to find out that the parent council were dedicating the benches in Thomas's memory. The plaque on the benches reads "Thomas Sorensen 1996–2014. A Friend to Anyone Who Needed One." The school had a special assembly to dedicate the benches and invited our family and Thomas's friend Gregg. A former principal came to speak about Thomas's impact on the students. He broke down in tears as he was speaking.

In November 2016, two years after Thomas's passing, we received a message from Santa Kim. His appearance on Christmas Eve was always one of Thomas's favourite parts of Christmas. Kim told us that he was being honoured at a Calgary Stampeders football game as one of their top fans. The Stampeders were doing a video about Kim as a fan, and as a thank you, they were allowing him to choose a charity of his choice to receive $3,000. Kim chose Easter Seals Camp Horizon in memory of Thomas. He invited Glenn and me to the game, where we had special seats to watch the game and to view the video in honour of both Kim and Thomas. It was special, too, as Jamie was also attending. In fact, he was working his last day as a security supervisor for that game.

We found out after Thomas's passing that a group of campers from Camp Horizon decided to hold an annual hockey tournament in Thomas's honour. Each year, at the beginning of the summer, the campers and staff have a hockey game called the Thomas Memorial Hockey Cup Tournament. I was privileged to attend the game a few years ago to see the involvement, the passion, and the memories. I mingled with so many of Thomas's camp friends, some of whom I'd never previously met. They were thrilled that I attended. One of Thomas's friends had some help in making a "trophy" for the winning team out of cardboard and silver spray paint. I hope this event will continue for years to come.

Thomas achieved character, built citizenship with his community through helping others, gained a vast amount of compassion, and became a better person because of all he did. He has left a legacy, touching more lives than we will ever know.

The time since Thomas passed has been difficult. There are reminders everywhere. In the beginning, when I was walking down a grocery store aisle it hit me—a certain memory of Thomas—and I started to cry. Other times, someone who does not know he passed asks me how Thomas is doing. And still, every now and then, out of the corner of my eye, I see something—a movement, shadows, a flash of light—and think it is Thomas sending a message. So many daily events and sights remind me of Thomas, and I know he is with me. It might sound odd, but that is how it is.

Glenn's final thoughts

When Kathy started writing this book, I decided to write my own chapter, so here it goes.

Raising Thomas was incredibly challenging for our family at times, and maybe some families like ours have equally or more difficult challenges to face. Trust me on this: throughout the years we have seen many families fall apart over having a sick child. Sometimes, one of the family members can't handle the stress. We've heard many excuses over the years like, "I didn't sign up for this," or "I want my freedom and my life back." Soon, we hear that one of the parents walks out, leaving one parent alone, perhaps with more than one child to raise and take care of. I had always assumed it would be the man who left, but I was wrong. We found that it's equally men and women who run away. Being left alone to raise a handicapped child compounds the difficulty that already exists.

Please believe me when I say having Thomas was worth every minute of every day. Watching your children grow up, even if one of them is handicapped, is the most rewarding experience life has to offer. There can be lots of laughter and joy watching them grow and mature, even among the challenges that every parent faces. We had many happy times. Even with the hard times mixed in and with their sometimes-shortened lives, raising a handicapped child *is worth it*! Kathy and I would go back in a heartbeat and do it all over again just to have Thomas back even for a short while. Yes, we truly value every precious moment we had with him.

As a family, Kathy, Jamie, and I have grown, matured, and learned to be humble and more positive in life. Our outlook on life, especially when we see other handicapped people or families, is so different now. I can't explain it; you likely wouldn't understand this perspective unless you could walk in our shoes. Our own family members think they understand, but, sadly, we know most don't.

Kathy is my soulmate. I think raising two kids together (especially Thomas) and sharing all these life experiences has made our love for each other stronger. Even after Thomas's passing, our love for one another has continued to deepen and be more fulfilling. We love being together. It's almost like we can read each other's minds. Yes, that might seem weird, but it's true. I love being together. Kathy and I have a wonderful, loving relationship.

Well, what more can I say? Writing my little bit from a father's perspective can't hurt, and hopefully, it will help you realize that as sad as it can be at times, life is still good. I would go back and do it all over, not changing a thing.

Writing my part of this story has been a long and challenging journey. Because some of the sections have been very emotional for me, I've had to leave it alone for weeks or even a good month at times. When I wanted to continue, I would read everything I'd written up to that point to get my head back in it so I could continue my story. I have really tried to give you an accurate account of our lives and hopefully a bit of understanding of what it's like to walk in our shoes.

I would really like to believe and hope that when you see handicapped people in your everyday life, you will treat them as human beings with the respect they deserve and not treat them like they have the plague. Some handicapped people just need a small helping hand to live a long and productive life and to be able to contribute to society. And some just need a smile in order to feel as though they've been acknowledged as a "normal" human.

Thomas was a true advocate and champion for handicapped people. He strived and worked hard right up to the last day of his life to change people's attitudes about those who are handicapped and to educate others that those with disabilities are people with feelings and dreams, as well.

Afterword

Thomas was a guest speaker at many galas and functions over the years in hopes of trying to bring this awareness to more people. He also did a conference call once a year for several years with all the bigwigs at the Safeway head office. He talked to everyone he could about what it is like being handicapped and what we can all do to make this world a better place. Thomas hated lazy handicapped people because he felt they made him look bad, and he really wanted to change their attitudes, as well. If they were lazy, he never wanted to be around them.

If you have a handicapped child, I strongly recommend you enroll your child from an early age in some camp or organization for handicapped children. It's good for them. It increases their self-esteem and gives them an opportunity to develop great relationships with other kids while enjoying activities they may not otherwise get to take part in. And you get a few hours of respite for yourselves, which you do need. You can't be "on" 100 per cent of the time. Thomas met so many wonderful and true lifelong friends at Camp Horizon—not only the counsellors but also fellow campers. He felt that he was he fully accepted, and he was also able to help out fellow campers in his own way. Easter Seals Camp Horizon built Thomas's confidence and challenged him to push his limits. Kathy and I got to meet the people there, and we also were able to find some wonderful future caregivers. Thomas's time at camp also allowed us to have a break—a moment to be able to just not worry about everything. It worked for us all.

I believe that Carleton University is the only university in Canada, and maybe the US, that is set up for handicapped students with specially-equipped dorms and 24-7 care. The university has proximity readers on the doors that allow the students in wheelchairs access to the buildings when they approach. Even though Thomas was handicapped and could not even scratch his nose, the faculty and other staff at Carleton made him feel like an independent, responsible adult. With their support, he could do anything. Even though Thomas would phone home almost every day to talk to his mother, he was happy to be there and loved every minute of it. We never had to worry while Thomas was there; the attendants were just that good. From putting the students to bed at night; getting them up in the morning; helping with breakfast, lunch, or dinner; even doing their laundry—whatever the students' needs were—the caregivers handled it all.

Although this university was a five-hour plane ride away from home, we felt comfortable and confident that Thomas was in good hands. We highly recommend this institution if your child wants to go to university. They will give you a tour, answer all your questions, and send you home with lots of literature.

Yes, your child can go to university! Why shouldn't they? Don't keep your child home forever because you want to keep them safe. All it takes is for you to say, "Yes you can," over and over, to your child from an early age. Yes, you can. We always told Thomas he could be anything he wanted when he grew up. We knew he would never drive a car. So did Thomas. He knew what his limitations were, but having parents who always encourage their kids to strive for their dreams and to be the best that they can make a difference. It's much better to say, "Yes, you can," instead of "No, you can't."

I haven't said a whole lot about our son Jamie in all this. I should at least mention that Jamie is, and has always been, a wonderful son and a fantastic brother to Thomas. Jamie and Thomas had a really positive and special relationship. There were many times over the years that Jamie went that extra mile for his brother and included him in almost everything. Even some of Jamie's friends would come and watch Thomas for a couple of hours if the rest of us had commitments. Yes, they were brothers and teased each other, but the love they had for each other was evident. Even in the last hours of Thomas's life when he was heavily sedated, Thomas spoke out loud and said, "Jamie, I love you!" As I recall, those were the last words we ever heard Thomas say.

We have asked Jamie if he would like to contribute to this story and write in his own words his memories and thoughts, good and bad, of what it was like growing up with a handicapped sibling. Jamie is very private and has told us that he didn't want to write anything for the book. We respect his wishes. However, he did give us permission to include the following section, which he wrote for Thomas's scholarships set up at Carleton.

Jamie Speaks.

Eighteen years is a beginning: the beginning of adulthood, of starting one's life away from the constraints of societal pressures to go to school and be a part of a system of limitation. At eighteen years, the world is your

Afterword

oyster, and you are free to pursue any path you wish to take. My brother, Thomas, passed away at eighteen. However, his eighteen years were not by any means average. Thomas had a rare form of muscular dystrophy. And though he was physically confined to a wheelchair from an early age, his mind was brilliant and his ambition limitless. He was defined but not *confined* by his disability. Thomas utterly refused to let his disease serve as an excuse. Instead, he wore it prominently for the world to see.

Throughout his life, Thomas was passionate in his quest for disability advocacy. He would never turn down an opportunity to educate anyone willing to listen, attending countless events and charity fundraisers as a speaker and representative. Thomas would not see life's challenges as such, but rather as opportunities to prove they could be overcome. He would not avoid or even find a way around obstacles, instead, opting to charge through them head-on. As high school was wrapping up, Thomas was determined to assert his independence and decided to pursue an education at Carleton University. Thomas's dream was to study viral vectors as a means to cure disease. He successfully petitioned the Alberta government for funding to allow him to attend university outside the province, which he deserved.

While Thomas's story is inspirational, there is more to it than his accomplishments. Thomas was an extremely caring individual. He would always find time for his friends and family, and he was never afraid to introduce himself to someone new and include them in his life. He was full of wit, able to make anyone smile on their worst days, and was not one to complain about the problems he was facing in his own life. Whether it was determination or sheer stubbornness, there is no denying his internal drive to make the world a better place. Even in his final hours, he was not ready to go. Not out of fear, but out of an undying will to accomplish more.

Eighteen years is a beginning … the beginning of the legacy of Thomas Sorensen.

Kathy's final thoughts

I am heartbroken that Thomas didn't live out all of his dreams. He wanted to do more. I am devastated that he didn't experience everything that could have been his first love and the relationship that goes with that, his dream of finding cures for diseases, and typical life experiences when you come of age and move through the various phases of adult life. He accomplished so much and yet, in many ways, he was only beginning. Most of all, I truly miss him everyday.

Glenn and I always wanted to be able to provide the best for our boys. At the same time, we didn't want to offer anything on a silver platter. With my parents being much older when I was born—Mom was forty-one and Dad was fifty—and me being the youngest of five girls, a strong work ethic was certainly a part of my life.

Although I feel no regrets about my own childhood, raising Thomas brought about many pangs of guilt. To begin with, Glenn and I were told we were both carriers of muscular dystrophy. When Thomas was about two-and-a-half years old, Glenn and I were told that our chances of meeting each other, each carrying the mutant gene, and having Thomas were one in millions. We were also advised not to have more children since our odds would be the same. We decided, sadly, not to have more children. We would have loved many more. When Thomas was seventeen and it was finally confirmed that he had LMNA, we learned that we were not both carriers of the genetic mutation after all. However, up to that point, we both felt responsible for passing on the mutant gene that caused Thomas's disease; we felt that having a child with special needs was "our fault." It was a very difficult mindset to overcome.

In addition, we were always concerned about Jamie. We constantly wondered if he was getting enough attention, getting enough parent time and family time. When planning events or trips, we always had to make specific considerations and decisions because of the wheelchair and the need for accessibility. We always felt guilty that Jamie was not getting a "normal" childhood, and even though he never indicated any such feelings to us, we feared that he felt he was missing out on opportunities because of the care required for Thomas.

I also feel bad about not always including Thomas. There certainly were many times when Thomas wanted to go grocery shopping with me, but I have to say, sometimes I just needed to get out on my own and get the list completed. I knew if Thomas came along it would take so much longer to get anything done. Just loading and unloading the wheelchair took additional time. That is one thing I now feel guilty about. Thomas so enjoyed getting out, spending time with me, and having an opportunity for input on groceries. Now, I wish I could take Thomas grocery shopping with me.

I also miss the wake-up calls. Thomas would call for me every night, from one to eighteen times a night. I always tried to tuck him in, as he always felt that I did it best. Because we lived by a lake and had year-round spiders, and with his fear of spiders, he insisted that his blankets be well-tucked leaving no opportunity for any spiders to get at him. It was always quite a process to get the blankets tucked just right and to adjust his favourite "arm pillow," a pillow that gave his permanently bent arms and wrists more comfort. Nine times out of ten, after arranging all of this and getting his BiPAP mask in place, I would brush my teeth and crawl into bed, and then two minutes later be called to go and readjust everything for him. You have to remember, I was pretty much always exhausted and just wanted to sleep. There were nights when I felt so exhausted that I was impatient with Thomas, and yes, a bit angry, after having been awakened. Again, I miss those days and feel guilty even thinking about the times when I was grumpy about them.

Many times Thomas was invited to speak on behalf of a variety of non-profit organizations. Most of these occasions were on weekdays. I couldn't always take time off work to attend and had to scramble to find a caregiver who was available to accompany Thomas. I felt bad that I couldn't go to support Thomas and recognize his accomplishments. I was always very proud of his devotion when it came to agencies he wanted to support.

Friends were always important to Thomas. We tried to keep him busy and involved with his friends, including inviting them over for sleepovers. It was easier for other parents to have their child come to our house than for them to have Thomas to their homes. I always felt bad for Thomas when a friend had a birthday party and he wasn't invited. I understand that some of the parents didn't know what to expect when inviting a child in a wheelchair and were sometimes intimidated at the responsibility that came with him. Whenever Thomas was invited to a birthday, I always accompanied him unless they were parents we knew and allowed Thomas to attend without me. I know Thomas was often left out of many celebrations simply because he had muscular dystrophy.

Ahh, the doctors ... there were many. Thomas had a few favourites, and as he got older, he had enough knowledge to ask the right questions of the many practitioners he saw. I sometimes felt that I, too, could receive an honorary degree in medicine after everything we went through. He disagreed with many doctors and shocked others with his vast understanding of their field.

Through all of the medical appointments and trips to hospitals and emergency rooms, our experience with the innumerable doctors caring for Thomas was mixed. Many had egos and thought they knew what was best even though we tried to voice our concerns. Some had no idea what they were dealing with, and others would simply go by-the-book. There were few doctors who actually listened to our concerns and thoughts as to what was best based on our daily interactions with our son. So many were afraid or wouldn't bother to ask other doctors who had experience with muscular dystrophy patients for their opinions.

I think one of my biggest sources of guilt stems from the time the doctor at the Children's Hospital slapped my wrists for questioning Thomas's heart. When she scolded me and told me that it wasn't his heart that was the problem, I lost a fight. Looking back, I see that I backed off from pushing other doctors about opinions after this incident. Moving forward, I was hesitant to question any doctor when Thomas was in the hospital, both in Ottawa and Calgary. As a mother, I believe you have a feeling in your gut that tells you what your child needs. If only I had questioned more, Thomas may have lived a longer life. We will never know.

Glenn and I attended one session with a grief counsellor who suggested for my well-being that I send a letter to the doctor. I did, not expecting a response, but I hoped that it made an impact on her. The letter was as follows:

October 20, 2015

Dr. _____

This is a letter that I have been meaning to write for a couple of years. I can only hope that you, as a doctor, can take some of it to heart.

Afterword

First of all, I would like to tell you that we were right. Our son's heart was the problem. Secondly, I want to encourage you to think more carefully when speaking with parents. I was insisting that Thomas's health symptoms were happening because of his heart. You, openly, in front of all the interns and nurses, told me to "mind my own business" and that you, as a doctor, knew what you were doing. You told us straight out that Thomas's heart was not the problem. You decided that his problem was not his heart and ended that search. My husband made me apologize to you. Wow. If only I had kept pursuing. Because of your "slap on my wrists," I was hesitant to pursue further questions with more doctors as Thomas's health deteriorated while being treated in other hospitals.

Our son Thomas was admitted to the ICU at the Children's Hospital just over two years ago. He passed away a year ago, due to his heart. Thomas had a rare form of muscular dystrophy called LMNA. You may not remember him. If you need a reminder, please google "Thomas Sorensen Calgary." You will be amazed at his accomplishments. You discharged Thomas saying he had "a mysterious illness."

It has been just over a year since his passing, and words cannot express our sorrow, anger, and emptiness. This should not have happened. I keep regretting, as a parent, after your "wrist-slapping" not speaking up more for our son's care.

I needed to write this letter to you. I am hoping it will help our grieving, and I can only hope that this may help other parents in the future. I only wish I could say this to you face-to-face.

I am sure you do great work on a day-to-day basis. Just know that this case was not your best. Yes, I am angry. Our son is gone. I needed to say this to make some peace with myself. I was advised by a grief counsellor to do so. Will it help? Perhaps. It is something that has been bothering me for a long time. I always tried to do the best for our boys. That was always my goal/job as a mother.

I hope you can take this letter with understanding. And again, give parents some space. Listen to what they say. A mother's gut has substance.

Kathy Sorensen

I didn't receive a response, but writing and sending it helped me feel a little better. I can only hope that the doctor would listen next time to a mother's gut feelings. I can only hope that my letter made a difference for another child.

To other parents of special-needs kids: Never give up! Do not take no for an answer. When there is an obstacle, find a way around it. Even though a child is "special needs," the challenges they face do not mean that is the end of living. Help your child achieve the most they can. Help them strive to reach their dreams. Discover what your child's passions and abilities are and help them in pursuing and developing those areas. Special-needs kids are just that! Very special. They can and will surprise you, especially if they know you have their back.

One disappointing fact is that Thomas's health file is just that. A file, hidden away in the archives. Glenn did ask one of the doctors at the Children's Hospital if the thousands of pages of information would or could be shared in any way for possible research. The answer was no. Thomas's kind of muscular dystrophy is so rare, we thought his history could help someone in the future. But the only information shared was on the CDs we sent to the specialists in Barcelona. We have never heard if any of that was valuable or not.

To parents of any child: get life insurance on every child you have, as early as possible! Glenn had the insight to do this with both of our boys. Why do I say this? Should you have a child and, God forbid, anything with serious implications is diagnosed at any time, they no longer qualify for life insurance. We took out life insurance for Thomas when he was a month old. When he was diagnosed with muscular dystrophy, the insurance company told us that he would never be able to receive additional life insurance but as long as we kept up with the payments, he would be covered. When Thomas passed, his funeral costs were well over $25,000. That was in 2014. Every year, burial costs increase 10 per cent. Because we had kept up his payments, the life insurance covered these costs. Jamie has been able to continue the payments on his life insurance since he turned twenty-one. If he had purchased a new insurance policy at twenty-one, his monthly costs would have been much higher than they are. He continues his policy today at a much lower rate.

Afterword

As far as giving advice to parents of special-needs kids regarding extended family, that is tough. Our family members knew what Thomas's needs were, and yet, overall, on a daily basis, we didn't always receive support. As we mentioned before, it would have been nice to have had someone come by to help in those days when Thomas was home from school for a day, or just to receive a call and say, "You two go out for a night, and we'll take care of things." We know our family was there, just perhaps not always when and how we needed them to be.

Finally, my most excruciating regret is knowing that Thomas didn't reach his potential. The grief counsellor Glenn and I met with pointed out that our grief was an indication that we knew that Thomas wanted to do more. In Thomas's words, "I have not finished." As a parent, you wish for your kids to meet their dreams, accomplish their goals, and make a difference in our world. I do know that Thomas made a difference, impacting so many lives. I have to believe that. Even among all of the different moments of guilt, there are wondrous memories. I know that we supported Thomas as much as we could, and I realize that even with the guilt and stress along the way, both Glenn and I tried our best to support, love, and guide our boys to be the best they could be. And Thomas was.

If someone were to ask me my proudest moment or memory of Thomas, I would have a tough time answering. I would likely say one of those moments was during Thomas's earliest years, the day he was able to walk. Although it was for a short time, and his poor forehead was covered in bruises, he had pushed hard through the physiotherapy to get himself on his feet. At the time, it was a sign of hope.

The second proud moment was when Thomas received five out of five on his grade 11 AP final exam in biology.

And one of *the* proudest moments was when Thomas received word that he won the Terry Fox Humanitarian Award. We were told that there were thousands of applications, and he was the only Albertan to receive the award. Wow.

But, overall, what I am most proud of Thomas for is his tenacity, his spirit, his selflessness. His determination to beat the odds. He never gave up. When I think of the many obstacles he faced, I am reminded that he always found a way around them. He strived to be his best. He had manners and respect for elders, always asking if he could have a cookie or watch a particular show. And he always took responsibility for his actions.

Thomas was exceptional, and he taught us, his parents, so much. He had spirit. He had dreams, and he believed. Thomas gave us hope and inspired us to live. He faced daily challenges that few could endure. No one could match his love for life. Thomas always found humour when there was pain. He always cared for others and always tried to make a difference for people with disabilities. I could not be any prouder of our son. I believe Thomas lived as full of a life as we could have ever imagined. He wanted nothing except more time.

I know in my heart that Thomas and I had a most extraordinary bond. I loved him fully and deeply, and he knew that. I know he did. We were as close as a mother and son could be. I miss him every day and every hour. With time, I hope it gets easier.

Forever in my heart, Thomas! Miss you, Magoo!
I love you so much!

Getting to Know More About Thomas

For those who did not know Thomas, here is a little about what he liked!

Television

When Thomas was young, one of his favourite shows was *Thomas the Tank Engine & Friends*. This love exploded into his life; he had wallpaper in his room, toy trains, tracks, and even a large tabletop of the Thomas the Tank Engine tracks and village. One of Glenn's friends, Steve, took the tabletop and made it reversible so we could use it as a coffee table when Thomas was not playing and spending time standing to increase his muscles. We also were given a beautiful book with hundreds of the Thomas the Tank Engine stories in it. This was a regular bedtime storybook over the years.

Little Bear was a cartoon about a lovely little bear and his adventures. Thomas was given a small stuffed bear at his christening, and this quickly became his favourite stuffy. He called it Little Bear. Jamie now has the bear.

As Thomas outgrew the above, *SpongeBob SquarePants* soon became a popular cartoon with him. He would happily sing along to the theme song anytime the show came on.

Thomas also enjoyed *DuckTales*. He and Glenn would watch these together. Glenn still watches on occasion to bring back the memories.

As Thomas matured, he loved watching *MythBusters*. He enjoyed seeing how different ideas were disclaimed. He especially loved watching experiments involving anything getting blown up, as any boy would!

Cash Cab was another show he enjoyed. I believe it was a challenge for him to see if he could beat the contestants to the correct answer.

Thomas would also watch *Whose Line is it Anyway?* He loved the comedy and the actors who performed regularly on the show.

The Big Bang Theory was a regular in our house. Thomas would comment on the different scientific theories that were discussed, and he enjoyed the humour.

During his hospital stay in Ottawa, Thomas was watching *The Liquidator*, a Vancouver-based show on a store selling items at discount prices.

Movies

When Thomas was only two, he would watch the video of *Riverdance* over and over. He loved the music and was mesmerized with the dancing. Our nanny at the time also enjoyed it, as well as me, so we may have had some influence there.

The Incredibles was always a favourite. He watched the first movie several times.

Harry Potter was a must. We would make it a family event to go to the theatre when a new movie came out. Each time there was a new one, we would always rewatch the previous movies at home before going.

The Mike Myers movies, with him playing Austin Powers, were always a go-to on a rainy day. *International Man of Mystery*, *The Spy Who Shagged Me*, and *Goldmember* were often watched as a marathon in our house when Thomas was older. The boys loved many of the one-liners from the movie such as "A smoke and a pancake," and "There's a turtle poking out."

Books

As far as books go, it was always tough for Thomas. He needed someone to turn the pages for him or read to him. As a child, he loved the *Thomas the Tank Engine* stories. He went through a phase of the *Bernstein Bears*, as well. I have kept all of those books for possible future grandchildren.

He enjoyed *Love You Forever* and other stories written by Robert Munsch. He also liked *ZOOM!* and *Stephanie's Ponytail*. I believe those books made a connection for Thomas with people who are considered "different." *ZOOM!* definitely made a connection. Look it up! So much fun for kids in wheelchairs!

He read all of the *Harry Potter* books and totally enjoyed the *How to Train Your Dragon* series.

As Thomas got older, it continued getting more difficult for him to read an actual paper book. He could not do it on his own.

Thomas "isms"

This is something we hold dear to our hearts. Thomas had certain words he loved to use. Sometimes he would just add -ish to a word. "It is about 10:00-ish." "It is deliciousness-ish."

If Thomas didn't like the way a conversation was going, he would try to change the subject by saying, "Anyways …"

His favourite word was the longest word in our vocabulary. He tried to use it whenever he could. The word is *antidisestablishmentarianism*. It means the "opposition to the belief that there should not be an official relationship between a country's government and its national Church."[29] Where he got that from, I have no idea.

Thomas loved the word *awesomeness*, and one of his favourite responses to something someone would say to him was *indubitably*.

And if he loved a food, he would sometimes moan and say, "Nom nom nom …"

Foods

Growing up, Thomas loved milk. As a baby, he would drink eight 8-oz bottles a day until we were told that caused an iron deficiency.

He loved pasta, pork, and ice cream. One of his favourites was fried hashbrowns with a runny, fried egg, covered in ketchup. He did love any kind of potato with ketchup.

Did I mention he loved ketchup on his ketchup?

He did not like anything that was "slimy" in his mouth, which included in his mind, lettuce in any form, or melons. And he would not eat any raw

---

29 Cambridge Dictionary, s.v. "antidisestablishmentarianism," accessed August 9, 2022, dictionary.cambridge.org/dictionary/english/antidisestablishmentarianism.

vegetables. He loved the mini-wieners, Kentucky Fried Chicken, a juicy burger with cheese and bacon, and definitely Nutella!

He was a typical kid and was picky to a point. We tried to encourage him to eat in a healthy way and introduce him to new foods. As he grew older and began to understand his intake, he was making wiser choices. He still never ate a salad with greens, though.

Timeline

1992

Kathy and Glenn met in May.
Kathy and Glenn got engaged in December.

1993

Kathy and Glenn got married in July.

1994

Kathy, Glenn, and Jamie moved to Kelowna, BC.
Kathy started a new teaching job; Glenn was working as a bricklayer; Jamie entered kindergarten.

1995

Kathy became pregnant with Thomas.

1996

Thomas was born on January 23.
Thomas started using a helmet in September to reshape his head.

1997

In May, Thomas was diagnosed with muscular dystrophy.
The family moved back to Calgary in July.
Thomas had his muscle biopsy in August.

1998

In January Thomas's Congenital Muscular Dystrophy (CMD) was confirmed.

1999

The family moved into a new house in January.
Thomas started kindergarten at daycare (three years old).

2000

In February, Kathy, Jamie, and Thomas took a trip to Nova Scotia for Grampie McNeil's ninetieth birthday.
Thomas attended kindergarten in Woodbine School.
Thomas received his first wheelchair.

2001

Daycare would not take Thomas.
Thomas entered grade 1 in September.

2002

Thomas began grade 2 in September.

2003

Thomas turned seven.
The family moved to a new lakeside house in Midnapore in May.

2004

Thomas turned eight.
Thomas was granted the Children's Wish trip to Denmark.
Thomas received his first power chair.

2005

Thomas began grade 5 in September.

2006

Thomas turned ten.

2007

Thomas went on the Dreams Take Flight trip.
Thomas began grade 7 in September.
At the Giddy Up Gala in October, "Back to the Saloon," Thomas was guest speaker and sang a song for the seven hundred attendees.

2008

Thomas turned twelve.
Thomas was Easter Seals Youth Ambassador for Southern Alberta.
Thomas won the Heart, Spirit, Legacy Award (grade 7) in June.
Thomas was guest speaker at the Between Friends Gala, twenty-fifth anniversary in September.
Thomas started playing hockey.

2009

Thomas turned thirteen.
Thomas was featured in a music video that had been filmed in the summer with Gord Bamford.

2010

Thomas was confirmed in the Lutheran church on April 25.
In June, Thomas won the Faculty Award (grade 9).
Thomas started grade 10 at E.P. Scarlett in the Advanced Placement (AP) program in Biology and Art.

2011

Thomas started grade 11 in September, age fifteen.

2012

Thomas started grade 12 in September.

Thomas was granted early acceptance into Carleton University.

2013

Thomas fought for government funding for university.
Thomas won the Terry Fox Humanitarian Award.
Thomas graduated from high school.
Thomas began studies at Carleton in September, age seventeen.

2014

In January, Thomas received an implantable cardioverter-defibrillator (ICD) implant for his heart.
Thomas made the Dean's List.
Thomas came home for a visit in July.
Thomas returned to Ottawa and was hospitalized.
In August, Thomas returned home and was hospitalized three days later.
September 1, 7:55 a.m., Thomas passed away.

Gratitude

When I began writing Thomas's story, I did not feel that I had the ability to compose it properly. I had the idea to include different voices to help relay how much impact Thomas had on others. My husband, Glenn, and I first thought that maybe we should hire a ghostwriter. Shortly after I began writing, the principal at my school gifted each member of the staff with the book *Wonder* by R.J. Palacio. As I read the book, I recognized that its layout was similar to what I had already planned. I contacted the author with no expectations that she would respond. Much to my delight, she emailed back saying that she had read the articles written about Thomas and felt that not only was it a story that should be told but that I should tell it. I want to thank Ms. Palacio for giving me the inspiration to continue my writing.

I must thank my husband, Glenn. Writing this was difficult but also therapeutic. Glenn was by my side always. When I was writing, he would come in and give me a hug, give me the push I needed. He helped wipe away any tears when working through a difficult part of Thomas's story.

I would also like to thank Angela, Peter, and of course Lorna, for their expertise in the layout, grammar, and final editing touches. Without their support, I could not have done this.

Thank you to the many friends and family who read all or sections of the book or through the many drafts and edits. Your feedback was very much appreciated.

To everyone who contributed to Thomas's story, thank you. So many individuals from so many different walks of life were able to get to meet and know Thomas, and so many friends of Thomas who have continued to be inspired by him.

Mostly, thank you to our son Thomas for such an incredible story. You made us better people. You showed us love, compassion, humour, spirit, humility, and forgiveness. We are better people today having had you in our lives.

Thomas, I truly feel that you have been with me every step of the way.

For Further Reading and Reference

"Alberta Aids to Daily Living (AADL)." Government of Alberta. 2021. alberta.ca/alberta-aids-to-daily-living.aspx.

"Attendant Services Program." Carleton University. 2021. carleton.ca/attendant-services-program/.

"Calgary Selects." The Official Site of the CPHL Calgary Powerhockey League. 2021. powerhockey.ca/page/show/38047-calgary-selects.

Colquhoun, Frank (ed.). *New Parish Prayers*. London: Hodder & Stoughton: 1988.

"Cure CMD." TREAT-NMD Neuromuscular Network. 2021. treat-nmd.org/organization/cure-cmd/.

"Dreams Take Flight Calgary." 2021. yyc.dreamstakeflight.ca/.

Easter Seals Camp Horizon, "Easter Seals Camp Horizon," YouTube video, 2:19, June 5, 2013, youtube.com/watch?v=w9u6cVB5wbo

Elliott, Tamara, and Jill Croteau. "Budget Cutbacks Keep Teen with Muscular Dystrophy from Pursuing University Dreams." Global News. Updated April 29, 2013, 6:17 p.m. globalnews.ca/news/520812/budget-cutbacks-keep-teen-with-muscular-dystrophy-from-pursuing-university-dreams/.

"Emery Dreifuss Muscular Dystrophy." *Rare Disease Database*. NORD: National Organization for Rare Disorders. 2021. rarediseases.org/rare-diseases/emery-dreifuss-muscular-dystrophy/.

Family Support for Children with Disablities (FSCD). alberta.ca/fscd.aspx

"FDA Approves Innovative Gene Therapy to Treat Pediatric Patients with Spinal Muscular Dystrophy, a Rare Disease and Leading Genetic Cause of Infant Mortality." FDA U.S. Food & Drug Administration. May 24, 2019. fda.gov/news-events/press-announcements/fda-approves-innovative-gene-therapy-treat-pediatric-patients-spinal-muscular-atrophy-rare-disease.

"First Human SMA Gene Transfer Therapy Trial Opens." ClinicalTrials.gov. May 29, 2014. institut-myologie.org/en/2014/05/20/first-human-sma-gene-transfer-therapy-trial-opens/.

"Healing Touch." University of Minnesota. 2016. takingcharge.csh.umn.edu/explore-healing-practices/healing-touch.

Komarnicki, Jamie. "A Legacy of Hope Left Behind by Calgary Teen." *Calgary Herald*. September 3, 2014. calgaryherald.com/news/local-news/a-legacy-of-hope-left-behind-by-calgary-teen.

"Ministry of Advanced Education." Government of Alberta. 2021. alberta.ca/advanced-education.aspx.

"Obituary of Thomas Voss Sorensen." McInnis & Holloway Funeral Homes. September 1, 2013. mhfh.com/tribute/details/4905/Thomas-SORENSEN/obituary.html.

"PowerHockey Cup." Electric Wheelchair Hockey Association, 2018. powerhockey.com/category/cup/.

"Primary Health Care Resource Centre: Self-Management." Alberta Health Services. 2021. albertahealthservices.ca/info/Page7733.aspx.

Remembering Thomas Sorensen. Facebook. facebook.com/thomas.sorensen.31.

Rick Hansen Foundation. 2021. rickhansen.com/.

Sant Joan de Déu Barcelona Hospital. "Neuromuscular Diseases." 2021. sjdhospitalbarcelona.org/en/children/neuromuscular-diseases.

Schmidt, Colleen. "Student Makes Dean's List Despite Funding Right and Physical Disablity." *CTV News*. Last updated July 24, 2014, 5:44 p.m. calgary.ctvnews.ca/student-makes-dean-s-list-despite-funding-fight-and-physical-disability-1.1930887.

Starlight Children's Foundation Canada. starlightcanada.org/.

"Starlight." Starlight Children's Foundation. 2021. starlight.org/.

Thomas Sorensen. Twitter. twitter.com/thomassorensen6.

"Thomas Sorensen Memorial Scholarship for Students with Disabilities." Future Funder, Carleton University. 2018. futurefunder.carleton.ca/giving-fund/thomas-sorensen-memorial-scholarship/.

"Thomas Voss Sorensen." Peter Foreman. YouTube video. 15:06. September 7, 2014. youtu.be/v_M6kb58X00.

Wood, Damien. "Teen with Muscular Dystrophy Dies in Hospital." *Toronto Sun*. September 2, 2014. torontosun.com/2014/09/01/teen-with-muscular-dystrophy-dies-in-hospital.

Wood, Damien. "Young Disabled Calgarian Who Fought Government to Fund Studies at Carleton University—and Won—Dies at Age 18." *Edmonton Sun*. September 2, 2014. edmontonsun.com/2014/09/01/young-disabled-calgarian-who-fought-government-to-fund-studies-at-carleton-university--and-won--dies-at-age-18.

White, Ryan. "Provincial Funding Stalls Teen's Carleton University Education." *CTV News*. Last updated April 28, 2013, 6:50 p.m. calgary.ctvnews.ca/provincial-funding-stalls-teen-s-carleton-university-education-1.1257964.

www.ingramcontent.com/pod-product-compliance
Lightning Source LLC
LaVergne TN
LVHW091436060225
803129LV00003B/343